REGARDING FILM

By Stanley Kauffmann

NOVELS
The Hidden Hero
The Tightrope
A Change of Climate
Man of the World

CRITICISM
Theater
Persons of the Drama
Theater Criticisms

Film
A World on Film
Figures of Light
Living Images
Before My Eyes
Field of View
Distinguishing Features
Regarding Film

EDITOR
(with Bruce Henstell)
American Film Criticism: From the Beginnings to Citizen Kane

MEMOIRS
Albums of Early Life

PAJ BOOKS

Bonnie Marranca and Gautam Dasgupta,

Series Editors

Regarding Film

STANLEY KAUFFMANN

Criticism and Comment

FOREWORD BY MICHAEL WOOD

The Johns Hopkins University Press

Baltimore & London

© 2001 by Stanley Kauffmann

All rights reserved. Published 2001

Printed in the United States of America on acid-free paper

9 8 7 6 5 4 3 2 1

The Johns Hopkins University Press

2715 North Charles Street

Baltimore, Maryland 21218-4363

www.press.jhu.edu

Library of Congress Cataloging-in-Publication Data

Kauffmann, Stanley, 1916–

Regarding film : criticism and comment / Stanley Kauffmann.

p. cm. — (PAJ books)

Includes index.

ISBN 0-8018-6584-0 (alk. paper)

1. Motion pictures — Reviews.   I. Title.   II. Series.

PN1995 .K297   2001

791.43'75 — dc21   00-042852

A catalog record for this book is available from the British Library.

To Bonnie Marranca and Gautam Dasgupta

Contents

"There's hope," Stanley Kauffmann wrote in *Living Images* (1975), his third collection of film criticism. He added, "There always *is* hope in the film world, of course, even when there's no immediate reason to believe it." Not many critics or viewers would subscribe to this claim now, and even Kauffmann has changed his tone. In 1974, in a essay reprinted in *Before My Eyes* (1980), he was still eagerly saying that "hope is more of a constant in film than in virtually any other art in America," but by 1980, in a piece reproduced in *Field of View* (1986), he was writing about "the poor state" of American films, and suggesting that even when the gloom lifted, he couldn't believe it would "stay lifted." Towards the end of his new collection, *Regarding Film,* he evokes "the dire conditions" of contemporary filmmaking, and says "the situation is inarguably dark."

But there always *is* hope, in Kauffmann's film criticism if not in the film world. To abandon hope, for him, would be to abandon his post and his faith in the art he has scrutinized and celebrated for so long—for a third of that art's existence, he said in his preface to *Distinguishing Features* (1994). Now he could say, if he wished, that he has been writing about film for closer to a half of its existence, since the traditional starting date of the cinema is 1895, and Kauffmann sent his first, unsolicited film review to *The New Republic* in 1958. Within a page or so of his remarks about the gloom of the American cinema he is saying that "the most inspiriting event in any art anywhere is the appearance of a good new film." He thinks this form of event is rare, and getting rarer, but rare is not the same as extinct, and "two respectable pictures in a year can keep hope alive." Even when Kauffmann talks about the darkness of the situation of film he is looking for the light. It's dark all right. "But is it black? I think not." And a little later: "Optimism is possibly too grandiose a term to use here. Persistence isn't." Of course the subdued terms Kauffmann uses in these later essays ("respectable," "persistence") have their own sadness and tell their own story. We are a long way from the excitements of the French New Wave and the heyday of Antonioni and Kurosawa, a long way even from the early and middle Steven Spielberg. But then this means that hope is a critical principle for Kauffmann, a measure to be sought and found, not simply a ready-made denial of gloom. "There's hope" is a phrase that will take many inflections. It may mean we have reasons for hope, and even plenty of them; it may mean our hopes are slender but they are what we've got; or it may mean we are clinging to the sheer idea of hope, playing for time till the reasons for hoping return. All these inflections occur in Kauffmann's criticism. They are signs not of changes of heart but of a deep immersion in the changing history of the movies and the world. What's important is that hope as a principle never vanishes.

One of the reasons for this fidelity to hope is personal and temperamental. In a revealing answer to a question about how many movies a week he sees as a critic, Kauffmann said, in a 1974 article, the number varied from none to twelve but was usually about three, and then added, "But the point is that most weeks it wouldn't have been less if I weren't a critic." In other words, he is that almost obsolete creature, the critic as moviegoer (or the moviegoer as critic). "The mere physical aspect of filmgoing is part of the kinesis of my life — the getting up and going out and the feeling of coming home, which is a somewhat different homecoming feeling from anything else except the theater. . . . To have my life unpunctuated by the physical act of filmgoing is almost like walking with a limp, out of my natural rhythm." In another mood, Kauffmann might want to distinguish coming home from the movies even from coming home from the theater, but the essential thing here is the journey out and back, the return with whatever surprises or failures of surprise the cinema turned out to hold. "No matter how much I know about a film's makers or its subject before I go, I never really know what it's going to do to me: depress me with its vileness, or just roll past, or change my life in some degree, or some combination of all three, or affect me in some new way that I cannot imagine." It's characteristic of Kauffmann that he should remember the chance of vileness, or of the film's just rolling past; even more characteristic that he should end on the idea of the new.

And here is where temperament turns into a kind of theory, something that goes well beyond the person. For Kauffmann one of the important features of film in the cinema, as distinct from novels or plays, or even films on television, is that it is inescapable. It doesn't move us "more grandly or deeply" than other arts — how could it and why would it? But it does get to us "more quickly and surely." "When two screen lovers kiss, in any film, that kiss has a minimum inescapability which is stronger than in other arts," both as visual fact and emotional symbol. This is why "when we sit before a screen, we run risks unprecedented in human history." There is a touch of overstatement here, no doubt, but Kauffmann is proposing a significant counter-truth to the suggestion we find both in Virginia Woolf and in Stanley Cavell, to the effect that film displays a world complete without us, a world we can only haunt, never enter or influence — the way we could interrupt a play, for instance, by throwing tomatoes or assassinating the hero. "We see life as it is when we have no part of it," Woolf said of the cinema. We can't get into the film, Kauffmann would agree. But we can't hide from it, either, and this new, unavoidable relation to the representation in front of us has all kinds of consequences. It makes the representation real to us in a way that enhances and transcends all traditional notions of realism. What we see on the screen, however fantastic, must be real in one sense because we have just seen it — we can doubt that such things exist anywhere else but we can't doubt that we saw them. And if the screen world is categorically separate from ours, we also picture it as weirdly continuous with it. In the present volume, Kauffmann cites a moment in Edwin S. Porter's film *The Great Train Robbery* (1903), where one of the passengers, forced to disembark from the train, runs toward us to escape from the robbers. "This," Kauffmann says, "is an evolutionary moment in the history of film. . . . The passenger doesn't run right or left: he runs, at a slight angle, directly toward us, toward the camera." If this had happened on stage, we would be expecting the character to crash into the footlights, fall into the audience. Here we expect nothing of the sort. "When an actor leaves a film shot, in any direction, we simply assume that he is continuing on in the rest of the world. . . . We conceive that the camera at any one moment is focused on one fragment of immensity. Porter's fugitive wasn't heading toward the end of anything: if he hadn't been killed, he might still be running."

The new relation also creates not only new audiences, but a new kind of audience, and when Kauffmann coined his famous phrase about "the film generation" in 1966, he was thinking not only of habitual, enthusiastic moviegoers but of people who had grown after the movies had grown up, "the first generation that has matured in a culture in which the film has been of accepted serious relevance, however that seriousness is defined." Weren't the images of film inescapable for the previous generation? Of course they were, but they were largely construed as outside the ambitions of art, and for the new generation, "most of them born since 1935," Kauffmann says, art and seriousness go hand in hand. What we can't hide from is the authority of the images but also a certain developing mastery of the image-makers.

But Kauffmann is not a purist about film, and thinks it's a mistake to elevate the "sheerly cinematic" above other values. To praise a film like Ophuls' *Lola Montès,* for example, for its composition and cuts and camera movements, which are indeed "superb," and yet ignore the banality of the story line and the poverty of the acting, is not to celebrate cinema but to let cinema off the hook, "a derogation and patronization of cinema," a settling for second best. For Kauffmann cinema is everything that can be put to work on film: angle, editing, and lighting but also writing, acting, music, what belongs to other arts as well as what belongs only to the movies. He was hard on Orson Welles, although he later relented to some degree, because after *Citizen Kane* he became "a scene and sequence maker, not a filmmaker." Michelangelo Antonioni, by contrast, is the complete filmmaker, "one of the finest artists in film history," and a "mistake" like *Zabriskie Point* causes Kauffmann something like physical pain. "How badly we need the best of Antonioni."

Kauffmann's finest local perceptions sometimes concern the framing or timing of shots, or overall visual effects, as in a whole series of wonderful comments to be found in *Regarding Film.* On Bergman, for example, who "always had a way of putting antagonists face to face . . . as if they were locked there, as if the quarrel had to be seen through to the bitter end, no matter how painful to the opponents. The pressing placement of the camera, the restrained editing, with as little cross-cutting from one face to another as possible, make us feel as if we were watching an epic encounter." On the screen world of Abbas Kiarostami: "Like Ozu and Antonioni . . . Kiarostami seems to look at film not as something to be made, but to be inhabited, as if it were *there* always, like the world, waiting to be stepped into, without fuss." On the contribution of Woody Harrelson and Juliette Lewis to *Natural Born Killers:* "It's not acting in any integrated, resourceful sense but the presentation of familiar planes off which the un-familiar lighting and frenzy can bounce." But of course Kauffmann loves acting in the integrated, resourceful sense as well. Of Marlon Brando in *A Streetcar Named Desire* he says "he irrupts into the film like history taking its revenge." Of Marilyn Monroe in a sequence of pictures, he says she is "not a mate but a protectorate." The same ecumenical love leads him into an adoration of Emma Thompson which is a little hard for the rest of us to share. Thompson is "miraculous"; "no prize is good enough for her"; "she is the first film actress since Katherine Hepburn to make intelligence sexy"—this last comment about her performance in Kenneth Branagh's wretchedly arch and whimsical *Much Ado about Nothing.*

We don't have to share Kauffmann's opinions–or his distaste for the American avant-garde film—in order to share his hopes, in all or any of their inflections. His interest in the film generation was an interest in people who could not only watch films but make them, either by be-coming moviemakers themselves or by helping to create a climate in which good new movies could flourish. "I believe the Film Generation has the power to evoke the films that it wants," he wrote in 1966. And when this belief began to fade, Kauffmann's diagnosis was a long way from nostalgia or elementary regret. The next generation—let's call it, for simplicity' s sake, the Rock Generation—lost sight of old movies be-cause it lost interest in new movies, and maybe the other way round too, although Kauffmann doesn't say this. He recalls showing Dreyer's *Passion of Joan of Arc* to his students, and getting the same bemused response, in-dependently, from two of them: not only had they not known this film, they had "never imagined the medium itself was capable of such heights." Kauffmann's point is that in the history of film "present tense and past tense are uniquely interwoven," and only the weave, rich or impoverished, makes cinema.

Is this texture of tenses really unique? It is if we accept Kauffmann's understanding, elided here but richly expressed elsewhere, that cinema is above all an art of uncertainty and surprise, an art of what hasn't hap-pened yet, an art of the future. However old the cinema gets, it will always be new or involved in novelty in this sense, and this argument provokes Kauffmann to one of his most difficult and ambitious propositions. This new-old art must constantly seek new audiences, and hope will die only when all possibility of an audience has vanished. At that time—and here

Kauffmann begins to sound like Emerson — America itself will have died, since this search for new audiences "is in some ways a search to discover whether America still exists in any prognosticable sense." It's not that only American films count, or that American films are best, far from it. It's that filmgoing, necessarily, has the nationality of its practitioners. We can speculate about what attendance at the cinema means in England, France, or Latin America and elsewhere, and we have Italo Calvino's marvelous *Road to San Giovanni* to help us understand the habit in Italy. But we know that in America moviegoing means the exercise of hope, the enduring and enchanting expectation, disappointed or not, of being affected, as Kauffmann says, in ways we cannot imagine.

MICHAEL WOOD

Preface

re•gard 1. To look at attentively, observe closely.
2. To look upon or consider in a particular way.
3. To hold in esteem or respect.
—*American Heritage Dictionary*

Hence the title of my seventh collection of film criticism, with the hope
that these definitions apply as well to the previous collections. The reviews and articles herein have been selected, from those written since
1992, because the film or topic or book is of lasting significance or
because the comments may be of continuing interest, or both.

As before, the order within sections is chronological unless there is
more than one review of a director's work, in which case the reviews of
his other films follow the first.

All but two of the pieces in this book first appeared in *The New Republic*. (The exceptions are noted.) To my friends at that magazine, profound gratitude for their support. Thanks, perennial, to Carl Brandt,
agent and friend. Thanks above all to L. C. K.

S. K.

REGARDING FILM

Reviews

Graham Greene, who was a film critic from 1935 to 1941, wrote during his tenure, "Life as it is and life as it should be: let us take that as the only true subject for a film, and consider to what extent the cinema is fulfilling its proper function." This principle, wildly inappropriate though it may seem in numerous instances, is nonetheless insistent. Let's add only that "life as it should be" is less defined by the critic than it is envisioned by the artist. That vision, in whatever species of film, breezy or grave, is the critic's basic concern. The following reviews, about films that vary precipitously in kind, continue more than forty years of inquiry into what this particular art implies about perfection.

Riff-Raff

FEBRUARY 15, 1993 | Britain has developed a kind of director that is relatively scarce in this country, the one who is centrally interested in the working class. In the United States we had the late Martin Ritt, who returned to that subject from time to time; and we have documentarians, like Barbara Kopple. But the British examples concentrate much more closely on working people, and they do it in fiction, thus are nearer to the mainstream. Mike Leigh, Terence Davies, and Ken Loach are hardly box-office bonanzas, but they are filmmakers of declared allegiance and, though they may briefly wander, they are faithful to it.

Is there anything new to be said about the working class as such—in Britain or elsewhere? Generally speaking, no; but as with most subjects in art, the question isn't novelty. Or to put it properly, the novelty arises not from the subject but from the fresh experience of humanity that's evoked.

Ken Loach does this dynamically in his new film *Riff-Raff*. Loach (b. 1936), whose earliest films shown here were *Poor Cow* and *Kes,* has found exactly the right material for himself in a screenplay by Bill Jesse. Jesse, since deceased, was a writer who supported himself as a construction laborer. His screenplay is virtually devoid of novelty, but it's a good deal more than sufficient in character.

On character, then, Loach has fixed, which in cinematic practice results in a particular texture. He works in close much of the time, often in close-up, often with hand-held camera, trying without ostentation to make that camera more of a companion than an observer.

A gang of workers is helping in the renovation of some old buildings in London. All of these men are, one way or another, likable; all the bosses, and their foremen, are bastards. But so engaging are these workers that the neatly assigned colors are not bothersome; they seem merely to mark out the grid on which the film will operate.

The story is minimal. One of the workers, a young Scotsman (Robert

Carlyle), meets a young Irish singer (Emer McCourt) through a coincidence connected to the renovation. They become lovers and live together —squatting in unoccupied premises as do all the other workers. The lovers get on famously for a while, though her singing career does not. He has to make a quick trip to Glasgow to attend his mother's funeral. He comes back to find her doing drugs, which for him is the finish. He has seen what drugs have done to close relatives. They part.

This story, however, seems no more than the thread on which the dailiness of the workers' lives is hung. Besides the Scotsman, the group includes a middle-aged leftie from Liverpool, a man from Bristol, men from other regions, three of them blacks. Two of the blacks are African, one is a cockney who dreams of going to Africa. The leftie gets fired for protesting safety conditions, and the film's ending proves that his protest was just.

The only real flaws are the first shot and the last. We first see, and we last see, rats scurrying around in rubble. As symbolism, this is so trite that it makes us stiff with apprehension at the start and irked at the end because we see how inapt it is. The men with whom we've just spent ninety-four minutes may be thought of as rodents by their bosses but certainly not by themselves. They are the opposite of self-conscious victims: they are lively and funny—and vulgar in a way that strips the lacquer off our own vulgarity. All the leading actors were professionals but were required to have had construction experience; the secondary players were all construction workers who now are, at least a bit, professional actors. They all acquit themselves with energy, precisely used, which is another tribute to Loach, who clearly had their confidence.

The film is in English *and* is subtitled. A good idea. The only previous example I can remember is *Sparrows Can't Sing* (1962), which was about cockneys. It's helpful here because of several regional accents, and it would in fact be welcome in some American films where Mumble is King. But the subtitles are the only relative innovation in a picture that prospers by dealing so chummily with an old topic.

Stolen Children

MARCH 22, 1993 | Two years ago Gianni Amelio made *Open Doors,* based on Leonardo Sciascia's novella. Now Amelio presents *Stolen Children,* and now his name must be inscribed on a particular honor roll—of those directors who have done extraordinary work with children.

Stolen Children—the Italian title translates more accurately as *The Thief of Children*—centers on an eleven-year-old girl and her nine-year-old brother, so perhaps Amelio's achievement was a bit easier than, say, Truffaut's with tots in *Small Change.* Still, the screenplay by Amelio, Sandro Petraglia, and Stefano Rulli calls for inflections and silences that are, or ought to be, beyond the comprehension of this pair; and they are so persuasive that we forget we're watching juvenile actors. It's right that we should forget; but later we remember.

The idea of the film was suggested by a newspaper story. The children and their mother are Sicilian, living in Milan. (Sicilians and other southern Italians are sometimes called "the blacks of Milan.") Impoverished, the mother prostitutes her daughter. After a time the police intervene, the mother and a customer are arrested and the children—played by Valentina Scalici and Giuseppe Ieracitano—are ordered to a children's home.

They are to be escorted to that home, a Catholic one near Civitavecchia, by two carabinieri. En route one of the officers cuts loose to visit a girlfriend in Bologna; the other, younger one, played by Enrico Lo Verso, is left in sole charge of the youngsters. We don't brace ourselves for a sentimental journey because the beginning is so ghastly, and we're right. Sentiment could not be the aim of this film. Verity is, including verity about Italy.

The home at Civitavecchia declines to accept the children, partly on the ground that they are Sicilian and will not fit in (a patent excuse to get rid of this unsavory pair). Lo Verso then has to take them to a home in Sicily. En route they stop at his sister's new restaurant in Calabria; then in Sicily he rents a car to expedite the trip.

The three stop at a beach for a swim and also in Noto (the incredible city where an episode of Antonioni's *L'Avventura* took place). There Lo Verso catches a thief who has snatched the camera of a French tourist. But this capture gets Lo Verso in trouble. When he takes the thief to the local carabinieri headquarters, he is reprimanded because he has dallied along the way with his charges. The three proceed in the car. They pull off to the side of the road for a brief snooze but sleep through the night. The film ends the next morning. Lo Verso still sleeps at the wheel; the girl and the boy sit by the side of the highway watching traffic zoom past. (*The International Film Guide* tells us that originally there was an overtly brutal ending.)

No, no sentiment, but during this journey of several days, a bond grows slowly between the taciturn, anorexic boy and Lo Verso; and from time to time the brutalized, suspicious, sullen girl lowers her defenses. Yet the picture is not a journey toward betterment. In fact, the children's realization that whatever has grown between them and Lo Verso must soon end is what underlies their quiet bitterness.

While all the gradations of temperament and response are being calibrated, we move through a series of landscapes that, excepting Noto, are as anti-touristic as possible: neon, poured concrete, tawdriness, new railroad terminals done with the blank coldness that proves Mussolini's architecture is not entirely forgotten. Indeed, the film can be seen as a contest between a harsh, new yet shabby Italy and the humane traditions embodied in the young officer. The scene in which he greets his grandmother at his sister's place is the warmest moment in *Stolen Children*. The rest is struggle: his for the children's confidence, theirs to be able to face emptiness.

Lamerica

JANUARY 29, 1996 | Newsreels show Italian armed forces landing in Albania in 1939. What joy in Albania (say the Fascist newsreels). What happiness to be joined to Mussolini's empire.

Then it's 1991 and there's another Italian invasion—two hustlers who hope to swing a deal in post-Communist Albania. Fiore, a middle-aged smoothie, and his young associate, Gino, somewhat less smooth, mean to set up a phony shoe factory with the aid of a corrupt Albanian official. It will pour money into their pockets. As a front, they need an Albanian to be chairman of this dummy firm, preferably someone who suffered under Hoxha. In a ghastly wreck of a former Communist prison they find Spiro, eighty, illiterate (he can sign his name, which is all that's needed); silent, stubborn, just sufficiently interested in life to prefer it to death.

This is the start of *Lamerica,* the new film by Gianni Amelio, who made the unforgettable *Stolen Children.* The screenplay by Amelio, Andrea Porporati and Alessandro Sermoneta suggests for a time Fellini's *Il Bidone,* which was about a post–World War Two scam. But *Lamerica* soon evolves quite differently. Fiore returns to Italy, leaving Gino to escort Spiro from Durazzo, where the story begins, to Tiranë, where the old man is to sign some papers. But Spiro runs away from the orphanage where he has been stowed overnight and boards a train.

Gino chases the train in his jeep and catches the old man en route to Tiranë. They stop for a rest, and the jeep's wheels are stolen. Gino can't telephone for help: few places out in the country have phones. Besides, the Albanians don't understand Italian, especially when they choose not to. Gino and Spiro continue their trip as best they can, by bus and other means. Thus, what started as the chronicle of a scam metamorphoses into the account of a difficult journey, shared by a relatively hip young man and an occluded old man.

Three themes develop. First, we see the destitution of Albania in the post-Communist era, so great that several people wish they had Communism back: things were better run. Second, we see that Albania is narcotized by Italian TV, which is watched in cafés and hotel lobbies and which feeds dreams of opulence through commercials, lush serials, girlie programs, game shows. Third, we see a melding of Albania with Italy that no one could have predicted. Spiro is an instance of a large phenomenon. He is not Albanian: he is gradually revealed as an Italian, a Sicilian named Michele. He was one of the Italian soldiers in those opening newsreels, many of whom defected and assumed Albanian identities. Jailed for fifty years, for reasons unspecified, apparently on suspicion of espionage, he kept his real nationality a secret out of fear.

These are social-historical matters. But Amelio, certainly struck hard by them, is an artist and is fundamentally concerned with people as such. So, beneath all the above, another theme emerges: illusion. Michele, somewhat blunted in mind, thinks that he will find his wife and son waiting for him in Sicily, the son who was born the day he left: he ran away from Gino to get back to Sicily. Gino has dreamed of getting rich easily;

but, predictably, the scam disintegrates. And all through this journey, he meets many Albanians, mostly young men, who think that wealth awaits them in Italy. At the end it is only Gino who is undeceived.

He is arrested for his part in the scam and is released on condition that he leave Albania at once. He tries to make Michele realize that no family can now await him in Sicily, and he pays a barracks-like hotel to lodge and feed him. Gino tells those Albanians who press him that the only future they can have in Italy is as car-washers. He boards ship for home.

On the ship, crammed in every crevice with emigrants, he discovers Michele, now possessed of another fantasy: this ship is taking him to America. (To him L'America is one word: Lamerica.) Surrounding them are hordes of people who don't share Michele's illusion; but they have their own. They think they are going to TV paradise in Italy. Only Gino, the hustler stripped of deception, sits shivering in reality. In a not quite subtle note, the ship is named *Partizani*. More subtly, bitterly, the film ends with numerous close-ups of passengers' faces, hopeful.

Though he doesn't think of it this way, history has smitten Gino. Fifty years of it, crystallized. He has seen how great power filters down from the top of the pyramid to bully the powerless at the base: how the chief consolation for impotence is illusion.

The one bothersome element in the script is the character of Gino—one aspect of it anyway. He doesn't seem quite experienced enough for Fiore to have made him his partner and to leave him in charge. For one point, after an attempt has been made to ransack his jeep, Gino trusts—much too easily—a local policeman to guard it while he and the old man go off to relieve themselves. A touch too patently, Amelio has arranged it to deprive Gino of his vehicle.

Yet Enrico Lo Verso plays Gino with an investment of self that carries the role over any bumps. In *Stolen Children,* Lo Verso, who looks like a moody fox, played the young policeman taking a boy and girl from Milan to Sicily. (In that film, too, a journey served as a medium for exploration.) Here he reacts so acutely to every stimulus—an official's questioning, a mob's threat—that he seems a quick barometer registering every fluctuation in the emotional climate.

If at the start we think the film is going to be the story of the scam, it's because Amelio has over-cast the role of Fiore, who dominates the opening but soon disappears. Michele Placido is a superb actor. (He was

Caliban in Strehler's *The Tempest*.) We're unprepared for an actor of his strength and personality to leave a film so early. Even those who know nothing of Placido may well feel this surprise.

Carmelo di Mazzarelli's performance as Spiro/Michele is the sort of miracle possible only in films. No one would choose an eighty-year-old fisherman for such a role in the theater, particularly if he had not even come looking for it. Amelio saw Mazzarelli in a Sicilian harbor. Only after he recruited him did Amelio learn that the old man had in fact been in the Italian army in Albania. The piecemeal procedures of film make such casting of complete amateurs possible—in the right hands. (Look at the leading role in De Sica's *The Bicycle Thief*.) Some part of Amelio's success with Mazzarelli must be directorial shrewdness; some of it sheer empathy—helped, I'd guess, because Amelio is a southern Italian who has worked in Sicily and presumably understands the old man's dialect. Anyway, the result is an oaken monument to stoicism, a life that has reduced suffering to taciturnity.

As director, Amelio looks for the shot that speaks silently: the crowd in the café watching the Italian TV program that they can't understand; the young man sitting on the floor of a jammed truck who doesn't ask for help although he's dying; the little girl in the hotel-barracks who has mastered disco dancing and is frenzied with it. Children, in fact, scurry throughout the film. Amelio uses hordes of them as if they were pestiferous insects. They cluster around Gino, brazenly begging and stealing; at one point they very nearly kill old Michele for his clothes. Amelio spares us nothing of their smiling malevolence because he expects us to understand its roots, which we do.

Much Ado about Nothing

MAY 10, 1993 | Silence. Black screen. Three words appear—"Sigh no more," the opening of the lovely song in the play. The rest of the words then follow, and Emma Thompson's voice begins to speak them. The film cuts to a glorious Tuscan hillside, with a picnic of ladies and a few old men spread upon it and with Thompson, nestled in a tree, reading the song from a book.

As she finishes, a messenger arrives to report that Don Pedro and friends are returning from the wars. Then far below we see a group of galloping riders. Patrick Doyle's score surges in. The ladies rush to bathe and prepare. Under the opening titles, the horsemen arrive and plunge into *their* baths. And Kenneth Branagh's film of *Much Ado about Nothing* is off to a marvelous start.

If Branagh accomplishes nothing better in his film-directing career—and why shouldn't he do more?—his *Henry V* and *Much Ado* will lodge him securely in the world's gratitude. *Much Ado,* for reasons given below, is not quite up to the level of *Henry,* but once again Branagh has adapted Shakespeare dexterously. Once again he has followed Granville Barker's advice about pace in Shakespeare, understanding that the essence of pace is not speed but energy. Once again he has excellent colleagues off-camera, most notably Doyle, that open-throated composer, and the editor Andrew Marcus, who knows how to tip in glimpses of others to give dialogues a balletic lift. Once again Branagh has his attractive self on screen. Once again—and may I live to type these words a hundred times more—there is Emma Thompson.

Much Ado, as many have noted, is a peculiar play. First, there's the title. It's both a modest shrug of the author at his own brilliance and an Elizabethan joke. "Nothing" was probably pronounced "noting," which was a synonym for eavesdropping. But the chief problem is that the two most interesting characters are only marginally in the main plot. That plot is about the Claudio–Hero–Don John tangle, which is less interesting.

Shakespeare began (we can imagine) with a woman and a man, Beatrice and Benedick, who duel verbally because they enjoy their antagonism and tacitly respect each other for it; and whose façade of mutual dislike is cracked by scheming friends so that the pair are forced to confess their love for each other. But if the author had left it at that, the play would have been less than half as long as it needed to be for his theater.

So, to fill it out, he adapted a plot from several previous works about a maiden, a cousin of Beatrice, falsely accused of lewdness. He interwove it with the Beatrice-Benedick story, using the false-identity device that he later used in *Othello,* adding the dead-woman-returned-to-life idea that he used again in *The Winter's Tale,* and working in some bits with a comic constable whose stupidity delays the truth about the maiden. Thus he put together a full-length entertainment for the Globe Theater.

But, in one sense, to no avail. The interesting characters are still Beatrice and Benedick. (Which is why Berlioz called his opera by their names.) In any production those two performances must carry the play; and in this film, the two performances are, in quite different ways, absolutely scintillating. Branagh is feisty, persistent, lucid, completely taking. The one thing he is not is elegant: he has few traces of a Renaissance gentleman. But he has the magical ability to blend a modern-day persona with consummate ease in Shakespearean language and action.

As for Thompson . . . . I'll try to restrain myself. She *has* elegance. She has the finest command of inflection and style. She has spirit and soul. She is the first film actress since Katharine Hepburn to make intelligence sexy. She lets us understand that Beatrice, much like Kate in *The Taming of the Shrew,* behaves as she does because she is employing the only means available to break out of the expected pattern—daddy's girl up for marital auction.

Thompson's Beatrice implies that, much as she loves her cousin Hero, the maligned virgin, she couldn't possibly behave in Hero's docile, male-determined way. She makes herself thorny to the man she wants, and she does it gaily. When Thompson says, "Then there was a star danced, and under that was I born," we can see galaxies wheeling.

There's more. After Hero's erstwhile fiancé, Claudio, has excoriated her (and we know she's innocent), Benedick asks the shocked Beatrice, loyal to her cousin, what he can do for her. Thompson then speaks the two words with which Ellen Terry is said to have stabbed the audience with ice: "Kill Claudio." Ellen, thou shouldst be living at this hour—to hear Emma.

The entire play/film, dark strands and all, is enclosed in an atmosphere of celebration, a festival for returning warriors. This festive air is well dramatized in Phyllis Dalton's summery costumes: most of the women's dresses and men's uniforms are off-white. Many of the actors, too, "furnish" the screen appealingly: Kate Beckinsale as the pretty puppet Hero, Richard Briers as her father, Brian Blessed as his brother, Imelda Staunton as Hero's attendant who is unknowingly used to entrap her mistress.

But there are four lapses in the casting, three unfortunate and one dire. All are American. Robert Sean Leonard, squint-eyed, plays Claudio not quite tolerably—pale both in love and in hate. Keanu Reeves, as the villainous Don John, knows all his lines and speaks them clearly and gives the sort of performance that makes parents beam at college productions.

Denzel Washington plays the prince of the returning warriors. I was advocating colorblind casting some thirty years ago, always with the proviso that a black actor in a white role should demonstrate by talent that the producer would have been misguided not to use him or her. That was in the theater. The proviso, for obvious reasons, is even more pressing in film. Washington is barely adequate, with little of the princely bearing that he showed in *Malcolm X*.

The disaster is Michael Keaton as Dogberry. I simply have no idea of what he was doing, what person he was trying to play. His painful performance proves yet again that Shakespeare's low-comedy characters need clowns, actors who are funny in themselves before they begin their parts.

Someone like Joe Pesci might possibly have had the shtick to do the thick-headed constable. But Keaton is just a straight actor, sweatily trying to be funny — with muggings, long pauses and an ire that may be meant as comic but seems Keaton's attempt to hide the fear that he is failing.

What was the reason for the casting of these Americans? Was it to "internationalize" the film, as a bow to the coproducers, American Playhouse? If so, it was self-evidently shortsighted. We could have seen the forest better without those four trees.

It's hardly a minor defect — four misjudged pieces of casting in prominent roles. But Branagh and Thompson and sixteen other actors, Doyle's enrapturing music and Branagh's cinematic grip of the play — inventive, lithe, somehow *Shakespearean* — are splendid. This *Much Ado* is a flawed gem. Certainly, regrettably, flawed; still, a gem.

JULY 19 & 26, 1993 | In recent weeks, whenever I've been feeling cloudy, a thought has come to cheer me up. Kenneth Branagh exists. Not only has he changed my formerly fixed conviction that Shakespeare cannot be filmed, he has made me happy at having my mind changed.

Now a book arrives — his second, in a way. (The first, a pro-tem autobiography called *Beginning,* is good reading.) This is a tie-in volume with the film of *Much Ado about Nothing.* It contains the screenplay, a congenial introduction by Branagh (including a witty letter from Lewis Carroll to Ellen Terry about the Hero-calumny plot), thirty-two pages of color photos and some production shots. The book sent me back to see the film again.

It's even better than I remembered. (However, the colors in the theater print seemed less vivid than those in the print at the press screening.) A few small changes or additions of opinion. It's now even more clear that Branagh's astonishing energy—as actor-director—makes him the Atlas on whom this world rests. As for Emma Thompson, I watched her carefully in the scenes where she's only an onlooker and saw how thoroughly she stays *in* a scene without mugging.

Two previously underprized performances: Phyllida Law (Thompson's mother), a woman in waiting; Jimmy Yuill, the friar on whose clarity much depends. If there's such a thing as an increase of blandness, Keanu Reeves and Robert Sean Leonard exemplify it the second time round. Denzel Washington seemed a bit more princely this time yet is not quite up to what he might have done. Michael Keaton is unchanged—still abominable. (Branagh's apologia for Keaton in his introduction cuts no ice.)

Under, beyond and above all is the way that Branagh's direction links the film to what might be called the Shakespearean motion. As does the play, as do almost all of Shakespeare's plays, the film seems to unroll and unroll and unroll, leading us on and on. One doesn't often cry for pleasure at a film. It happened here.

Anachronism Note. Bruce T. Johnson of Mill Valley, California, an admirer of this film, writes to point out two slips. He wonders whether Benedick could have had a lawn chair in Renaissance Italy but is willing to overlook the matter "since Shakespeare himself is guilty of harmless anachronisms." I agree: clocks in ancient Rome, for instance. Then Johnson adds that, early in the film, "we see the women of the estate stripping for their baths. There's a very quick rear view of a deeply tanned extra with a pale white triangle on her backside, clearly the imprint of a bikini bottom." I missed it. My mind was on higher things.

Hamlet

JANUARY 27, 1997 | Kenneth Branagh wins two victories in *Hamlet*. He has made a vital, exciting film; and he has triumphed over the obstacles he put in his own way.

Let's first rejoice in the virtues. Branagh confirms what was known from the opening shot of *Henry V:* he has fine cinematic skills. His directing keeps *Hamlet* flowing, endows scenes that might become static with germane movement. Many of his touches illuminate. One of them: Hamlet comes into a huge mirrored room in the palace, sees himself full-length and, after a moment, begins "To be or not to be." Two selves speak that speech and give it an added edge.

Then there's the text itself. Branagh has used the complete First Folio text and has included a scene from the Second Quarto that is not in the Folio, to make a film that runs four hours plus intermission. I could find only a few alterations, trifles compared with the chopped, twisted, insulting text that Olivier used in his 155-minute version. Branagh's film looks splendid. He sets it in the mid-nineteenth century—with Blenheim Palace serving as the exterior of Elsinore—and Alex Byrne's costumes fully exploit the period. The cinematographer, Alex Thomson, using 70-mm wide-screen format, has nonetheless created lighting that seems naturally evolved from the hundreds of candles. And as for the music, Patrick Doyle again does wonders. He wrote the scores for Branagh's two previous Shakespeare films, and here again he provides music that rises unobtrusively to benefit scene after scene.

Every supporting role of significance has been superbly cast. I can't imagine a better Claudius than Derek Jacobi, who brings to it force and cunning and manipulative charm. The sequences in which he converts the furious Laertes from enemy to accomplice are masterpieces of guile manifested as honesty. (Jacobi, by the way, was the first Hamlet that Branagh ever saw; and years later Jacobi directed Branagh in a theater production.)

Jacobi is no surprise: Julie Christie is. This Golden Girl of the 1960s virtually disappeared for a while, then reappeared in a London production of Pinter's *Old Times*. She was so dull that I thought she was being used just for her name. But here, as Gertrude, she is emotionally rich. She brings to the role the apt quality of overblown sex object, and, presumably with Branagh's help, she completely fulfills the woman. In Gertrude's key moment, the closet scene, Christie bursts with the frightened despair of a guilty woman who thinks that her behavior may have driven her son mad.

Kate Winslet, dear to us already through *Sense and Sensibility* and *Jude,* gives Ophelia the kind of vulnerability that almost invites the man she loves to wound her. Polonius gets the obtuse officiousness that he needs from Richard Briers. It's immediately clear why Horatio, done by Nicholas Farrell, is Hamlet's dearest friend: anybody would want him for a friend. Laertes, a role always in danger of being as much of a blowhard as his father, Polonius, is realized in his confusions by Michael Maloney. Branagh, as he did in *Much Ado about Nothing,* has sprinkled some American actors through his cast. The best of these is Charlton Heston as the Player King, sounding and (even) looking plummy, home at last.

Hamlet is unique in Shakespeare. I can think of no other role in the plays in which an actor is so compelled, commanded, to present *himself.* Macbeth, Othello, Iago, the Richards and the Henrys—run through the roster, and always the actor selects and nurtures what there is in his imagination and experience and technique that will make the man come alive. No such selections for Hamlet. The whole actor is the whole character. So, when we see a Hamlet, we are looking at an actor in a unique way.

Branagh's Hamlet—or, one might say, Hamlet's Branagh—is attractive, keen, nobly intended, tender with regret for Ophelia, torn with disgust for the chicaneries of the world, fiery, quite susceptible to cracking into frenzy. (In appearance, he is fair—not Olivier's platinum blond— with a somewhat darker moustache and goatee.)

This is a man we could meet and understand. What this Hamlet lacks is what possibly we could not understand: his sense of falling upward into the metaphysical. This is what is sometimes called the "poetic" nature of Hamlet, this linkage with a spirit walking the earth in quest of purgation; and this linkage, in mystery and awe and uncertainty, leads to what Granville Barker called "a tragedy of inaction." Branagh's Hamlet doesn't attain this quality: it doesn't quite seem to be in him. Not long ago Ralph Fiennes, burdened with an unworthy director and cast, nevertheless did a Hamlet on Broadway that took us out into the spheres. Not Branagh. Every word he speaks is true. But in Hamlet that is not quite enough.

Now the lesser aspects of the film. First, the obverse side of Branagh's directing skill. He is too eager for spectacle, even if it's pointless or harmful. When Gertrude and Claudius exit at the end of the first court scene, confetti rains down on them. For the moment, it's startling, pretty. Then we wonder who planned it and who threw it. Answer: the director. When the Ghost speaks to Hamlet, the earth splits and flames leap. Is this God overseeing unpurged souls? Or the special effects department? Rosencrantz and Guildenstern arrive on a toy locomotive. Who put that model train and tracks on the palace grounds? Old King Hamlet? Claudius? Or the director? When Hamlet and Laertes duel, the civilized sport explodes into Errol Flynn antics, with ropes and chandeliers—another directorial intrusion. Branagh sets the whole film in winter, which allows for some breathtaking vistas but makes us wonder why the old king was sleeping outdoors in his snow-covered orchard on the afternoon of his murder and how the brookside flowers could be present when Ophelia drowns.

Another obverse side, one that may sound odd: the use of the complete text. Admirable though it is in Branagh to aim at "classic" status, not every word is helpful today, especially in a film. To hear Marcellus discourse on "the bird of dawning" at Christmastime, just after the Ghost's second appearance, is a soft indulgence in Elizabethan folklore. To hear Gertrude include a small dirty joke, about "long purples," when she tells Laertes of his sister's death is to coddle the lad from Stratford who couldn't always keep rustic humor out of his plays. And the sad fact is that, when Shakespeare takes time out from drama for moral commentary, the result is sometimes mere homiletics. Hamlet's speech about "the dram of evil" is not only a brusque lapse in the action, it captures perfectly the quality in Shakespeare that Bernard Shaw called "the atmosphere of the rented pew."

Sex. Branagh has searched for chances to get it into the film. While Polonius is warning Ophelia to be careful in her behavior with Hamlet, to avoid the prince completely, Branagh includes flashback shots of her and Hamlet naked in bed together. Presumably Branagh takes his license from the bawdy song that Ophelia later sings when she is mad—"Young men will do't if they come to't," etc.—a song that is usually viewed as the raving of a sexually repressed virgin. Whether or not Hamlet and Ophelia actually had an affair is possibly arguable, but what seems clear is that, if they have made love, it detracts considerably from the fierce, Savonarola-like outburst of the "get thee to a nunnery" passages.

Then, too, Polonius is given a visiting whore in the scene with Reynaldo, who is apparently her pimp. (Ophelia bursts in without knocking—fortuitously, just after Reynaldo and the whore leave.) Branagh's purpose is to lend irony to the old man's instructions to Reynaldo, about checking on Laertes's behavior in Paris, but the episode smacks of opportunism.

Politics. Of course *Hamlet* is, among other elements, a political play. One cause for Hamlet's hatred of Claudius is that his uncle has "popp'd in between th'election and my hopes." Branagh's use of the mid-century period affords the ambiance of the "Age of Metternich," but it misplaces in time the Denmark–England–Norway–Poland relationships of the original. Further, Branagh distorts the political action of the closing scenes. Early in the play we learn that the young Fortinbras of Norway wants to reconquer some lands that his country lost to Denmark, but the Norwegian king dissuades him. Fortinbras swears never to attack Denmark, but he will ask for the right of passage through Denmark to attack Poland. Toward the end of the play Fortinbras leads an army into Denmark and sends a messenger to Claudius to ask for that right of passage.

Incomprehensibly, in Branagh's film, Fortinbras then attacks Elsinore. (Real reason: Branagh wants to heat up the film's closing moments.) Shots of this violence are intercut with the Hamlet-Laertes duel. Just as Hamlet dies, the Norwegian soldiers burst into the court, destroying as they come. Fortinbras ought to feel a bit foolish, not only having broken his word but to find out that, just before Hamlet expired, the prince named him as his successor. ("He has my dying voice.") Instead, Fortinbras is shown as a glowering conqueror moderately disturbed by the prince's death. The very last shot is of old King Hamlet's statue being toppled and smashed. Why did Branagh choose that shot as the moment toward which the entire film moved?

Some other points might be called matters of interpretation—Claudius's slapping of Hamlet in anger at the chaffing about Polonius's corpse, the straitjacketing of Ophelia in a padded cell—but one Branagh touch seems just plain misreading. Claudius (in Act III, Scene 1) says he has "closely sent for Hamlet" so that the prince can meet Ophelia while Claudius and Polonius are hidden and watching. They do hide. Hamlet enters, finds the chamber empty though he has been sent for, muses aloud while waiting ("To be or not to be"). Then Ophelia enters—the girl who, for days, has been forbidden to see him. And it was the king who summoned him here. Surely, in simple reason, Hamlet must be suspicious that this is a set-up from the moment she appears. Instead, Branagh plays it merely petulantly until, after the nunnery speech, he hears a noise behind the door and the deception dawns on him. Branagh's treatment not only makes Hamlet less acute than we are, it takes the bite out of "Are you honest?"

Interpretations and innovations have different weights in a Shakespeare film from such matters in a theater production. When I saw Ingmar Bergman's production of *Hamlet,* with his sluttish Ophelia wandering through scenes in which Shakespeare forgot to include her, I was relieved that Bergman had not filmed it. Branagh's film, warts and all, will be with us for some time to come.

On the whole, this is good news. Though his *Henry V* and *Much Ado about Nothing* were closer to perfection, *Hamlet* is more difficult in every way. Flaws, problems, bumps, yes; but the film surpasses them finally through Branagh's talent and the talents of his colleagues. And, not to be slighted, there is Branagh's infectious joy—the right word even for *Hamlet*—in doing Shakespeare.

The Story of Qiu Ju

MAY 17, 1993 | What do Idrissa Ouedraogo, Ousmane Sembène and Zhang Yimou have in common? Each is a highly gifted filmmaker who in his own country—Burkina Faso, Senegal and China respectively—deals with the culture that he knows. Each is aware that his films will be exported, but in an intrinsic sense, none of them makes films for export.

Yet each film by these directors is two films: one that his country will see and one that is seen abroad. This is of course true of French or Finnish or, to us, any other foreign films, but the wider the cultural-social differences between the country of origin and the United States, the more binary the film becomes. Each of the directors above may be amused or offended—he certainly can't be surprised—to realize that, after he has invested so much of art in a work, its first function elsewhere is as a superior travelogue.

Zhang's latest, *The Story of Qiu Ju,* is a sharp case in point because it's his first contemporary picture to reach us. (*Ju Dou* and others were period pieces.) So social contrasts are more striking. *Qiu Ju* is based on a novel called *The Wan Family's Lawsuit,* a much more pertinent title, and is set in Shaanxi province during the winter. A sturdy young peasant woman, Qiu Ju, fights for justice. Her husband was kicked in the groin in a quarrel with the political chief of their village. His quest for justice falters, but Qiu Ju persists in carrying the complaint to higher and higher officials, finally to court.

This pursuit entails arduous travel, to towns, to a bustling modern city, all of which Qiu Ju, seven months pregnant at the start of the story, undertakes with her sister's help. At the end she and her husband get justice, somewhat more than they want.

Now whatever else this picture accomplishes—and the "else" isn't very much—it's a fascinating account of the lives and customs, the dailyness, of all the people in it. More: after our first visit to the chief's house or to the city, our return has the effect of a ballad, with cumulative verses about survival in a cold climate, troubles in traveling, finaglings of bureaucrats and stubborn courage. But without this ballad-documentary quality, would the film hold? If the film were set in, say, Arkansas, the exotic elements would be much thinner and the story might soon pall.

Yet Zhang was not counting on the strangeness of Shaanxi abroad, no matter how much this may help him with us. His talent, never remarkable in narrative or drama, is manifest in sheer cinema. He frames lovely pictures without self-consciousness. He edits succinctly. He states themes quietly: under the opening credits, crowds stream past us on a city street; then Qiu Ju and family emerge from that flood like flotsam snagged on the bank. Out of the billion-footed mass, says Zhang, here are a few individuals whose story we'll follow. We might have followed any of the others, whose story might be just as interesting.

Gong Li, usually the leading woman in Zhang's films, plays Qiu Ju (all but two of the others in the cast are nonprofessionals), and once again she acts principally with her mind. Her attractive, blunt-cheeked face rarely changes expression; but through the pauses for thought and decision, and her quick actions after the pauses, she tells us what Qiu Ju has been feeling and thinking. And she does it with tenacity and humor.

After all, a kick in the groin—not, heaven knows, in itself but as a cause for legal action—has its funny side. (Near the beginning she tells her husband, "If we can't fix your plumbing, we're stuck with the single-child policy for good.") And before the film is half along, she has us chuckling at her terrier grip on the trouser-leg of Communist authority, more concerned about her husband's cause than he is.

It's obviously to the good that Zhang doesn't consider that he's making a documentary when he works, but, for us, it's also to the good that his film's fictional art brings documentary benefits along.

OCTOBER 25, 1993 | Nine of Raymond Carver's stories and one of his poems are *not* transferred to the screen in *Short Cuts*. Robert Altman, who directed and cowrote the screenplay with Frank Barhydt, is quite explicit about that. Altman says, "I look at all of Carver's work as just one story, for his stories are all occurrences, all about things that just happen to people and cause their lives to take a turn." This was not an offhand remark: it's in his introduction to a special edition of those stories and that poem. Licensed by this odd view — on the same ground, all of Dickens's novels are just one novel, etc., etc. — he has boiled the original material into what he calls elsewhere "Carver soup."

But he doesn't serve it. With little more than a Carver aroma in the air, he serves up his own 189-minute offering. This offering — let's put food metaphors aside — is structured much like *Nashville* (1975). Set in Los Angeles, *Short Cuts* tells nine stories involving twenty-three people and presents them in intermingled form. Before very long, we're aware that we're meant to be impressed more by the dexterous mingling than by the stories themselves. The fates of most of these characters seem of less concern to Altman than his cinematic virtuosity. In some ways he certainly displays this virtuosity, but over the whole (intended) dazzle looms the figure of Altman the Devourer.

Carver admirers will recognize the antecedents of the film's narratives. A couple order a birthday cake for their small son who is then killed by a car ("A Small, Good Thing"); a man goes on a fishing trip with some pals and later reports to his wife that a woman's body was in the water upstream the whole time ("So Much Water Close to Home"); a man takes out the pesty family dog and deliberately loses it ("Jerry and Molly and Sam"): these are some of them. All of them have been altered — not, alas, beyond recognition: just to the point where they are still recognizable. One of the film stories — about a fading jazz club singer and her sensitive cellist daughter — is original, contrived by Altman and Barhydt in their idea of the Carver mode.

But there's no point in indicting Altman for changing Carver: he has already pleaded both guilty and not guilty, the latter because he made the changes in aid of his own art. Well, how far has he aided his art? Let's note at once that some moments in *Short Cuts* strike home. The scene between the parents of the dead boy and the baker of the birthday cake is quietly moving, as the irritated baker learns why the cake was not picked up. Bonds between two married sisters—in which, without saying much, they laugh together about some sexual matters—have insight and charm. A reconciliation between a bullied hash-house waitress and her boozy husband is an oasis in the midst of grunge.

Some of the filmic devices spin the several narratives along. At the start, for instance, helicopters fly over nighttime L.A. and environs, spraying insecticide against the medfly. The film cuts from the 'copters to the beginning of Story A, then back to the 'copters, then to the beginning of Story B, then back to the 'copters and so on, as the spraying itself evokes reactions from the residents of each story and helps to get them going. (No matter that the device is a reminder of the opening of *La Dolce Vita:* Altman invisibly tips his hat to Fellini with thanks for the assist.) Throughout the film, its parts click into place.

Still, the clicks sometimes obtrude. Just after the fisherman-husband tells his wife that the woman in the stream was dead, we cut to the young mother of the just-expired boy. Sometimes the Altman of *McCabe and Mrs. Miller* shows his italicizing hand: when two unhappy couples settle down for a drunken barbecue and game-playing, we get a close-up of the game they will play—a box marked Jeopardy. When the dead boy's grandfather leaves the hospital, he walks past an attendant who is—so significantly— mopping up. And for all his deftness, Altman sometimes seems foxed by the wide screen he's using. That's when we get immense close-ups, plunked right in the center—utter visual banality.

And after the film traverses its three hours and ten minutes, what *is* it? Well, we can say fancifully that if there had been no Raymond Carver, *Short Cuts* might look much better. (The same fancy would help lots of films: if there had been no Nabokov, Kubrick's *Lolita* would be first rate.) But when significant literary antecedents are involved, comparisons with their film versions must press on us—if not for complete fidelity of detail then certainly for similarity of tone.

Carver's pervasive quality, under his terse style, is compassion. He sees ordinary twentieth-century Americans battling circumstance, and he sees the odds against them. The struggle is not so much with the specifics in any one story: it's a profound struggle for purpose and relief, though they are strapped to the harshness of our times. Carver's people have their visions deepened by small epiphanies: a couple, apartment-sitting for neighbors, tries on the figurative garments of another life; a wife discovers things about herself when her fisherman-husband tells her that he managed to ignore a body for a few days. Not all of the stories depict large crises; sometimes it's the very smallness of the event that shows how easy it is to split lives to the core.

In Altman, however, compassion extends only to plainly terrible moments, such as death. Most of the time, unlike Carver, he merely observes, often satirically. In addition, he misses no chance to exploit sex. Sex is very present in Carver, but generally it's treated as a constant unfathomable mystery in otherwise prosaic lives. Altman seizes every sexual moment to move from mystery to flaunting. Often it's not amplification of Carver, it's invention. He gives one of Carver's characters a wife who earns money doing telephone sex while holding a small child on her lap. It's the kind of smirk that Altman knows he can't be reproved for in these liberated times.

Probably the worst aspect of *Short Cuts,* vis-à-vis Carver, is the most successful of the film devices—the interweaving of the stories. One of Carver's best attributes is his sense of form, and that form can be seen only when the story stands alone. To read a Carver collection is to walk through a gallery of beautifully formed objects. To blend his stories into "soup," no matter how smartly, to see them "as just one story," is to vandalize good art, to rationalize filmic opportunism as aesthetic principle.

Two of the actors in the large cast are unbearable. Robert Downey Jr., playing a Hollywood make-up artist who specializes in horror effects, patently sees himself as floating on a sea of hip appeal. He sinks. Jack Lemmon plays the grandfather of the dying boy; Altman and Barhydt haul him into the hospital on thin pretext and then give him a fat monologue. It's about the long-ago infidelity that wrecked his marriage, and he tells it to his son who at that moment is more concerned with his own son. The whole part is a vulgar concept, and Lemmon acts it accordingly.

Almost all the others fill their parts to bursting. The women are especially vivid: Madeleine Stowe as a harried and betrayed wife, Jennifer Jason Leigh as the telephone-sex mom, Andie MacDowell as the mother of the dying boy, Julianne Moore as the artist-wife of a jealous husband, Anne Archer as a woman who supports her unemployed spouse by clowning at children's parties, are all outstanding.

But the humanity with which they fill their roles can't prevail against the fact that they are trapped in Altman's gimmicky stories and that the sheer quantity of those stories is supposed to distract us from their quality. Throughout the film, the feeling grows that these good actors are merely being exploited by the director; the object of the film is not empathy but his self-celebration. All the nominal subjects—agony, affection, passion, hate, remorse—are finally congealed by Altman's mechanistic cleverness.

It's All True

NOVEMBER 15, 1993 | Another sadness about Orson Welles. *It's All True* is a documentary about *It's All True,* the three-part film on Latin American subjects that Welles started in 1941. This assemblage contains all that is left of the project—footage rediscovered in 1985—introduced and concluded by excerpts from interviews with Welles at various points in his life, along with the comments of still-surviving people who are in the Brazilian segments or were concerned with them. All in all, we see what was attempted and how it was blocked.

Welles went into the project at the behest of the State Department, which, in those early years of World War II, wanted to enhance relations with Latin America and decided that a film by the newly emerged American wunderkind would help. *Citizen Kane* had recently appeared; *The Magnificent Ambersons* was being concluded; Welles was producing *Journey into Fear,* in which he performed, directed by his friend Norman Foster.

As a condition of accepting the Latin American venture, Welles got a promise from his studio, RKO, that they would send his editor and the *Ambersons* footage to Rio de Janeiro so that he could work on it there while making *It's All True.* This promise was broken. (*Ambersons,* magnificently directed, had its ending deformed in other hands.) Power shifted at RKO; the new president left Welles stranded in Rio with almost no money or equipment. He did what he could, came home and found that the whole matter had been taken out of his control.

For years he tried to get possession of the footage and edit it, but it never happened. The footage was presumed lost (so, naturally, every time it was mentioned in absentia, it was exalted). Then in 1985 it was discovered—what was left of it, anyway—and after more tribulations, this new film arrives, encasing it.

We'll never know what (the original) *It's All True* might have been in Welles's hands, and it's certainly some sort of sin against art that his hands were slapped away from the project. But though he might have edited this footage more subtly, with a keener sense of rhythm, he couldn't have improved the footage itself in the editing room. What we get here are not remotely the bits and pieces of an aborted masterpiece. The completed work might have served the State Department's purposes vis-à-vis Latin America, but there is almost no trace here of the Welles who preceded or came after it (except that the influence of Eisenstein, apparent here, continued).

The first section, "My Friend Bonito," is about a Mexican boy and a bull. It was directed by Foster; Welles supervised, mostly from afar, and was going to edit it. It's a commonplace piece of sentiment, photographed in what can be called Latino Luxe—lots of low angles shooting upward to monumentalize humble folk, faces against the sky, long shots of small figures against low-hanging clouds, all rendered in velvety blacks and dulled whites. It's the texture that was employed earlier by Eisenstein in *Que Viva Mexico!* (another "lost masterpiece") and by Paul Strand in *The Wave*.

Welles used it again in the second segment here, "Four Men on a Raft," which he directed. It recounts the actual story of four fishermen from northeastern Brazil who had traveled by raft down the coast to Rio to present protests to the government. The third segment was to be "The Story of Samba," the Brazilian dance and music that captivated Welles. In a Rio studio he re-created the February *carnaval* (later memorably used in Marcel Camus's *Black Orpheus*); he sometimes gives it Dionysian heat but it is mostly predictable stuff.

The sadness mentioned earlier is less about the uncompleted film than about the uncompleted man. Such a fine frenzy of energy surrounds this Latin American project—so much that he was doing, so much that he was planning. This new film is a poignant reminder of the force of the Welles explosion in the performing arts. Thus it's a reminder, too, that, for a complex of reasons, this force never truly fulfilled itself. What a blessing it might have been for American theater and film if this lively, imperious genius had flowered to the fullest.

Schindler's List

DECEMBER 13, 1993 | Steven Spielberg has made his own Holocaust museum. In *Schindler's List,* an adaptation by Steven Zaillian of Thomas Keneally's book, Spielberg has created a 184-minute account of the fate of Kraków's Jews under the German occupation, centered on the German businessman and bon vivant, Oskar Schindler, who devised a ruse to save 1,100 Jews from the Auschwitz ovens. A closing note tells us that in Poland today there are fewer than 4,000 Jews but in the world there are 6,000 "Schindler Jews," survivors and descendants.

For this film Spielberg has done the best directing of his career. Much of his previous work has been clever and some of it better than that, but *Schindler's List* is masterly. He has, with appropriate restraint, shot it in black and white (except for two closing sequences in color). Janusz Kaminski's superb cinematography uses shadows like prosody—*illuminates* with shadows. Michael Kahn has edited with intensity and line, never breathless, always fast. (One demurral: the intercutting between a Jewish wedding in a camp, a wild German officers' party and a German officer's boudoir romp is heavy.) John Williams has arranged a score, with Itzhak Perlman doing violin solos, that for the most part is quiet: Jewish melodies on woodwinds or a small children's chorus under scenes of inhumanity.

Liam Neeson plays—no, inhabits—Schindler with the authority of a roundvoiced, juggernaut con man. Neeson bears himself like a Middle European, a comment I can't quite explain but that may be understood by many. He drives forward like a sensualist whose pleasures are food, drink, women and money. And Ben Kingsley—O rare Ben Kingsley!—is the Jewish accountant whom Schindler plucks from a condemned group to run his business and who combines gratitude with disdain, subservience with pride. (Actors who want to study the basis of acting—concentration—should watch Kingsley.)

Spielberg has not used one trite shot, one cheap tear-jerking assemblage. Tears are evoked, but honorably; his aim was to make a film that gripped us with authenticity. To this end he often uses newsreel angles and newsreel cutting. Yet he is not hand-held-camera nutty: where a panorama is needed—Jews in a long street assembling for deportation, Jews in a (seemingly) mile-wide file coming over a great field toward liberation—he understands how to present it and leave it alone. (Most of this picture was filmed in Poland.) Imagination, talent, commitment shine in every frame.

Now come two dreadful words: and yet. Is there a need for another film about the Holocaust? Especially after *Shoah?* Presumably there are at least some people who have never seen a Holocaust film and may see this one because it's by Spielberg and will have mainstream promotion. Let's hope there are many such.

But others may be aware of two bothersome connected points. Both of them demonstrate yet again how good work can be victimized by previous work, good or less good, on the same subject. First, the German commander, played by Ralph Fiennes, though based on fact, is by now something of a film cliché—smooth, cultivated, monstrous. Second, the film takes about two hours to reach the event that the title promises, Schindler's (not quite predictable) rescue operation. Everything up to then, vigorously done though it is, is—in two senses—terribly familiar.

Still, this film is a welcome astonishment from a director who has given us much boyish esprit, much ingenuity, but little seriousness. His stark, intelligent style here, perfectly controlled, suggests that this may be the start of a new period in Spielberg's prodigious career—Part Two: The Man.

JANUARY 24, 1994 | If a film has genuine worth, it's more than one film. It changes with further viewings. The second time you see it, it's larger. This time you aren't "distracted" by the story, by discovering what happens next. You can concentrate on the qualities that made you want to see it again, usually acting or felicities of vision or both. (Third and later viewings—of especially fine films—have an even stranger effect: as you learn more about them, you simultaneously feel you're seeing them for the first time. This happened to me recently with *Grand Illusion* and *Citizen Kane,* each of which I've seen upward of thirty times. Though I now saw even more in them, I had a feeling of fresh arrival.)

I don't know how many times I'll see *Schindler's List,* but ever since my first viewing, I've known that I wanted to see it again, soon. For two kinds of reasons. First, personal. I'd expressed concern that people who know something about the Holocaust might find the earlier portions—ghetto enclosure and labor camps—overly familiar. Well, I know something about the Holocaust, and I wanted to examine more carefully what had happened to me, what might happen again, while watching the film. This second time, I was again so taken by Spielberg's insistent honesty, by the heightened factuality, that I saw how my familiarity *helped,* made the film a confirmation and a deepening.

Then there were sheerly cinematic reasons. I wanted to see the "second" film; and throughout, I noted subtle compositions, astringent editing, overall vigor of construction that had certainly affected me the first time—I had thought it superbly made—but now seemed even more astonishingly fine.

But with the second viewing of *Schindler's List,* some other things became clear. The film rests on two large motions of change, one within the film and one, so to speak, behind it. The first is Schindler's metamorphosis, from hustling opportunist to self-disregarding savior. Some viewers have objected that Spielberg and his screenwriter, Steven Zaillian, didn't articulate the change vividly enough; but to have done more would have been to tamper with history. Thomas Keneally, from whose book the film derives, is specific about the unspecificity:

> One of the commonest sentiments of Schindler Jews is still "I don't know why he did it." It can be said to begin with that Oskar was a gambler, was a sentimentalist who loved the transparency, the simplicity of doing good; that Oskar was by temperament an anarchist who loved to ridicule the system; and that beneath the hearty sensuality lay a capacity to be outraged by human savagery, to react to it and not to be overwhelmed. But none of this, jotted down, added up, explains the doggedness with which, in the autumn of 1944, he prepared a final haven for [the Jews who worked in his Kraków factory].

Recurrently, beginning in the middle of the film, we see Schindler being shocked beneath his poise by the blacker and blacker wolfishness of the Nazis whose party pin he wears. But never is there a Moment of Truth, together with an angelic choir on the sound track. Spielberg's artistic triumph here is that he refuses to explicate, to interfere with what is actually known. He leaves the mystery of Schindler's goodness as finally inexplicable as the mystery of the "human savagery" around him. (This, for me, is the true subject of the film.)

There's another instance of this avoidance of italics. Near the end, when Schindler assembles his 1,100 Jewish workers on his plant floor to tell them that the war is over and they are free, the German army guards, fully armed, assemble on a sort of balcony above. Schindler addresses the guards: says he knows that they have orders to liquidate his workers; and asks them whether they want to go home as men or as murderers. After a moment's pause, one of the soldiers leaves—and is soon followed by the others. Spielberg's exquisite touch is that he never shows the face of this first soldier, no twitching, no making up his mind; after the pause we simply see the soldier pass the camera. Yes, we soon see the guards' commander wavering in decision, but he had become a character who needs finishing off. The bellwether soldier is a particle of history.

The second major change is the metamorphosis of Spielberg himself. It's not possible to compare the horror itself with a film about it; still, we might venture to compare the effect of the Holocaust on Schindler with the effect of knowledge of the Holocaust on Spielberg. We know from much recent interviewing that the Holocaust has long been a presence for him (as it was with Schindler) but how he has concentrated for the most part on ingenious commerce (as did Schindler). Then (again like Schindler) the force of the horror burst through to alter him.

How is that alteration manifested? Initially, with the choice of subject. Still, the filmmaking might have been Spielberg-clever. All the cleverness was renounced. Among the new powerful austerities, including the use of black and white, two elements stand out as warrants of gravity. First, the faces. Face after Jewish face appears, most of them only once, and each of those faces is a testament. By filming in Poland, Spielberg was able to use faces engraved with knowledge, inheritors of grief, that certify and magnify his story. Though they are faces of our contemporaries, they are nonetheless faces of the past.

The best compliment to Liam Neeson, the Schindler, and Ben Kingsley, the Jewish accountant, is that they don't obtrude as actors. Their faces fit. This is also true of Embeth Davidtz, as Helena, the camp inmate selected by the Nazi commandant to be his housemaid.

Then the second element, the children. There are many, as there must be, and some of them are centered for a few moments each. They never seem to act. Spielberg has worked well with children before but always in childish matters. Here the children cannot possibly understand much, but they are convinced of *something*. Spielberg has brought these children up to the film's level of truth.

The small boy fleeing the German army's roundup of Jews in the Kraków ghetto for deportation and death, this boy who dives through the toilet seat in an outhouse, this boy who surfaces in the ordure and discovers that three other children are there already, this boy I'll remember. There's a notorious German army photo of a small Jewish boy, arms upraised, being marched out of the Warsaw ghetto by soldiers—Bergman used that photo in *Persona.* The Warsaw boy's face is in the world's memory—in reality. This Kraków boy's face, ordure-streaked—Spielberg's attempt to bear witness fifty years later—may join that earlier photo in the world's memory.*

Amistad

DECEMBER 22, 1997 | Uniquely, attractively, Steven Spielberg's career is scored with deep changes of intent. Mostly he has worked in the realm of popular pictures, sweeping the world with success after success by realizing juvenile fantasies with a mature talent. But sometimes he employs that talent on mature subjects. *The Color Purple,* to some degree, grasped troubling matters in black American society. *Schindler's List,* to the gratifying surprise of many of us, dramatized monumentally the mystery of good in the midst of the mystery of evil. Now Spielberg presents a film out of nineteenth-century American history that again demonstrates his extraordinary gifts.

Amistad tells a story so significant that its relative obscurity up to now is hard to understand. (After famine, a feast: an opera called *Amistad* has just

*See p. 190.

appeared in Chicago.) To compress it: in 1839, on board the Spanish ship *Amistad,* bound from Havana to a slave port with a cargo of black Africans, the recently captured slaves revolted, led by a man called Cinqué, killed most of the Spanish crew, and ordered the two survivors to return them to Africa. Before very long the *Amistad* was commandeered by an American naval vessel and taken to Connecticut. After a hearing, the slaves were put on trial. The U.S. government's argument was that the slaves were property and should be returned to their owners. The defense, quick and hot, was that they ought to be returned to Africa.

The case tangled with a Spanish-American treaty and with sharp domestic controversy. It drew immense attention in this country, along with visitors to the New Haven prison to see the blacks, as a burning issue for both pro- and antislavery forces; and President Van Buren tried to walk a tightrope to avoid offending either group in his upcoming election campaign. The Federal District Court held that the slaves should be returned to Africa, a ruling upheld by the Circuit Court. The government then appealed to the Supreme Court to reverse the decision, and the defense was joined by John Quincy Adams, aged seventy-four, the former president, and now a member of Congress. The defense won. The blacks were returned to Africa (where, in fact, ironies awaited).

To deal with this complex story, Spielberg had of course to condense it. With a screenplay credited to David Franzoni, which adds at least one fictional character and alters some real ones, the result is inevitably incomplete and in some regards hyperbolic. But the film conveys the mass and weight of this national, international, yet scorchingly personal drama.

Without in the least slighting Spielberg's concerns with the materials as such, for me a chief benefit of the screenplay is that it offers splendid opportunities for his filmmaking gifts. Clearly, he was building his film on texture. Aided by his superb cinematographer, Janusz Kaminski, who did *Schindler's List,* and by his designer, Ruth Carter, who provided almost palpable clothes, Spielberg puts people before us, not costumed actors, and he puts us among those people.

The very first shot, an intense close-up of a black man, dirt-caked and wet, as lightning flashes, as he struggles to pull his shackles loose in the ship's hold, not only crystallizes the theme; it seizes us with verity, the sense that a vital filmmaking talent is striking toward the truth. Scene after scene confirms this feeling—small deployments of groups that vary the patterns we didn't know we hoped not to see, large swells of pleasure like the first shot of a courtroom in afternoon light, which persuades us that the world was real and people had eyes back then, too. I can't remember a stronger sense of my presence in the past since Bergman's *The Virgin Spring*.

As agon, as embodiment of the struggles involved in the slave trade, in its meanings for American and European civilization, the film depends greatly on the performance of Cinqué, and here Spielberg's choice can only be called brilliant. Djimon Hounsou is a native of Benin who has been living in Paris and has had small roles in French and American films. He is a magnificent-looking man, but it is his spirit, more than his physique, that fulfills the role. Courage, anger, the dignity of a slave who despises his masters—all these come from Hounsou as emanations, not "creations." If you think the film exaggerates Cinqué's bearing and being, read William Cullen Bryant's contemporary poem about him, which begins "Chained in a foreign land he stood, / A man of giant frame." Hounsou becomes the Atlas on whom the cosmos of this drama rests.

The only other character of comparable importance is, naturally, John Quincy Adams. The writing of this role has been touched, invitingly though visibly, by theater. Some of Adams's qualities have been shaped into what might be called a George Arliss part. In the 1930s Arliss used to play crotchety older men, including historical figures (Disraeli, Wellington, Richelieu) who were seemingly out of things but who were discreetly observant and who stepped forward at the end to settle all difficulties. Anthony Hopkins plays that role here, cleverly clothed in Adams-ness, and from his first moments we get the savor of a fine actor relishing a damned good part. Our first glimpse is of Adams dozing in the House yet making a keen reply when it's needed. We see him at home fussing with the plants in his hothouse. After the defense wins the New Haven trial, we know the government must appeal because Adams has so far appeared only peripherally. The structure of the film, as well as the facts of history, require that the case go to the Supreme Court so that Adams can flourish. He does. He argues. He wins. Hopkins, as Adams and as himself, is magisterial.

Morgan Freeman shines—he's an actor capable of reticent shining—as an ex-slave who now is head of an anti-slavery group in the North. Nigel Hawthorne (of *The Madness of King George*) is smilingly obsequious as Van Buren. Pete Postlethwaite (of *In the Name of the Father*) bites like a bulldog as the principal prosecutor. Matthew McConaughey does what he can with the sketchiest main character, the first defense lawyer.

The only women visible in the film are some of the missionaries who come to the prison to save the black men's souls. A questionable sequence results from the gift of an illustrated Bible to one of the black men, who figures out, from the picture, the relevance of the story of Jesus. The contradiction in a Christian society that owned slaves would have been lucid enough without this sequence. But Spielberg's weakest choice is the John Williams score, which sometimes floats wordless choruses under big moments. The moments might have been even bigger with less music.

Nonetheless, *Amistad,* shortcomings and all, is solid, engrossing. While it's in progress, it envelops us; paradoxically, when it's finished, it seems to stand free, like a strong sculpture. Spielberg, the master of film-world success, shows yet again that he is master of much more than that success. In both aspects, and because of both aspects, he is invaluable.*

Saving Private Ryan

AUGUST 17 & 24, 1998 | Steven Spielberg's new film begins as a monumental epic; then it diminishes; and, by its finish, is baffling. *Saving Private Ryan,* written by Robert Rodat, is about World War II in Europe. It begins on D-Day, June 6, 1944, at Omaha Beach in Normandy, an invasion for which the term "gigantic" shrinks. Then, not long after the Allies win a position in France, a U.S. captain named Miller is sent with a squad of seven to find a certain Private Ryan, a paratrooper who has landed farther inland. Ryan's three brothers have been killed in combat; he is the sole surviving brother. General Marshall himself has ordered that Ryan be found and sent home.

After some rugged difficulties, Ryan is located by Miller and his squad, two of whom were killed en route. Ryan's reaction to the news about his brothers is what we would expect. His reaction to his proposed rescue is not. The last long sequence is a fierce battle, in which Miller and his

*See p. 205.

squad join Ryan's unit in an attempt to stop German forces from securing a bridge.

The war action of this long film is enclosed between two brief, cushiony present-day episodes in an American military cemetery in France. At the start an elderly man visits the cemetery with his family. At the close we learn who he is. He salutes; and the last image, like the first, is of the cemetery's American flag fluttering in the breeze.

The D-Day sequence, about twenty-five minutes long, is certainly one of the most powerful battle scenes ever put on film. D-Day has been recreated before, in *The Longest Day* (1962). I can't precisely compare the two versions, Spielberg's and Andrew Marton's. The latter's account was immense and gripping, as I recall it, but Spielberg gives us much more of the suffering, the slaughter, and the unflattering detail. (American soldiers shoot surrendering Germans whose hands are in the air.) Spielberg constructed his version with large and small waves of action, great tides alternating with intimate pain and will. His usual colleagues, the cinematographer Janusz Kaminski and the editor Michael Kahn, have helped him to make the whole battle, no matter how much we already know about it, newly astonishing, awesome, awful.

For me, who was glued to a radio on that June 6th, ankle deep in newspapers, no honor, no tribute, no regard can possibly be too much for the men who went ashore that day. But the film wasn't made solely to recreate that invasion, which is where the bafflement sets in. The film acts as if, from that large beginning, it moves to a special point; but it doesn't. Spielberg has said, "How do you find decency in the hell of warfare? That was what attracted me to the project." But every World War II film I can remember, and many other war films, have dealt with comradeship and sacrifice. *Saving Private Ryan* leaves us with the sense that a master director made a film while searching for its unique point and never quite found it.

The mission to find Private Ryan is, inevitably, smaller than the opening battle, but we expect it to reveal some large theme. The only element remotely like a theme is the question of whether the lives of these eight men should be risked in order to save the life of one man, but that is a very specific instance, confined to this action, not a matter of general relevance and depth.

Once the Private Ryan mission starts, the picture becomes a good war movie, not much more. Some novel twists—a duel between two snipers, an accident that discloses a roomful of Germans, a crisis with a little girl—spark the action, but on the whole we feel that we are once again in Movieland. And we don't know why. It's baffling.

Add to the disappointments the performance of Tom Hanks, usually an engaging deputy for us all, as the captain. His dialogue is a bit starchy—because he was a schoolteacher in civilian life, I guess!—but, unlike the men around him, he never seems to have quite burrowed into the earth of battle. Edward Burns, himself a filmmaker (*The Brothers McMullen*), gives Brooklyn sass to a recalcitrant member of the squad. Matt Damon sheds some sympathetic light on Private Ryan.

The Wonderful, Horrible Life of Leni Riefenstahl

MARCH 14, 1994 | Leni Riefenstahl is a monster. The first definition of that word in the OED is: "something extraordinary or unnatural; a prodigy, a marvel." It fits her. Of course other definitions follow, and a new documentary, *The Wonderful, Horrible Life of Leni Riefenstahl,* acknowledges in its title that one definition will not suffice. The film arrived last fall at the New York Film Festival almost simultaneously with the publication of Riefenstahl's 669-page autobiography; it's about to play at the Film Forum in New York and will soon open in several other cities.

The director, a German named Ray Müller, has made a well-knit work interweaving past and present and justifiably three hours long. A number of sequences show Riefenstahl arguing with Müller about angles, lighting and movement in the present-day sections, so this is quite consciously a film about a filmmaker. At the end Müller asks her some stringent questions about her past and leaves her, so to speak, face to face with us to answer. Thus, all in all, this is very far from a rounded account of her life. It is—very strongly—*her* version.

As is the case with some other monsters, the basic matters in her story are credible only because they actually happened. No fictionist would have dared to invent them. Riefenstahl was born in Berlin in 1902, and at the time of Müller's filming two years ago she was ninety, doing underwater photography in tropical seas. Here are some of the highlights that we see in between.

She was a beautiful young woman. When she was in her early twenties she was a dancer and was engaged by Max Reinhardt to appear at his Berlin theater and to tour. (He must have seen something other than the gauche dancing of which there are glimpses here.) She decided to enter films and was engaged for a leading role on the basis of a photo that she sent to a well-known director, Arnold Fanck. Her debut was in one of the mountaineering films for which Fanck was famous, and Riefenstahl, as we see in clips, did a great deal of very scary climbing in the film, much of it barefoot.

With *The Blue Light* (1932) she moved into writing and directing, and she also starred as a mountain girl who dared to climb where others would not go—a sort of prefiguring of heroic "Aryan" symbolism. Hitler admired *The Blue Light,* and after his ascendancy in 1933, he persuaded her to make a film of the Nazi Party congress in Nuremberg. This resulted in a short documentary about which, as an artist, she was not happy (the first instance of her vaunted ability to separate aesthetics from political morality). The following year Hitler persuaded her again—despite her reluctance, she says—to film the Party congress again. The result was *Triumph of the Will* (Hitler's title), a masterpiece of propaganda as art in which Nazi principles and fervor are so powerfully, even beautifully, presented that the most antagonistic are still shaken by it.

Four years later came *Olympia,* a documentary about the 1936 Olympics in Berlin, also a masterpiece, less overtly propagandistic, in which the human body is rhapsodically celebrated. During World War II she made *Tiefland,* another symbolic work—with "Aryan" resonance—about the superiority of those who live high in the mountains as against lowland dwellers.

After the war she was de-Nazified by the Americans but was nonetheless interrogated and detained by the French over several years. Since then, she has had two principal interests. First, she spent long residencies among the Nuba people in southern Sudan and published picture books about them. (Susan Sontag memorably attacked one of them as further evidence of Riefenstahl's fascist beliefs. Riefenstahl responds to Sontag in this film, briefly.) Second, she has done much underwater photography together with her constant companion, a man forty years younger. She has not yet edited this oceanic footage into a film. No hint is given about the source of her money for these various expeditions or for her comfortable home.

About her films there is room for adverse comment. In *The Haunted Screen* Lotte Eisner traces Riefenstahl's physical images to German eugenics films of the 1920s. Anyone who has seen Fritz Lang's *Die Nibelungen* (1924) knows that some of Riefenstahl's visual ideas in her symbolic films had antecedents. She tells Müller that De Sica and Rossellini both praised her for being the first director to shoot on actual location. If they did, they were thoroughly mistaken. (Just one instance: André Antoine, the French theater director who began to make films in 1915, did most of his shooting on location.)

About her political accounting, there has naturally been much more dissent. She says that she never joined the Nazi Party. (If true, what difference does it make? Bertolt Brecht, the prime dramatist of Communist causes, never joined the Communist Party.) But in *Nazi Cinema,* Erwin Leiser reports that in 1935 Riefenstahl published *Behind the Scenes of the Party Rally Film,* a book about the making of *Triumph of the Will.* The first sentence: "My personal involvement in this project overcomes all doubts, all misgivings, all obstacles."

Toward the finish of Müller's film, he tells her that everyone seems to be waiting for her to apologize. Riefenstahl, still trim and lithe at ninety, responds vigorously. She asks what she should apologize for. That she was born at a certain time in a certain place? This answer, though drastically incomplete, is far from irrelevant.

For me, it's superfluous, almost silly, for her to defend herself, for others to seek out holes in her defense. The key point is this: if Hitler had won, Riefenstahl would now unquestionably be a radiant star in the Nazi firmament. Hitler lost; she survived into another age and now tries to trim her record in the Nazi era to fit subsequent standards. (She now says she thought that the Nazi aim was to bring peace, and supplies a few clips on that theme. She didn't know about the camps. Etc.) When the simple criterion of Hitler's fate is applied, the whole issue seems settled. No matter how she defends herself, she committed vivid actions that aided the Nazis. No matter how she is attacked, she does have exceptional talent. If she had been just another Nazi hack filmmaker, she would never have become a center of controversy.

The three great Soviet film masters, Eisenstein, Pudovkin and Dovzhenko, had the bad luck to live past the Lenin era into the Stalin era and suffered for it. Riefenstahl's misfortune was much more gentle; yet it's the same sort of historical banana peel on which she slipped. We continue to admire the Soviet masterworks for their art despite the heavy irony of their now blood-drenched enthusiasm. Under that rubric Riefenstahl's best films can live.

In any case Müller's documentary presents her version of life fascinatingly; and, at the least, proves that she's a first-definition monster.

Thirty-two Short Films about Glenn Gould

APRIL 25, 1994 | On the title page of the *Goldberg Variations* Bach said that they were "Composed for Music Lovers, To Refresh Their Spirits." The French Canadian writer-director François Girard used the *Goldberg Variations* as a (very general) guide to his film about Glenn Gould, and Girard, in his own measure, refreshes us.

He felt, he says, that any conventional narrative approach to Gould's peculiar life and prismatic personality would be inadequate. Gould was celebrated for his playing of the *Variations*. For Girard and his script collaborator, Don McKellar, it followed logically that a Goldbergian approach would be best. Thus *Thirty-Two Short Films about Glenn Gould*.

Girard's variations go two pieces past Bach's thirty, and, though they all have the same basic theme — Gould — they have nothing like the complex relationship with one another that Bach's pieces have. Still, the mosaic approach is quickly engaging and increasingly winning, especially since no promise is made, or kept, that the mosaic will add up to a complete picture.

Under Girard's hand we get teasing yet satisfactory glimpses — vivid, funny, cranky, passionate, eremitic, humane — of an artist who viewed his exceptional talent as a means to explore the relation between talent and the world. Gould says, in one episode, that he dislikes the artist-audience relation. One reason that he gave up concertizing was that, with the aid of technology, he could play for himself; those who wanted to do so could listen later, through records and tapes. Gould was almost as interested in destroying the "heaven-storming" public pianist, the virtuoso who, like Liszt, could make women faint at his recitals, as he was in exploring masterworks.

Girard, who has made two previous features and a number of videos about art, is more interested in vis-à-vis connection than Gould was, yet his film manages to breathe some of its subject's ascetic air. First, the quintessential: he found an actor whom we could believe as Gould. Colm Feore, born in Boston of an Irish family, was trained at the National Theater School of Canada, has done much TV and some films but has been busiest at the Stratford, Ontario Shakespeare Festival. There he has ranged from Dionysus in *The Bacchae* through the Prince in *Hamlet* to John Worthing in *The Importance of Being Earnest*. He has a craggy face and a musical voice. He doesn't greatly resemble Gould physically, but he captures much of what we are told was the inner man: Feore is an actor with confidence in quiet. Before the film is very far along, he persuades us that the quandaries and quiddities and aspirations of Gould are being realized before us.

The opening — one long take without a cut — establishes the ascetic risk of Girard's directing, along with its complimentary confidence in our collaborating. An immense Arctic vista. Ice forever, like a frozen Sahara. Far on the horizon, a figure walks toward us. All that happens in this first segment is that he keeps walking toward us while we hear Gould playing Bach. At last he comes close and stops, a man in hat and overcoat and galoshes, obviously not lost, glad to be where he is. The title of this episode (all of them have titles) is "Aria."

Every sequence except one has Gould's piano under it. The exception is the very next sequence, "Lake Simcoe," which is accompanied by Toscanini's overwhelming performance of the *Tristan* prelude. The episode is about the boy Glenn and his parents at their house on a Canadian lake. The use of *Tristan* seems strange, particularly in the scenes with the boy and his mother — is something Oedipal being suggested? — until we see the boy absorbed by a radio broadcast of the prelude. (The sound track adjusts to the relatively tinny quality of the radio when we see it.) This, the only music in the film not played by Gould, is one clue as to what made him a musician.

The following thirty episodes are indeed variations. Some are brief statements about Gould: by Yehudi Menuhin, a French violinist named Bruno Monsaingeon, a friend called Margaret Pacsu and a cousin, Jessie Greig, with whom he used to have long phone conversations. (Gould was a telephone junkie.) One segment, "Forty-Five Seconds and a Chair," is just that: Gould sits in a chair and listens to a recording of his. Another, "L.A. Concert," shows Gould signing a stagehand's program just before he steps on stage. Then the stagehand sees what Gould has written: "This is my final concert." After that L.A. concert—in 1964—he only made recordings until he died, at fifty, in 1982.

"Truck Stop" shows Gould going to a roadside diner where they know him and know what he wants. Until his scrambled eggs arrive and he douses them with ketchup, he listens—*listens*—to all the conversations going on around him. Another episode sets a fragment from the work of the noted Canadian animator, Norman McLaren, to a fugue from *The Well-Tempered Clavier.* Another segment sets close-ups of the assorted pills that Gould takes against a passage from Hindemith. The episodes swing from bustle to isolation, from eccentric aloofness to a mundaneness so intense that it, too, is eccentric. (There is, by the way, no hint of any kind of sex life.)

Near the end we see a close-up of the liftoff of a space missile in the United States, and we're told that *Voyagers* 1 and 2, launched in 1987 and 1989, contained messages of mixed sorts that might connect with beings in outer space. One of those messages is a brief Bach piece played by Gould. No word has come back yet. Stay tuned.

Girard's highly selective yet empathic technique has reminders of the late Derek Jarman's *Wittgenstein*—a coincidence, merely. Alain Dostie's camera work, too, combines reticence with pleasure. At the end the film reiterates Gould's love of the north, and Dostie's camera dramatizes Gould's ideal of isolation. Chiefly, however, it is Girard's form and his relish of it that consummate the film. Following along considerably below Bach but mindful of him, Girard has composed variations that refresh the spirit.

Sunday's Children

MAY 16, 1994 | Ingmar Bergman, who retired from film directing twelve years ago, has not retired from filmmaking. Since 1982 he has written two screenplays, *The Best Intentions,* directed by Bille August (1992), and *Sunday's Children,* directed by his son Daniel and just released in the United

States. (In addition he has published two books, an autobiography called *The Magic Lantern,* which is a Bergman work of art, and *Images,* a sort of supplemental volume. Some retirement.)

Like many another artist, Bergman is obsessed with his father—with his mother, too (about whom he made a short documentary in 1983), but principally his father. The autobiography delved into his childhood and youth and his father's courtship of his mother and the early, rocky years of their marriage. *Sunday's Children* is about the eight-year-old Ingmar and also the man he became at fifty and the relations that the two Ingmars had with his father in 1926 and in 1968.

The film is even more intricately familial: the director is Ingmar's son by his pianist wife, Käbi Laretei. While watching, I kept wondering about Daniel Bergman. He had been through plentiful seasoning in film work and had directed a short and some TV; still, this was his feature debut. That's nerve-racking enough for anyone, but this debutant had added burdens. The screenplay had been written by one of the greatest directors in film history, and Daniel's directing was inevitably going to be compared with his. More: that writer was his father. Even more: the leading characters were his father and his country-clergyman grandfather, along with his grandmother and assorted relatives. We might imagine that Daniel's first reaction, to the suggestion that he direct this film, would have been to jump out the window. Or, at least, leave Sweden.

However, it's good for all of us that Daniel took on the job. The film he has made, like August's Bergman film, is not an Ingmar imitation, it's his own. There is much more savoring here of natural beauty (with Tony Forsberg's camera) than Ingmar would have done—lovely woods and lake shores and old bridges. Perhaps one reason that Ingmar didn't want to make this film was that the panoply of nature was essential but was not his directing métier.

Yet this indulgence, this remembrance of lakes past, is not the prime point of the enterprise. The author is in fact underscoring our self-deception in art about nature. Pantheists and other romantics have often given us the equivalent of these rustic idylls in Sweden, 1926, implying that the beauty of the world is an order to which mankind might aspire. "Every prospect pleases and only man is vile," said Bishop Heber. Nuts, says Bergman père. Nature is just part of the decor against which man is vile and is also a lot of other things.

The boy Ingmar learns that his clergyman father and his mother have a deep rift between them. He needs reassurance from them, reassurance that he is safe, that the world around him—so beautiful—is safe. One Sunday morning in summer he accompanies his father to a somewhat distant village where his father is to preach. On the way back, father and son strip and swim in a lake. It's lovely. What could be more reassuring, more comforting about the future, than that this boy and his father, who truly loves him, share this idyll. But idyllic moments guarantee nothing.

The numerous flash-forwards that weave through the film before and after this moment, sequences set in 1968 when the fifty-year-old Ingmar visits his dying father, show that the communion of this idyll and of others has worn away. Increasingly Ingmar has seen that idylls are easy, that they don't counterbalance or obliterate grievous actions, betrayals and disappointments. The memory of the idylls becomes almost ironic.

Daniel Bergman has perceived this point. In fact he emphasizes it by making the 1968 scenes, all in the old father's apartment, visually attractive in their own way. The rooms are as rich and mellow in city style as the country kitchen and living room are in Vermeer style. Both city *and* country beauties, says the film, are merely decor, not ethical imperatives.

It's tempting to speculate on whether Ingmar helped Daniel (now thirty-two) in the directing; but even if we assume that Ingmar kept hands strictly off, Daniel still couldn't avoid Ingmar influence. That would have been silly and wasteful. The scenes least like Ingmar are the enchanting pictorial ones, of which there are many. The scenes most like Ingmar are quarrels, particularly between husband and wife. Ingmar always had a way of putting antagonists face to face—he did it often—as if they were locked there, as if the quarrel had to be seen through to the bitter end, no matter how painful to the opponents. The pressing placement of the camera, the restrained editing, with as little cross-cutting from one face to another as possible, make us feel as if we were watching an epic encounter. (I've just seen it again in *Persona*.) Daniel has captured some of that feeling here.

Some of the elements in the picture seem, to an outsider, as much components of Swedish film as of Swedish life. I don't question the accuracy of Ingmar's memory—how could I?—I note only that other period films have prepared us for what were apparently Swedish universals: the jolly, bibulous uncle, for instance, who secretly hates his life; the nubile maid who loves the little boy and cares for him; the kindly country station-master.

But most of the screenplay is Ingmar territory, not least the fantasy elements, which remind us of *Hour of the Wolf, Fanny and Alexander* and more. A child born on a Sunday, as both Ingmar and his father were, is said to be gifted with special sight, the ability to see ghosts and fairies and such; and once the boy Ingmar is told that he possesses this power, his imagination does the rest. This gift remained with the artist. It enabled the grown man to see the ghosts inside living people.

As the young father, Thommy Berggren, once the ardent lover in *Elvira Madigan,* is firm yet pitiable; as the aged father, he is only the latter. Lena Endre is reticently strong as the wife and mother. The boy Ingmar (nicknamed Pu) is played by Henrik Linnros, who has imagination, and the director has found it. Per Myrberg, as the mature Ingmar, has the right face and air. It isn't a matter of resembling Ingmar, which he does not; tacitly, he conveys the sum of the years.

Daniel Bergman uses music well. There isn't much of it (nor is there in Ingmar's films), mostly a guitar. This helps the (deceptively) lyric quality of the film. Occasionally, however, there is a passage from Bach, possibly serving the same purpose as the Bach in *Persona.* It's more pertinent than nature as a standard for humankind because it is man-made, and its perfection is therefore all the more galling and humbling.

Spanking the Monkey

AUGUST 1, 1994 | Talent is announced in David O. Russell's *Spanking the Monkey.* The announcement is all the more ringing because this film, Russell's first feature, tackles two big problems head-on and does well with them.

The first is structural. *Spanking the Monkey* begins with forty-five minutes or so of relatively familiar material. A college student has to give up his good summer job because his mother has broken her leg. He must care for her, in his family's suburban home, while his father is off on an extended sales trip. The young man's frustrations, the domestic details, are, in essence, TV fare. But as the film moves to graver matters, we realize that it had to begin that way. Russell simply had to bite the bullet of seeming banality; and he succeeds in holding us. No trickery. He doesn't begin later in the story and then flash back to the necessary details with the promise of stronger stuff already in our minds. Russell *wants* us to feel the itch of familiarity: it's part of his tonal plan. And he survives this structural hazard because he casts all the roles so well and gives his actors dialogue as fresh as the familiar situations would permit.

The second problem is thematic. Russell's main subject is incest. Ray, the student, is around twenty; his mother, Susan, is an attractive woman in her early forties. In the course of things, Ray must massage her legs, must help her (with his back turned) to shower, must scrub her back and so on. He has the natural heat of his age. The picture's title is slang for male masturbation. (Russell gets some laughs out of the family dog's intrusions into the bathroom.) Ray's vexations, plus his mother's various discontents, lead one night to consummation. The next morning they wake up in bed next to each other, he in his shorts, his mother naked.

Russell treats this episode without prurience, almost with a tone of inevitability. But it raises a question I'm not competent to answer. I don't know, can't imagine, how a mother and son behave after incest. A social worker once told me that she and her associates were inured to incest, that it occurs in every sort of family and that mother-son incest is the second most common. (Father-daughter is first, she said, brother-sister third.) I certainly don't maintain that we must have personal experience of a subject in order to comment: anyone can feel the horror of Oedipus's discovery. What I have to take on trust here is the lack of horror.

These two people show no embarrassment or regret. They don't even mention what happened. They behave as if it had never happened or if it did, as if they were not mother and son. Possibly their behavior is a mode of denial, but we don't sense that they feel a need to deny anything.

What then happens in the film precludes any repetition of the act. During a telephone quarrel with the traveling father, Ray lets slip a remark acknowledging the act. The father flies home, but even then, the general air is as if Susan had slept with another man, not her son. Later events show that the matter rankles in Ray; Susan seems unruffled.

Russell, too. The incest, for him, is one more element in the picture's texture, a texture so skillfully contrived that, in a somewhat frightening way, it nearly "normalizes" the incest. Dailiness has been the film's motto.

The slicing of fruit, the clunking of ice cubes into a glass, similar actions, are shown close up as the film winds along. I doubt that Russell wants to imply that incest is as common or unremarkable as the whittling of pineapples; but he wants to show life in that house flowing along, bearing in its stream trivialities and crises.

This approach quietly dramatizes the film's really fundamental theme. Incest is the most unsettling act, but we see that it is only the most trenchant element in a general fabric of sex. Ray gets involved with a neighboring high school girl, and their encounters lead to more puzzlements and discoveries. Several sequences in the father's hotel rooms show that, like that other salesman, Willy Loman, he finds female solace on the road.

Sex itself, repressed or steamy or insidious, thus becomes the real venue of the film. The title promises it, the picture fulfills it. The prettiness of the house, the banality of the chores, are important as, in a sense, disguises. The well-kept houses and lawns are all the more well-kept, we come to feel, as defense or protest against what cannot be so well-ordered in behavior.

When Louis Malle made a film about incest, *Murmur of the Heart,* the atmosphere was fairly stormy from the start. When Bernardo Bertolucci flirted with the idea in *La Luna,* operatic extremities set the key. Russell shucks all this apparatus, apparently in the belief that it is antiquated and false to make the environment adumbrate the theme. What he gives us is middle-class tidiness, in the midst of which mysteries are tugging.

But—a looming antithesis—the ending lets the film down. I won't describe it: I'll merely note that it's as if Russell had concentrated so intensely on everything up to that point that the need for an ending came as a surprise. The finish is a fiddle. It lacks even a clearly intended ambiguousness.

Praise, however, for Russell's colleagues. Michael Mayers, the cinematographer, renders the house as if he were doing layouts for *Good Housekeeping.* As for the cast, I've rarely seen better actors in a low-budget film. Jeremy Davies, who is Ray, has not a whit of Matthew Broderick or Michael J. Fox about him. He sulks and simmers like someone trying to find an interior road map and not having much luck. Alberta Watson, as Susan, radiates sexuality in a nonaggressive, almost humorous way. Benjamin Hendrickson has what might have been the really thankless part, the salesman father, a role written in different shades of desperation. Hendrickson plays it like someone trapped within his life. Carla Gallo gives the high-school girl gentle pride.

All of them, and others, have helped to make *Spanking the Monkey* the sort of film we always want, one that improves with afterthought. Except for that ending. More from Russell soon again, I hope, and next time completed.

Barcelona

AUGUST 15, 1994 | Whit Stillman's first film, *Metropolitan* (1990), was about upper-class Manhattan yuppies and their amorous tribulations, which were heightened at Christmas time. Brooks Brothers was the décor of look and of mind. The intricate, sometimes witty dialogue had one classic aspect: as in Restoration comedy, the articulate exchanges seemed an attempt at vitality on the part of people who were otherwise rather languid.

But the verbal fireworks were not enough, in this case, to rescue the whole from general languor. The chief interest of *Metropolitan* was in its territorial claim. Stillman was seizing a corner of the American film world for this social class, holding it against the middle-class or working-class or ghetto-class, racially mixed, gutter-spoken majority of new American pictures. Wryly enough, this was just the opposite of the situation early in this century when unrefined characters had to elbow their way into theater and film past the soigné well-to-do.

Stillman's second film, *Barcelona,* makes *Metropolitan* look retrospectively like a warm-up. First, it is immediately apparent that his sheer cinematic fluency has taken a great leap forward. In the earlier film I frequently felt that Stillman had shot scenes with no prior vision of them. He just got them into the camera one way or another so that he could move on. Scene after scene in *Barcelona* is quite the reverse: the way that we see is relevant to what we're seeing. And scenes are often finished with a quick fade to black, which gives the film a smart, astringent tone.

But the great advance is in the film's embrace. It is about something more than the mere existence of its people. At first, there's only one small clue of depths ahead. In this respect Stillman's screenplay resembles David O. Russell's *Spanking the Monkey:* for a while, it seems to be about engaging but light matters, but they turn out to be only the necessary prelude to a deep plunge.

The time is "the last decade of the cold war." Stillman takes two young men of, figuratively, the *Metropolitan* set—played by two of the *Metropolitan* cast—and puts them in Barcelona. (A city that Stillman knows because his wife is Barcelonan.) One of the young men, Ted, is a sales rep for a Chicago firm. The other one, his cousin Fred, is a lieutenant j.g. in the Navy who arrives to do advance public relations for a visit of the Sixth Fleet. Fred barges in on Ted unannounced, takes the spare room in the apartment, soon moves into Ted's social life and soon borrows Ted's clothes so that he can get out of uniform when off-duty.

All this leads to some quite funny, quietly cantankerous dialogue between the two men, Ted irritated, Fred Teflon-coated, both dueling without anger. (Stillman's actors play it well, with *sforzandi* that quickly subside.) They join, however, in attention to attractive young Spanish women. Ted is also concerned with job security and with religion: he reads best-sellers on improving himself, and he reads the Bible concealed within a copy of *The Economist*. Both he and Fred sometimes discuss Large Questions, like the relation between beauty and true worth, which make them sound—quite deliberately—like Holden Caulfield a dozen years later.

Then the darkening comes. True, the very beginning of the film signals it: almost the first thing we see is the bombing of the American Library in Barcelona. But no one is hurt, and Ted and Fred never discuss it. Then anti-Americanism swells, both in Barcelona generally and specifically against Fred when he is in uniform. This puts the man-about-town behavior of the pair in a different light.

The local USO is bombed, and an American sailor is killed. Fred has to officiate at the dockside ceremony with the coffin (but Stillman keeps it from being maudlin by having it take place in a loading shed with Taps among the crates). For various mistaken reasons, a newspaper begins running stories about Fred as a CIA agent. The tentacles of the world tighten, and Fred is shot in a taxi by a man passing on a scooter.

Ted puts in a long, long vigil at Fred's hospital bedside. Ted has heard somewhere that the sound of a familiar voice helps a comatose patient to recover, so he reads *The Scarlet Pimpernel* aloud to the unconscious Fred. When he isn't reading, he kneels by Fred's bed and prays. A Spanish girlfriend, who hasn't figured much up to now, also comes to the room: she offers *War and Peace*—in English, of course.

Fred recovers. Mostly. This recovery doesn't seem false. It seems the truth of a romance, certainly bitter, certainly self-aware, but a romance. Any grimmer outcome to the shooting would have been as if a truck had slammed into one of the film locations in Barcelona and killed the cast: it would have nullified everything that had already been filmed. This view is amplified by the ending of the film in which almost everything is set to rights.

Nevertheless, Stillman's film functions as a warning—bright, sexy, funny, yet a warning. The best members of the social set that he knows are proceeding into the twenty-first century as if they could shape it like the twentieth, which was itself in some part a failure to repeat the nineteenth. Stillman hears his people asking: Why *can't* high spirits prevail? Why can't questions about Beauty and Worth still occupy young men's thoughts? Why can't spurts of religious schwarmerei sufficiently warrant faith? And, in some sort of nebulous analogy with all this, why can't the rest of the world see the benevolence of America's intentions, blunted though they often are by clumsy execution? These questions seem to underlie the film, and Stillman is shaking his head sadly.

Heading the cast is Barcelona itself, which Stillman presents gorgeously and without Gaudí. None of the three leading young women—Tushka Bergen, Mira Sorvino and Hellena Schmied—is in fact Spanish, but who's complaining? All are appealing and adequate: Bergen as a woman who entrances both cousins but who never quite leaves her original boyfriend, Sorvino as a moralist whose ideas on property are malleable, Schmied as the faithful Tolstoyan.

Taylor Nichols (Ted) and Chris Eigeman (Fred) play parts that were, says Stillman, written for them, and all three knew what they were doing. They give us Congreve or Vanbrugh characters of today. Tomorrow may be another matter.

The cinematography by John Thomas, who did *Metropolitan,* is teasingly lovely about Barcelona. Christopher Tellefsen, who too worked on *Metropolitan,* is the keen-eyed editor. I hope their presence, as well as others', means that Stillman is assembling a team for the long haul. Along with Hal Hartley and David O. Russell, he helps to cheer up American film prospects.

OCTOBER 3, 1994 | Oliver Stone's *Natural Born Killers* is mainly about itself. It has a narrative, quite commonplace. It has characters, all of them stock. It has dialogue, most of which is either banal or straining not to be. It has themes, with which we are all too familiar. What makes this film an explosive event is the way it is made and why. It's as if Stone deliberately chose material that is run of the mill because he didn't want to be distracted by novelty of plot or character. To do justice to such novelty would have diverted him and us from the central matter, the film's very being as film.

Its texture can be called collage in forward motion. Here Stone brings to full frenzy a stylistic approach that was signaled in *The Doors* and *JFK*. He mixes every kind of technique—color and black-and-white, blunt verism and animation, historical quotation and computer distortion are only some of them—and mixes them continuously, in order to blast us out of our usual film-viewing coziness. The surrealists of the 1920s wanted to shock expectations so sharply that the artist's real purpose could slip past the surprised sentries of convention. Except that the term "surrealism" now has other resonances, *Natural Born Killers* might be called surrealist. If we can imagine surrealism blended with expressionism, as if *Un Chien Andalou* were folded into *The Cabinet of Dr. Caligari* and then boiled, we get near to Stone's intensity.

Even before the full intent of the film becomes clear, we sense tremors. Stone is agonized by the same frustrations that tormented Godard in his early films. When his film leaves his hands, it is finished, but he wants it to be as wild, as unpredictable, as seemingly spontaneous as anything can be that is put in cans and shipped to thousands of theaters. In very great measure, in what could almost be called appalling measure, he succeeds.

The subject, or at least the foreground subject, is coarse film-world fodder: maniacal violence. (Stone almost chuckles as he puts these clichés before us.) The structure is still another variation on the Bonnie-and-Clyde form. Somewhere in the Southwest, young Mickey and Mallory encounter each other when he comes to her family's home to deliver meat. (Remember Stanley's first entrance in *A Streetcar Named Desire?*) Mallory's home life, with a lascivious father and a non-protective mother, makes her hungry for break-out and adventure. Mickey's home life, as we learn later, has primed him for the same outburst. They begin by drowning her father in a goldfish tank and incinerating her mother in her bed. Then they cut loose in a red roadster, killing blithely in diners and service stations and convenience stores. Fifty-two deaths in three weeks. At last they are captured.

A year later, when they are both lifers, the host of a TV program called *American Maniacs* gets the right to interview Mickey in prison. Mickey's behavior on camera ignites his fellow prisoners to riot. Mickey seizes the chance to grab a shotgun, kill guards and escape. He also seizes the chance to break Mallory out of her cell; she grabs guns and joins him. Through the storming riot, accompanied for a time by the TV host who is trying to keep the event on the air, they make their way out together and flee.

The screenplay is by David Veloz, Richard Rutowski and Stone, from an original story by the new guru of gore, Quentin Tarantino. But the screenplay cannot possibly have mapped the film in detail: what we see, in all its whirligig horror and humor and fascination, must have been created by Stone as he proceeded.

Which is what makes my synopsis above misleading. The action is not sequential: the film begins well into the three weeks. The telling is not orderly. Almost always the camera is tilted one way or another, a shot is interrupted with the same shot in black-and-white and/or by the addition of backgrounds that amplify—glimpses of jackals and snakes, of great betrayers (Stalin, Hitler, Nixon), of pop and film quotations (a bit of *The Wild Bunch* inevitably). Each figurative note of the film is an implicit chord, just as each moment of our consciousness is more than what we see or say immediately. Each screen moment dramatizes Stone's feverish struggle to mine every possible visual reference and connection before he is forced to move on to the next shot.

This lightning-stroke exploration of the couple's minds discloses more than they knew was in them. One element dominates—the tyranny of television. Not just the usual flashes of TV news with the fugitives watching and relishing the reports about them. Stone saturates his film with our society's media saturation. Mallory's home life at the start is seen as a sitcom, in a phony setting, with exaggerated makeups, with canned studio laughter and with a credit crawl at the end. At one point in the Mickey-Mallory rampage, their adventures are re-enacted by look-alikes on TV, with the words "A Dramatization" superscribed. Layer after layer of media degradation is piled upon us. If we feel at first that Part Two of the film, in prison a year later, may be overextended, we soon see that it was necessary to show how their lives and TV really connect—TV causes a riot—and I use "really" here just as porously as possible.

Stone suffers from a sentimentality, one that often plagues the ruthlessly tough—a belief in the grand simple wisdom of nature and of those who live close to it, like American Indians. The opening of his film, like that of *The Doors,* is set in the desert, with animals; the very last image, under the closing credits, is an immense close-up of a rabbit. The only regret for a killing that the killer-pair express is for an Indian seer.

But Mickey and Mallory are not visionary. They are driven by demons—the word is sometimes flashed on their chests—that are specified only by their upbringings. (Mickey's father was an oddball who killed himself.) But no clinical attempt is made to justify their homicides. They live in a time piled higher with temptations to mindlessness than any age in history. These two people are simply unable to bear the beguilings of quick animalistic gratifications that most of us are still able to resist.

Stone's cinematographer was once again the superb Robert Richardson. The editors, sine qua non, were Hank Corwin and Brian Berdan. The music itself is a collage—of many contemporary numbers and cool "references." Examples of the latter: after the opening murder sequence in a diner, the lighting changes (it changes constantly), and in a soft glow, Mickey and Mallory waltz to *La vie en rose.* The prison riot rages over a background of *A Night on Bald Mountain.*

Woody Harrelson and Juliette Lewis play the leads and supply all that is wanted. It's not acting in any integrated, resourceful sense but the presentation of familiar planes off which the unfamiliar lighting and frenzy can bounce. Robert Downey Jr. plays the TV host with his usual painfully revved-up energy. Tommy Lee Jones plays the prison warden with a calculated exaggeration that condemns all previous performances of smilingly brutal wardens.

This brings up the matter of satire. The term has been used by some, including Stone himself, to describe the film. Trusting the tale and not the teller (who may just have been supplying a term to mollify critics), I disagree. Jones's performance isn't satirical: it's a cultural comment on that long line of wardens who have helped to make phony artifacts of so many prison films. *Natural Born Killers* is much closer to free-flying fantasy—

on grave themes—than to satire. Under the closing credits, for instance, we see a comfily furnished van, with Mickey driving and Mallory pregnant, accompanied by small children. This isn't satire, it's a peripheral lost dream. But the ultimate element that distinguishes the film from satire is the position of Stone himself. He doesn't hold Mickey and Mallory at arm's length, looking down at them. He moves with them, fantasticates with them, rages with them. He himself, we feel, is one of the Dante-Doré creatures.

This is also what distinguishes *Natural Born Killers* from the avant-garde work that has used comparable collage methods. Stone isn't investigating techniques. He's on fire. He *means* it. His film slashes its way back into the dark jungle in our brains from which it sprang.

Nixon

JANUARY 22, 1996 | Let's begin discussing *Nixon* with what is usually put last, or peripherally, in an Oliver Stone review: his directing talent. It's most easily identified by his attitude toward linear narrative. True, several of his films, including the recent *Heaven and Earth,* were made in relatively conventional narrative style: but when Stone is most himself, the self he has apparently been working toward, he is too impatient for mere linearity.

The Doors, JFK, Natural Born Killers are the work of a man infuriated by the fact that he can show us only one image at a time, can have us hear only one line, or combination of sounds, at a time. It's obviously odd to compare Stone with James Joyce, but they do share one impulse. Joyce moved in his art from the monadic to the polyphonic, the chordal, trying to encompass the teeming complexity of the human mind in every split second. Something of the same rage at his art, at the fate of being able to present only one image at a time, gnaws at Stone.

Nixon assumes that a film biography cannot rightly be linear because everyone carries his entire life with him all the time. The backpack, ever present and always growing, is invisible in life but need not be so in film. An instance: when Nixon's path to the presidency is made easier by the Kennedy assassinations, someone remarks that the two deaths have helped him. Nixon says, "No, there were four." Then we get visual references to the early deaths of two of his brothers, which made it possible for him to go to law school.

Most of the film is much more densely woven than this episode: with contrapuntal time strands, lightning play of black-and-white renderings against full color for emphasis, with repetitions of shots from different angles to suggest how different minds will remember the moment—all volatile, scintillating. (Also a few stylistic bows to *Citizen Kane.*) Sometimes a reference is banal, as when Nixon's dead mother appears to him near the end of the film, but mostly the texture of this three-hours-plus film is exciting as we feel Stone trying to open, open, open.

Next, the acting. All the supporting roles are adequately played, but if they were done even better—which would have been unnecessary—they still couldn't have been much more than supportive of the central figure. Anthony Hopkins's performance as Nixon consummates all their work, all of Stone's work. We very soon forget that Hopkins, despite hair and dental touches, doesn't look like that too-familiar face and figure. Hopkins plunges straight for the core discomforts in Nixon, the conflicts in a man ravenous for power who not only is uneasy in public but who patently dislikes most of those who are closest to him.

Hopkins creates the manic, insistent, pumped-up energy, plus the almost calculated obtuseness about defeats. (The one fissure in that obtuseness—"You won't have Nixon to kick around anymore"—is the result of a promise to his wife to leave politics: a promise that he, alas, breaks.) Hopkins overwhelms us with the conviction that everything about this man is fabricated except that drive for power, a drive that sometimes seems to hag-ride Nixon himself. Hopkins made me remember that, when Nixon was on TV with his wife, I used to think that he was twisting her arm behind her back to make her smile; and that, looking and listening to him, I used to wonder if everyone else thought he was as mentally ill as I thought him.

For Robert Richardson, the cinematographer, for Brian Berdan and Hank Corwin, the editors, all of whom are Stone veterans, only sheer admiration will suffice. About the score a few questions. What John Williams wrote was helpful, but I didn't understand why Schubert's second symphony was quoted at one point or why, at the Lincoln Memorial, "John Brown's Body" was slammed in so heavily.

And now, the element that most others will consider first, the screenplay by Stephen J. Rivele, Christopher Wilkinson and Stone—which is to say, the biography as such. In candor, I note first that it would be hard to loathe Nixon more than I do. I'm aware of his accomplishments—the accord with China, for prime instance. I'm aware, too, that as Tom Wicker says, Nixon's punishment for Watergate may now seem too hard after "Savingsgate," the savings-and-loan outrage "for which neither Presidents Reagan nor Bush suffered banishment." Nonetheless, from the very start of his political career, Nixon stained himself with guile and calumny made all the worse by his righteous rhetoric. (Wicker reports that, as early as 1950, Averell Harriman walked out of a supper he was supposed to attend with Nixon, saying, "I will not break bread with that man!") His opportunistic progress right up to Watergate, his grim maneuverings in Vietnam, his smarmy schemings to reestablish himself in the years between his resignation and his death—these put him well beyond the furthest pale. The historian Joan Hoff says in her study of Nixon that he was not unprincipled but aprincipled, meaning that he had "no apparent awareness of conventional moral or ethical standards." This strikes me as generous.

All of the above is to underscore that I went to Stone's film with one question uppermost in my mind: Why? Even acknowledging Stone's understandably persistent concern with Vietnam, why this long film about Nixon? To some extent, Stone answers this question, which he clearly foresaw.

Nixon begins with a disclaimer, stating that the film uses dramatic license, including condensation, that some scenes "have been hypothesized or condensed." I'm unequipped to check all the rearrangements, though one of them struck me forcibly. The weird scene at the Lincoln Memorial at 4 a.m. one morning during the Vietnam War has patently been fiddled with: the confrontation with students, which here ends pensively, in fact ended with ugly gestures on both sides. As this film moves along—races, despite its length—we see that it is neither an attack on Nixon nor a defense. Nor is it a tragedy. Large pronouncements have been made, some of them by Stone, using that word: but *Nixon* is no tragedy. The protagonist's fall causes no catharsis. For the kindliest viewer, it is pathetic; for the rest of us, it is high time.

The picture is a case study. It examines Nixon's insecurities and his resultant aggressions; his firm beliefs at one moment and his equally firm dismissal of them later; his combination of overweening complacency and defensiveness; his grabbings and his near-shock when some of the grabbings succeed; his desperation to attract people and his failure to do so. (After Nixon's fall, Kissinger says, "Can you imagine what this man would have been if he had ever been loved?") However, despite Stone's mercurial gifts, the film does not become an artistic whole; it remains an examination of characteristics.

What's missing is what Stone's best films have had: a subtext, a large theme evoked by the action on the screen. With *JFK,* it was a numinous atmosphere of uncertainty that has haunted this country since that murder. With *Natural Born Killers,* it was the fusing of life and media reports of life, so that we all swim in a sea of horrific electronic assault. But with *Nixon* such a theme is not discernible. This leaves the film not much more than the series of events presented—thus, in any deep sense, purposeless.

Two last points. We get only a few glimpses, and then they are unidentified, of the garish uniforms for White House guards that Nixon ordered when he became president, a juvenile fantasy that apparently was too much even for his admirers. And Stone never touches the basic mystery of those Oval Office tapes. (Of which there are four thousand hours: only sixty-three hours have been made public.) They were the only real proof of his complicity in the Watergate cover-up. Why didn't he destroy them before the public knew that they existed? My own guess is that, through his Quaker upbringing, there lingered a small potential for guilt in the "aprincipled" Nixon, a tiny damp hunger for punishment. His virtual rebirth after resignation, after punishment, seems to confirm this.

Well, *Nixon* goes forth now to run the gauntlet of historians and biographers. So it should, although the history-and-film relation can be more complex than accuracy tests indicate. One actual statement, however, lingers in the mind. In the clips here of Nixon's funeral service, we see Senator Dole predicting that the second half of this century will be known as the age of Nixon. A shiver ran through me. It may turn out to be true.

FEBRUARY 5, 1996 | Another visit to *Nixon* confirmed my admiration for it as filmmaking but also made me ashamed. Reviewing it a few weeks ago, I hadn't praised Anthony Hopkins enough. His performance is immense in two aspects: huge in its acting resources, huge in the Atlas-like way, without strain, that he supports the whole film. And his acting has a strange uniqueness. I can't remember another performance that triumphed so fully through the portrayal of discomfort. Hopkins's Nixon is uncomfortable when victorious or defeated, when joyous or worried. He even embraces his wife clumsily. Hopkins creates a man unhappy in his body and being, struggling throughout for ease in himself, wrecking conventions and ethics in this struggle. Former associates of this president are now telling us that the film does not portray the "real" Nixon. Few of us have knowledge of the private man. What we can say is that Hopkins's performance fits the man who was publicly visible for all those years.

Vanya on 42nd Street

NOVEMBER 7, 1994 | A group of actors gathers for a rehearsal of *Uncle Vanya*. They will work on a platform built in the orchestra of a dilapidated, formerly elegant theater just off Times Square, a venue that time and accident seem almost to have designed for the play. Today the cast will do a run-through without interruption. They wear street clothes; they carry coffee containers with the red heart that loves New York.

An elderly actress and an actor around forty sit next to each other and begin chatting about odds and ends. Then she asks him if he would like some tea or some vodka, and with a sense of slipping deliciously into beauty, we realize that the play has begun. The woman has become the nanny, Marina; the man is now Dr. Astrov. We are in Russia, on a country estate, around the end of the last century.

A generally wonderful two hours then follow. To begin with, it's Chekhov, who can seem wonderful even in mediocre performance. But this "rehearsal" is, for the greater part, exquisite. It's the result of work that has been going on, with some interruptions, since 1989. This performance is the fruit of genuine exploration, of the play and of actors' selves, a golden instance of a much-mooted, rarely realized goal.

For the past five years, the most open secret in the New York theater has been this production's preparation, though that last word is not quite precise. A group of actors was chosen for this play by the director, André Gregory (the André of *My Dinner with* . . .). They rehearsed. From time to time during the past five years, Gregory allowed a few "public" performances of the work-in-progress for invited guests. Then the cast would go back to rehearsing, would break for a time while the actors did other jobs for income, then would reassemble to work further under Gregory, then disperse again, then reassemble. And so on.

In September 1991 Louis Malle, who had filmed *My Dinner with André*, saw a run-through of *Vanya*. Two years later—time was not of the essence here, or at least it was differently of the essence—Gregory and Wallace Shawn, who plays Vanya and who had the dinner with André, asked Malle to film their production. This year the film was made. My worst worry about it is that the company may now stop rehearsing. I can't believe that these actors, most of them anyway, have reached their limits under this director. How about another film of the production after another five years?

This film is called *Vanya on 42nd Street,* which is literally true, but I hope it's not misleading. Nothing has been done to modernize the play. There are no costumes, no scenery, not even a samovar (there *are* disquieting touches of jazz in the act breaks), but in every remotest cranny of spirit, this is Chekhov. It is not a flawless production, but it glows with affinity.

Start with Malle. For me, his film career has been streaked with unsuccessful seriousness (*Lacombe Lucien; Au revoir, les enfants*). My favorite Malle film was the Shawn-Gregory dinner; there he was given an already achieved work—a play that had been performed—and had only to film it suitably. Which he did. He has done it again here. He understood the simplicities of Gregory's theater directing, the richness of the performances, and has transposed them to the screen without cinematic fol-de-rol, thus with utmost cinematic effect.

For instance, a great deal of the first act is done without much movement by the actors. They enter, sit near one another, leave, come back. Malle's camera, though far from static, doesn't try to compensate kinetically for these patterns: he accepts them as the prevailing dynamics of the sequence. This subscription to the performance is maintained throughout, and Malle's large film experience effortlessly keeps it from being "canned theater."

Gregory himself is only briefly visible. He doesn't "direct"; he makes a few remarks at the start and between the acts. I first got to know Gregory's work when he was the head of the Philadelphia Theater of Living Arts:

nothing conventional was done at that place. Subsequently I saw his unique *Alice in Wonderland* in New York (some of the *Vanya* actors were in it) and his numerous small parts in films; but this is the first Gregory directing that I've seen in years. Clearly, like Jerzy Grotowski, whom he studied, he now believes that the theater lives in the art of the actor—the traditional actor, not the performance artist—and that the disclosure of actors' art through a play that is worthy of them is the director's primary function.

The Gregory productions that I saw some years ago were radical in the immediately obvious sense, disruptive of convention in several ways. Now that theater fashions have turned that sort of radicalism almost into the norm, Gregory has become radical again simply by returning to tradition—by concentrating on actors and on fidelity to text. This bare-bones production isn't a stunt, it's an economic necessity. (But Declan Quinn, the cinematographer, lights it delicately.) Yet this mode of presentation helps to throw the emphasis on the quintessential: acting. Real acting.

I've seen most of this cast before, though not all have registered strongly. Gregory, however, divined what is in them and brought it out. Brooke Smith is Sonya, unrequited in love, left at the end with her equally unrequited uncle to spend the rest of their lives managing the estate together. The entire play moves to Sonya's closing speech, which is basically as ambiguous as Chekhov finds all certainties. Sonya promises her uncle that, "beyond the grave," they will find rest, will find their sufferings "bathed in a perfect mercy." With subtle bleakness, Smith conveys that Sonya must say *something* here: she must offer some consolation, some purpose, for all that has happened and will not happen. Sonya, Smith tells us, may or may not have religious faith, but she loves her similarly bruised uncle and, by comforting him, can also partly comfort herself. With Smith, the lines are tinged with hope—rather than belief—that they are true.

Larry Pine, the Astrov, has dignity and weariness as the country doctor filled with resignation who nonetheless plants forests for future generations, an activity that is analogous with Sonya's utterances about heaven. Julianne Moore, familiar from films, is perfectly cast as the beauteous, wasting Yelena. At first her recurrent laughter seems an actress's attempt to do a "different" Yelena. Then, as the role develops, Yelena's laughter becomes her defense against her stupid marriage, against the irruption of hysteria. George Gaynes, an old-timer, plays her elderly husband, the ego-maniacal Serybryakov, self-pitying, selfish. Gaynes is more than credible as the aging, ailing man who cannot understand why his ex brother-in-law, Vanya, whom he carelessly exploits, hates him.

This brings us to the tenderest element, Vanya himself. Wallace Shawn, who helped organize this production and this film, is a talented writer who has been acceptable in some small film roles, usually comic. With Gregory's help, he has found absolutely all there is of Shawn to bring to Vanya. He works to the top of his powers. But it's like a stripling strug-gling with a heavyweight. When Vanya exclaims that he might have been a Schopenhauer or a Dostoyevsky, we ought to feel that the claim is poi-gnant, pathetic. With Shawn, it doesn't get near pathos. The best one can say is that Shawn, with utter commitment, provides what he can of the Vanya needed for the weaving of the play's fabric; and his commitment helps the play/film to exist.

The adaptation is by David Mamet. To judge by one hearing, it's flex-ible and live. Though some cuts and adjustments have been made, Mamet is faithful to a fundamental quality in the work. He understands that, like all great writers, Chekhov stubbornly tells the truth about us, only the truth, but that, of all great writers, he is the gentlest.

Pulp Fiction

NOVEMBER 14, 1994 | By now everybody knows that Quentin Taran-tino is the happiest man in the world. Not so many years ago he was a clerk in a California video store, devouring film film film. Then he tried to break into filmmaking himself, first by writing scripts. It took years to get in. But those video days and the buff-dom of his boyhood sustained him, and now he is where he dreamed of being. He is making the films that will stock those video stores. Some younger aspirant will sell Tarantino tapes.

About his grit and passion, no question. About his achievements so far, some doubts. His first film was *Reservoir Dogs,* which drew particular attention because of its tidy frame and its offhand violence, which seemed to me shrewdly opportunistic—a subject and style carefully chosen by a man who wanted to get into filmmaking, who had tried various keys in the lock and had at last picked the right one. Then, along with other work, he wrote a story that Oliver Stone used as the basis for *Natural Born Killers*. (Composers often write virtuosic variations on simple tunes.) Now comes his much-trumpeted second film.

Pulp Fiction is *Reservoir Dogs* rewarded. Because of the first film's success, the second had a larger budget, thus has greater length, more stars, more lavish production, more violence—and certainly more room for the blackish humor that was visible in Tarantino's first. But, like the first film, *Pulp Fiction* revels in an underworld of menace and violence, of crime as cosmos, of sleaze. Tarantino of course wrote his own screenplay, and he tries to license his moral locale with an opening title that quotes two dictionary definitions of pulp. The first one is literal; the second is the figurative usage, derived from magazines of the past that were published on cheap pulp paper and specialized in lurid fiction of several genres.

He interweaves three stories. The film opens in a diner. A pair of petty crooks, played by Amanda Plummer and Tim Roth, after some dejected conversation decide to change their luck by robbing the very diner in which they are sitting. Just as they pull their pistols, we shift to the second story. John Travolta and Samuel L. Jackson are hit men for a drug czar, on their way to a hit. They converse casually, like telephone repairmen on their way to a routine job. They arrive where they're headed and do their killing.

That evening Travolta, under orders from his boss, escorts the boss's wife for the evening—dinner and dancing. The wife is Uma Thurman in a black wig. (A reference to Louise Brooks? Jeanne Moreau in *The Bride Wore Black?*) Thurman's greed for drugs complicates Travolta's evening with her.

The third story concerns a boxer, Bruce Willis. That same drug czar, Ving Rhames, apparently a heavy bettor, orders Willis to take a dive in the fifth round of an upcoming fight. Willis double-crosses him. This leads to his pursuit by the czar, more killing and the capture of both the boxer and the czar in a homosexual S&M den. (By now—no, before this—we are ticking off the film sources that Tarantino has been remembering.)

A further episode involves several of the above people—and Tarantino himself, passable in a small role—with Harvey Keitel, who repeats his performance in an earlier film as an efficient clean-up man for hit men in trouble. The picture closes at the diner where it began. Travolta and

Jackson arrive just as Plummer and Roth stick it up. (There's a time bend here—one of the picture's better gimmicks. We already know the fate that awaits Travolta elsewhere.)

At the center of most of the action—actually, it's just off-center—is a black attaché case, highly valuable for some unrevealed reason. Whenever it's opened, it lights the face of the person looking in. (Derived, perhaps, from the mysterious box in Buñuel's *Belle de Jour*.)

In one tangential way, Tarantino resembles recent Woody Allen: almost every one of his characters is a (presumably deliberate) cliché. The exception is in a flashback, a Marine officer just returned from Vietnam—and he's not really a character, just one long deadpan comic speech, laid in like a mosaic by Christopher Walken. All the others are familiar: the portentous gang chief, the workaday hit men (one of whom quotes the Bible), the pug with a streak of sentiment and so on.

Some of the action strains belief in a picture that dwells mostly in the naturalistic realm. On her night out, Thurman takes a life-threatening overdose of heroin, is revived at someone's house with a jolt of adrenalin straight to the heart, then is taken home by Travolta and dropped off as if it had been an ordinary date. I suppose there's meant to be some burlesque edge to this sequence, but even so, it's pretty farfetched. More matter-of-fact glitches: guns are fired in residential areas, and no neighbors seem to hear them. Willis kills a man, wipes the gun free of his fingerprints and then puts his prints on a doorknob. During the diner holdup, a couple of dozen people are ordered to lie on the floor. Not one of them makes a sound or a move—they become cardboard cut-outs—during long conversations among the principals.

Travolta, only seventeen years after *Saturday Night Fever*, has lost his looks but not his appeal: he is still quietly, modestly appealing. Jackson grows as he goes, a solid actor. Willis proves again that, when he has something other than an action-film dummy to play, he can act. Thurman is better as this tough cookie than as her usual Miss Winsome; still, it's hard to believe that she's an object of desire. Rhames, her husband, has taciturn depth. Plummer and Roth are beneath comment.

The designer, David Wasco, gave the settings the right gloppy postcard look, which Andrzej Sekula's camera exploits. Karyn Rachtman's music track buzzes the picture along very helpfully. And there's no doubt that director Tarantino's long film immersion has given him the eye and ear to do what he wants to do here — not only to pack the punch of the good Hollywood crime directors but to tease out the backhand sting that some of them had. Perhaps in the future he'll emulate other kinds of directors and films.

Meanwhile, however, what's most bothersome about *Pulp Fiction* is its success. This is not to be mean-spirited about Tarantino himself; may he harvest all the available millions. But the way that this picture has been so widely ravened up and drooled over verges on the disgusting. *Pulp Fiction* nourishes, abets, cultural slumming.

So much of what inundates us these days — in film, in various kinds of pop music — is calculated grunginess, of climate and temper. So much of what goes on in (what I hear of) rock music revels in the lower end of every kind of spectrum, grungy ideas and diction delivered by grungy people. So much of modern film seems to compete in grunginess. Very little of this stuff seems to have anything to do with the lives actually lived by its avid public. Most of it seems designed as guided tours of an underworld for people otherwise placed — career-oriented students, job-holding others. Escapism always has been one function of theater and film, and for ages it was cloyingly pretty-pretty. Boy, has the pendulum swung.

DECEMBER 19, 1994 | Several readers have complained about my complaint about *Pulp Fiction* — that Bruce Willis, after he kills the hit man, wipes his prints off the gun but then grabs the doorknob. Correspondents point out that this was Willis's apartment. Yes, but he leaves his prints on top of the hit man's, which means of course that he was there after the murder.

Oleanna

NOVEMBER 21, 1994 | David Mamet dazzles. Here are a few selections from his crowded career (and he's not yet fifty). Film: *House of Games,* which he wrote and directed; the screenplays of *The Verdict* and of *Hoffa.* Theater: *The Water Engine, American Buffalo, Glengarry Glen Ross, The Shawl,*

Speed-the-Plow, a version of *Uncle Vanya* (now filmed, reviewed here two weeks ago). He has published books of essays, and his first novel has just appeared. He has taught acting in several universities.

His plays and his original screenplays differ in style and intent, but most of them share some characteristics: a sense of life as tangle, of truth as prismatic and mercurial, of secrecy and deception as contemporary dynamics. Now a change arrives. His most hotly discussed play—recently filmed—has almost none of these qualities. *Oleanna* is a two-character work about a fortyish university professor and a female student, which tackles the subject of male attitudes toward women, of women's changing attitudes toward themselves. It is much leaner, more two-dimensional, more argumentative than most of Mamet.

Possibly this was inevitable because *Oleanna* attempts to deal with concrete social ideas. Perhaps, too, that's why he stripped his characters of the mysterious or quasi-mythical qualities that often attend his people. But if he did indeed tell himself that he had to put aside his characteristic art in order to do this job, he paid a price for the choice.

I saw *Oleanna* last year on stage and much admired Mamet's courage in confronting this thorny issue—one that's complicated both by oppressive tradition and bumptious innovation. But the play left me uncertain, distanced. I hadn't expected a "solution," but I had expected to be more greatly involved. Now the film medium has done ruthlessly to *Oleanna* what it often has done to other plays. This film, directed by Mamet himself, exposes what was ungainly in the play.

Let's look first at the writing, and we might as well begin with the title. As epigraph, Mamet quotes a folk song in which Oleanna is a place where the singer would rather be than "be bound in Norway / and drag the chains of slavery." I dare to question the title's relevance. It's no more relevant than *Speed-the-Plow* is to a play about the pyrotechnics of Hollywood deal-making.

Unlike the earlier play, however, this fancy title is the only non-prosy element in *Oleanna*. At the start, the student, Carol, comes to the office of John, a professor of education. She has read his book, which is the text of his course, but she can't understand what is happening in class, and she thinks she is failing. He is the one with power; she is the suppliant. The play's action, over several days, brings about a reversal of positions: at the end John needs Carol's help. Her persistence in her feminist views, as a base for her relations with this professor, her corkscrewing into his code of male acceptances, her newly realized insights about the (often unconscious) chivvying and patronizing of women, eventually unsettle John drastically—a man who had thought he was decently behaved and who finds that the social territory in which he has lived is slipping under his feet.

A highly promising subject for a play. But from the start Mamet loads his characters with broken dialogue that does nothing but impede character and thematic development. It seems an attempt to give these people familiar Mamet verism but without the inner counterpoints that so often take his dialogue past stenography into revelation. From the opening scene of *Oleanna:*

John: Don't you think. . . ?
Carol: . . . don't I think. . . ?
John: Mmm?
Carol: . . . did I. . . ?
John: . . . what?
Carol: Did . . . did I . . . did I say something wr. . .

John hasn't interrupted her; there's a pause before he replies.

Now, since this kind of writing seems inflicted on the characters, rather than internally generated by them, we're made to feel that Mamet is uneasy in this new territory, that he must "Mametize" what otherwise might have been pungent straight dialogue. Thus, from the very beginning, the dialogue itself suggests that the author is ill at ease.

Oleanna suffers, too, from distention. Mamet had here the material of a substantial one-act play in three scenes, but he wanted more bulk to provide more sense of the passage of time and possibly for practical reasons of theater production. (A long one-act play is, pragmatically, a white elephant.) So throughout the play, he braided long telephone conversations for John with his wife and his lawyer about the possible purchase of a house to celebrate his expected promotion to tenure. The telephone has long been suspect as a dramaturgic device, and it rarely has been used so blatantly to pad and to vary.

The prospective purchase of that house and the real estate agent's pressure might have made a good accompaniment to the onstage action if

Mamet hadn't used them so baldly. (Worse, at the one moment in the play when Carol reaches a point of self-revelation — "I have never told anyone this" — the phone interrupts her, and John goes into still another long phone aria. Her story is never resumed, which makes us think that Mamet is teasing: he didn't really know what Carol was going to say.)

Other bothersome matters. Early in the play John quotes a wisecrack about copulation so obviously out of character that it seems thumpingly planted for Carol's later accusation of abuse. Later, when she is about to leave, John grabs her by the shoulders and forces her to sit, an action that is extremely hard for us to believe — again a plant for later citation. And John's closing explosion, which finishes the story and him, comes after another phone talk with his wife in which he calls her "baby" a couple of times. When he hangs up, Carol tells him not to call his wife baby. This ignites him. I could believe her noting to John that he had used the word but not her ordering him to stop it. It's another contrived provocation. Add further that Carol, who in the early scenes had to ask for definitions of some common words, becomes competently articulate when Mamet needs her to be so.

Several commentators have said that *Oleanna* forces us to take sides. Exception, please. I felt tugs of sympathy for both characters from time to time, but the blunt mechanics of the work intruded between me and conviction either way. *Oleanna* seems to me a chunk of ore that needed greater refinement. Mamet, I'd say, needed to live longer with this idea before he began to write.

His direction of the film gives it some suppleness of movement without egregiously "opening up" a theater work. Debra Eisenstadt has more color as Carol than Rebecca Pidgeon had in the New York stage production. W. H. Macy repeats his theater performance as John. Mamet is devoted to Macy and often has used him in plays and films. This devotion may be understandable as friendship but not otherwise. Macy is a modestly adequate actor without distinction of face or voice or presence. He seems born for secondary roles at best and is out of place in larger ones — especially when he is half the cast.

Pidgeon, who is Mamet's wife, wrote some old-timey songs for the soundtrack, and Mamet supplied old-timey school-song lyrics. Their intended satire on the action before us is only mildly helpful.

Colonel Chabert

DECEMBER 26, 1994 | In one respect Gérard Depardieu is the Georges Simenon of French film: he supplies more work than America can handle. Simenon produced novels so plenteously, the Maigret series and others, that, though French publishers rejoiced in them, American publishers had to pick and choose to avoid glutting the market. Depardieu, in a slow year, makes three pictures, too many for the U.S. market. Some of his films have never been shown here.

Of course, not everything Depardieu does is at his best level. Unlike Simenon, who rarely wrote a clinker, Depardieu has fumbled from time to time. (I'm speaking only of the films that have been imported; the others I don't know.) In the poor ones he has usually relied on bluster, the oceanic energy that carries him along even when he is not really acting, as in *Camille Claudel* and *Cyrano de Bergerac*. But in very many pictures he has given acute performances that range awesomely in temper and that ring with every resource a talented actor can find in his imagination and body.

Consider: the anarchic hedonist in *Going Places;* the medieval peasant in *The Return of Martin Guerre;* the city man turned farmer in *Jean de Florette;* the ascetic, transfigured priest in *Under the Sun of Satan;* the ebullient yet shadowed hero of *Danton*—just a few from the Depardieu gallery. It's not leniency to infer that, in order to do his best work, he needs to do his lesser work. Prodigality is his mode of being: to pause and ponder for long stretches, as many leading actors do, would be to tamper with his artistic metabolism.

In a recent interview Emma Thompson, miraculous herself, said, "The essence of acting is concentration." This is not news (it has even been mentioned in this column), but it is simply, resoundingly true. The line lit up in my head at the first sight of Depardieu in the title role of his new film, made from Balzac's story *Colonel Chabert*. A wonderful, familiar double response thrilled through me. First, without any crevice for doubt, Chabert had arrived—a man, not an actor who had prepared. Second, it was Depardieu, *concentrating*. Once again he showed the power to transform himself at the same time that (which adds to the pleasure) we know it is Depardieu who is doing the transforming.

The year is 1817, the place a bustling law office in Paris. A knock at the door. A clerk opens. A heavyset man stands there, his face grim with expectation of trouble. He wears a coachman's coat and the oddly shaped top hat of the day. The clerk asks him who he is.

"I am Colonel Chabert."
"Which Colonel Chabert?"
"The one who was killed at Eylau."

We're off. A man has returned from the ghastly Napoleonic battle ten years earlier, alive despite beliefs to the contrary, clearly intent on re-establishing his life against odds. No one in the audience is likely to yawn at this point. (Or later, in fact.)

Since the story is by Balzac, it is about money. Certainly he treated other subjects, but centrally, as the greatest novelist thus far of the risen bourgeoisie, he focused on that class's chief arena of engagement, its chief concern in family relationships as well as in business. Chabert wants to recover his money from the wife who inherited it and who, believing him dead, remarried. (Says V. S. Pritchett: "The struggle to recover an inheritance is a theme to which Balzac continually returned.")

Chabert's existence is an unpleasant shock to his widow, now Countess Ferraud, and her husband. The countess, extremely rich, likes lolling in luxury; and her wealth has been one of her attractions for the count, who relies on her money to help him to a peerage under Louis XVIII. So Chabert has first to establish his identity, then face the effort to bilk him.

His lawyer, Derville, who (oddly enough) is also the countess's lawyer, is nonetheless a fair man. Though he is ferociously busy, his days and nights consecrated to money deals, Derville has a cynical view of the post-Revolution, post-Napoleonic society in which he lives, a society in which honor has sunk very low on the list of priorities.

He is played by Fabrice Lucchini, one of those actors whose initial appearance promises little but whose skill and intelligence, rather than power, make them appealing. The count is André Dussolier, most recently seen as the husband in *Un Coeur en Hiver*. Another polished performer. (And what voices French actors have. One reason I'm against dubbing, though I don't really understand French or any foreign language, is that I enjoy listening to the actors.) Fanny Ardant, the countess, has been problematic for me, with greater self-confidence than self. But maturity is bringing her more color, more understanding. These qualities help her performance of a woman who, under the blandishments, is venal.

As for Depardieu, I'll cite only his last scene. He has given up the fight for his money, he has given up the money world. (Pritchett again: the colonel has decided "to return to beggary because of his contempt for the vulgar meanness of his wife.") He sits on a bench in a hospice, leans on his walking stick and remembers Eylau—which we have seen earlier and now revisit. His eyes speak for him. Balzac's story is about transition. He has no illusions about the passing chivalric age, which Eylau symbolizes: Balzac knows its vanities and horrible cruelties. But it's the mercantile world that is swirling up around him, and it's the stench of that world that sickens him. Depardieu's Chabert comprehends all this.

Depardieu says that he wants to play the role of Balzac himself eventually. Speed the day. Perhaps that film can be directed by Yves Angelo, who directed here. Angelo, b. 1956, first took a degree in music, then studied film and worked for a long time as an assistant cameraman. He became a cinematographer and shot *Tous les Matins du Monde, Un Coeur en Hiver* and *Germinal,* among others. *Colonel Chabert* is his directing debut, and he was ready.

He understands movement and space—how to exploit small and large spaces—a crowded law office, a salon, a vast wintry battlefield after the battle. Angelo's cinematographer, Bernard Lutic, had the advantage of working for a man who knows precisely what he wants and knows how the camera can get it.

Angelo's musical background also enhances *Colonel Chabert,* reticently. Only chamber music is used. The Eylau scenes, with snow and dead men and dead horses, are silent except for a Beethoven trio, musing but not melting. Later, Mozart and Scarlatti and, with apt anachronism, Schubert and Schumann, add facets to this small gem of a film.

Through the Olive Trees

MARCH 20, 1995 | A couple of years ago, prompted by a friend, I went to see two Iranian films being shown in a special series. I remain grateful to the friend and to Abbas Kiarostami, the director of both films. Do we still need reminders that human connections, conveyed in art, persist through political differences? We still can use such reminders, I guess, especially when they come through truly good art.

I didn't write about those two films, *Where Is the Friend's Home?* and *And Life Goes On . . .* because (to my knowledge) they were not released here. Now comes Kiarostami's *Through the Olive Trees.* According to this year's *International Film Guide,* Kiarostami's latest was "the most note-worthy international success for Iranian cinema." It has been shown at a number of festivals and has won several awards. All this is somewhat surprising because of the film's quality.

Through the Olive Trees (1994) may be the quietest film I've ever seen. It takes even further the tone of the previous two by this director. They were of course composed for the eye, but they have the effect of tales told, of spoken narrative. Because they are gentle, meditative, immersed in the tempo and relations of the life they portray, they make us feel that we are listening to a village bard. They have a certain kinship with the films of Sembène and Ouedraogo. The local culture hasn't moved up to film-speed, so to speak, and the artist has used film as part of the local culture.

Kiarostami says that when he had finished *And Life Goes On . . . ,* which took place in northern Iran after the terrible earthquake of 1990, he be-came interested in a young pair who were in the film. They were not actors—he had used them more or less as themselves—and he noticed that they were not getting on very well together. Hossein wanted to marry Farkhonde, but she declined. Hossein was illiterate; she wasn't. He was able to provide; she didn't care. He wanted her very much; she was silent. (Taciturnity touches all these people. Hossein, the eager lover, isn't exactly loquacious.)

In *Olive Trees* Kiarostami goes back to the young pair's village to inves-tigate how they got together in the first place. All the people in the film play themselves—they are the persons in the story or members of the film crew—with the exception of Kiarostami, who is played by a professional actor. (The director says he can't function on both sides of the camera.) To describe what happens in the film is to make it sound almost parodic. It isn't, though it is a serene comment on the myriad films that sweat so hard to be gripping.

After he selects some extras, Kiarostami sets up his camera outside a markedly unsplendid house. He shoots a scene. On a balcony Hossein proposes to Farkhonde who is reading a magazine and doesn't even look at him as he speaks. Hossein then comes downstairs and speaks to another man. Here he makes a mistake. The director asks him to repeat the scene from the top. Again Hossein makes a mistake. Several times—I lost count—the scene is repeated from the beginning. Hossein never gets it quite right, and at last Kiarostami settles for what he has.

This whole section is the main part of the film! It is not remotely satirical, of Hossein or anyone else. It is a quintessence of the values of all the people concerned: the value of time, of amity, of shared beliefs, of filmmaking itself.

Farkhonde, waving off the offer of a ride, starts to walk back to her home. Hossein follows her, still talking, still proposing, still getting not even a glance, let alone a word. The camera then falls back and lets the pair walk into a long shot. Hossein follows her up a long zigzag path across the face of a hill, then over the top of it. Then, from the top, we watch him, still talking, follow her across the valley. We watch from a great distance as they make their way across a field. When they are very far off, he gets fairly close to her. They do not touch, but there is a moment's pause. She continues on her way; he turns and heads back toward us. The end.

Did she accept him? Yes, apparently, since they were together in the previous film, which takes place later; and *The Film Guide* says "the boy receives a positive response." But the quiet of the film pervades even his success. Whatever happened, I felt that for 103 minutes I had been in a different world of film. Neorealism? *Cinéma vérité?* Labels are more intrusive than helpful.

Here is a quotation from an interview with Kiarostami:

When I come on the set in the morning and I notice that my camera operator hasn't slept well, I avoid complex camera movements without letting him know. I do the same with the actors. If an actor has to play a sad scene and I notice that he is in a better mood than on previous days, I alter the shooting schedule.

With another director, this might be pretentious hogwash. With Kiarostami, I believe it—at least in intent. His films seem familial enterprises.

APRIL 13, 1998 | Like much that he has done, Abbas Kiarostami's *Taste of Cherry* is so simple that initially it's difficult. The latest film by this fifty-seven-year-old Iranian writer-director begins with a close-up of a middle-aged man driving slowly around Teheran in a Range Rover, past men who are waiting to be hired for anything and who offer their services. Mr. Badii (as he's called) shakes his head and drives on into the countryside. He speaks to a man who collects plastic bags for a living. He picks up in turn a young soldier, a security guard, a seminarian, and—the oldest of the lot—a taxidermist. To each he makes the same offer.

Mr. Badii will pay the person well if, next day, that person will come to a place that he points out, a hole in a hillside. Mr. Badii will be lying in that hole. If he is dead, the other man will bury him. If he is alive, the other man will help him out. In either case there will be plentiful money in the car. An advance is offered. All the men refuse the job. In fact, the young soldier runs away when Mr. Badii stops the car.

Suicide is a proscribed subject in Iran, which is why, presumably, Mr. Badii puts his offer in that odd way. He is quite serious in his intent, though he doesn't state it unequivocally, and wants to be sure that he is buried. Most of the men he picks up try to dissuade him. The taxidermist even tells him that once he contemplated suicide but changed his mind. He climbed up a tree to fix a rope. It turned out to be a mulberry tree, says the taxidermist, and the taste of one mulberry altered his view, brought him back to life, to living. (Later on, only in passing, he mentions cherries. Mulberries are the important fruit.) But Mr. Badii persists. Without having found a collaborator, he nonetheless drives back to the hole in the hillside, lies in it, and watches a storm over Teheran.

There is more to come, but here let's look at what has happened so far, which is the bulk of the film. Through the first minutes, through the first interview (and despite what we may know of Kiarostami's past work), we wait for something to develop out of Mr. Badii's request, some explanation of his motives for suicide, some increment of story. None of this comes about. Before long, we understand that this calm journey *is* the film—Mr. Badii's quest among the living for someone who will assist in his ritual of death. This slow search in a Range Rover takes on aspects of a medieval morality play like *Everyman,* in which a protagonist, open almost to the point of naïveté, finds answers that enlarge his questions. And, as the film's design becomes clear to us, a quiet spaciousness begins to inhabit it.

On this hillside Mr. Badii watches the moon sail through the clouds. Then comes morning, and a change. We see the morning *on film:* the view of the city below is presented in that grainy texture that filmmakers use to convey the sense of looking at a TV screen. Then, in usual focus, we see a film crew on the hillside, with the actor who plays Mr. Badii moving amidst the cameras and mike booms.

I have no compunction about revealing this conclusion. In fact, having experienced it, I still feel this change as a surprise and know it will surprise me again the next time I see *Taste of Cherry.* Besides, this switch from observation to observer, as we quickly remember, has often been used by Kiarostami.

Gilberto Perez says that Kiarostami's work moves "with remarkable naturalness . . . from the representation of reality to the representation, as part of reality, of the means of representation." (The section on Kiarostami in Perez's new book, *The Material Ghost,* is the best comment I have seen on the subject.) This perception helps to shift us from familiar Pirandellian ambiguity to latter-day holism. Characters are no longer in search of an author; authorship is now part of character. Observation of ourselves in the world is now part of being in the world. The appearance of the camera and crew is a reification of that truth, which exists whether or not a camera is present.

Kiarostami's work, as far as I know, has rarely had narrative or dramatic complexity. (I've seen five of his features, plus *The White Balloon,* which he wrote for another director.) Like Ozu and Antonioni, with whom he has rightly been compared, Kiarostami seems to look at film not as something to be made, but to be inhabited, as if it were *there* always, like the world, waiting to be stepped into, without fuss. Neither Ozu nor Antonioni used the camera's presence to underscore this concept. But at their best, both of them made film disappear—in any of its cajoling modes. It simply dissolves into being. So with Kiarostami.

Consequently the actors in *Taste of Cherry* don't make actors' points (something that many of us relish in other contexts). This director wants little more from them than wholeness of self. Homayoun Ershadi, as Mr. Badii, gives us a man whose harsh decision came from some place far beyond dramatics. Ali Moradi, the soldier, has the right air of growing discomfort as he hears more and more from Mr. Badii, as if he were discovering that he is riding with an infected man. Abdolhossein Bagheri, the taxidermist, gives his role the seasoned humanity of a man who loves life despite what he knows about it.

One fact in the press kit is not discernible in the film itself. The chief actors did not work with one another. Most of the film takes place in the front seat of the Range Rover; Mr. Badii drives, and his passenger responds. But the two segments of each sequence, driver and passenger, were filmed separately. In each case the sequence was filmed with Kiarostami himself (unseen) doing the driving and asking the questions, while the other man, on camera, answered. Subsequently, this footage was intercut with shots of Mr. Badii at the wheel asking the questions.

This method has a tinge of Godard's device of asking questions of his actors while he was off camera, through invisible ear devices, in order to keep them attuned to the world around the shot; and it also suggests Bresson's hatred of acting. A Bresson anecdote has him, at a rehearsal, saying to his actors: "If you all don't stop acting, I'm going to leave." One can imagine Kiarostami using this (invisible) split-screen device as a guard against acting in any conventional sense.

How Kiarostami has had a career in such a straitened country as Iran is another miracle. (*Taste of Cherry* was blocked from export because of its topic, suicide. Extreme efforts by people outside Iran got it to the Cannes Film Festival last year, where it was awarded the Palme d'Or.) Censorship is only one of the obstacles. Yet Kiarostami, along with other Iranian directors, has been creating a film culture in the last decades that is engrossing beyond much that is being done in less constricted countries, a culture that is deep and pure, revelatory of a people he loves. And like all national art that is sufficiently truthful, his work is illuminating for us all.

POSTSCRIPT | A second viewing emphasizes, among other matters, some details in that last film-conscious section on the hill. A squad of soldiers is seen training on a road below. Also below, a group of children play in a schoolyard. The soldiers remind us of the one we have met and his innate fear of Mr. Badii. The children remind us that the taxidermist had mentioned the sound of children playing as a simple, important pleasure.

The soldiers are ordered to fall out, and as they relax, grinningly aware of the camera's presence, we hear the "St. James Infirmary" blues. A soldier's pocket radio? In any case, life insistently burrows in.

Stalingrad

JUNE 5, 1995 | In the summer of 1942 Hitler seemed headed for triumph in World War Two. The Mediterranean had become an Axis lake; German armies were slicing through Russia; an Allied invasion of Europe seemed remote, perhaps impossible. Yet by February 1943 the balance had swung. Two events had altered Hitler's prospects: the Allied invasion of North Africa and the horrendous battle of Stalingrad. That battle, which involved about 1 million men, was a pinnacle of bloodshed. After six months of some of the most slaughterous fighting in history, the Russian forces not only stood firm at the Volga, they crumpled the German armies. Says Eric Hobsbawm: "From Stalingrad on everyone knew that the defeat of Germany was only a question of time."

Four years ago German producers decided to make a long and detailed film about this pivotal defeat. It's not a documentary but a fiction film, in the sense that characters have been created who are portrayed by actors; yet the facts that underlie the film seem accurate, as far as they go.

Stalingrad was co-written and directed and photographed by Joseph Vilsmaier, who has made two previous features (unseen by me). His 150-minute work begins at an Italian beach resort in the summer of 1942 where a company of German soldiers is resting and convalescing after African campaigns. Then they are shipped to Stalingrad as specialists who can help break the stalemate. In the following months, marked especially by the arrival of snow, we follow their decimation and the eventual collapse of morale.

Vilsmaier's cinematography is excellent: the colors don't glamorize, they confirm. (The film was mostly shot in Czechoslovakia.) His directing is competent, controlled. His actors are entirely credible. His contrasts between small huddled groups and vast wintry landscapes are telling, his plunges into combat are expert. The basic trouble with *Stalingrad* is that, as film, we have seen it before. The data are different, naturally, but we know from past war films that friendships will be ended by bullets, that some hothead will fire at the wrong time, that one or two men will simply crack under pressure, and, in a German film, there will be some soldiers who despise Hitler. Except for an episode with a Russian woman, Vilsmaier's film is honest; but honesty is not quite enough to enliven the familiarity.

And there are contextual matters. No one could expect this film to be anything like a complete history of the event, yet two salient facts are omitted. First, no hint is given of Hitler's attitude toward this battle. He insisted maniacally, despite the incredible losses, that the army push on; then, when the futility of that command became at last clear even to him, he insisted that the army fight to the last man. When the German commander Friedrich Paulus surrendered the 91,000 men left out of his more than 300,000, Hitler excoriated him. Second, there is no hint that tens of thousands of Axis forces were not German: there were very many Italians, Hungarians and Romanians. Both of these important facts could have seeped into the film.

When *Stalingrad* was released in Germany in 1993, storms broke in the press. Pulling no punches, the producers gave the film its premiere on the fiftieth anniversary of the German surrender. Reactions were, foreseeably, mixed. Vilsmaier and his colleagues maintain that the picture was made as a reminder of the horrors of war, especially for those tempted by neo-fascism today. We can of course hope it has that deterrent effect. But there's another effect. The film portrays the (historically unquestionable) courage of the German troops. We can't help wondering about the results if that courage had been rewarded. How much admiration or compassion can we feel for an army whose defeat was crucial to any chance that civilization may still have?

The courage—at least equivalent—of the Russians and the appearance of some of them in the picture remind us of another question, one that historians have pondered. The tenacity and sacrifice of the Russians at Stalingrad have never been surpassed. (In just one German air raid on the city, 40,000 civilians were killed. Total Russian casualties were estimated at 700,000.) Yet the Russians already had endured almost twenty years of Stalin's terror and were, essentially, fighting here to maintain it. What underlay their courage? The fear that Hitler's terror might be even worse? The powerful image of Mother Russia?

An irony is added to this puzzle. Eight years after Stalin died, the name of the city was changed to Volgograd.

Sister My Sister

JULY 17 & 24, 1995 | Murder inspires. The list is long of films, plays, novels, ballets begotten by real-life killings. Two of the more fertile murders, in that sense, occurred in 1933 in Le Mans, a French town otherwise noted only for auto racing. Two young sisters who worked as maids for a well-to-do Le Mans family murdered their mistress and her daughter— butchered them, in fact. Stimulated imaginatively by the story, Jean Genet wrote *The Maids* in 1946, a jewel in the crown of that fantastic genius; in 1964 Nico Papatakis, a French filmmaker, produced *Les Abysses* from the same material; and a few years ago the American playwright Wendy Kesselman used the material for her play *My Sister in This House*. Nancy Meckler, an American resident in Britain, directed the play in London; and now, with Kesselman's screenplay, Meckler has directed the film— called *Sister My Sister*.

Every aspect of the filmmaking itself is superb. Ashley Rowe, the cinematographer, has found exactly the right balance of light and shadow, the right temper of color, to make every shot look both natural and careful, the everyday put before us as evidence of strangeness. Even in those scenes where little happens, our eyes can discern some sort of imminence.

As for the directing, no one on earth could tell that this is a first film. Meckler has been directing in the British theater for twenty years (including a production of *Macbeth* with Julie Walters, who is in this film) and has run her own company, the Shared Experience Theater. In her film debut, she seizes us at once. Before the credits we see, over music and without voices, a sequence of the two sisters as children, happy together, the older one caring for the younger—shot in gray and white like a faded photograph. After the credits, color manifests the passage of time, as the camera moves slowly down the staircase in a prosperous house. We see no one. We see great blood smears on floor and walls. Then, following this Before and After prelude, the film begins.

Throughout the picture, Meckler directs with jeweler's precision, reflecting her work with actors in the theater, yet her film never becomes cinematically static. Neither does she fall into the debutante's error of pouring on cinematic tricks just to prove that a theater director knows all about film. (A fault that snagged even the early Bergman.) What we are conscious of constantly, in a gripping rather than a constricting way, is design. Everything that Meckler chooses to show us, every move of her characters, every elision, every variation of pace is part of that hard, quiet, compelling design, moving toward murder.

Good small touches aid this design. When the two sisters go to a photographer for a picture, we never see him. We only see them posing, while his mellifluous voice keeps trying to winkle information out of them about their employer. The fact that we never see the man even though they are in his studio underscores their isolation. When a faucet drips in the kitchen where the sisters work, we may tense a bit at the cliché, but Meckler amplifies it into a motif.

Joely Richardson plays Christine, the older sister. Unlike her own older sister, Natasha, Joely looks more like her father, Tony Richardson, than her mother, Vanessa Redgrave; but, like Natasha, Joely has inherited an electric talent from her mother. Redgrave, in her autobiography, says of one of Joely's theater performances that it had "fresh spontaneity," "gaiety and gentle gravity." (And why shouldn't a mother review her daughter?) Redgrave would have to alter her terms of admiration here. In this film Richardson is a coiled spring, first sexually, then homicidally.

At the start, when her younger sister Lea joins Christine for service in this house, there is the joy of reunion. Christine's only anxiety is for Lea to learn and succeed in her work. Then, as their employer Madame Danzard becomes more peremptory, as the girls' loneliness and proximity to each other begin to work on them, as sisterly love becomes incestuous, Richardson dramatizes the changes in Christine. Not with crassness but with restraint, a restraint that finally fails, Richardson's face and voice tell us of fires and fears and a sexual storm about to break. When the sisters' security is threatened, hot incestuous passion bursts into maniacal frenzy.

As Lea, Jodhi May is the perfect partner. Where Richardson is incisive, May is tremulous, supine, abject. Lea spends most of her waking life in some kind of terror, and, as the prologue predicted, she depends on her sister for protection and control. Latterly, she also depends on Christine for sex. When Christine goes amuck, Lea is of course transmuted with her. May is so desperately subservient to Richardson that we understand why, as the closing titles tell us, Lea was sentenced to only twenty years while Christine was sentenced to the guillotine. (After her prison term Lea worked as a hotel chambermaid until her death in 1982. Christine's death sentence was commuted; she died four years later in an asylum, a mental and physical wreck.)

Julie Walters very neatly draws the character of Madame Danzard, without caricature but with an aplomb based on bank accounts. Sophie Thursfield, too, avoids caricature as her lumpy, bored and boring daughter for whom marriage is a continually receding goal.

However, there is a trouble with the film—Kesselman's screenplay. It's skillfully constructed and written, but it's sheer pathology, nothing else. The film is thus only a case history, not a drama, with nothing ultimately to offer other than a chronicle of breakdown, the fracturing of two minds under psychosexual pressures. As with Papatakis's film of some thirty years ago, Kesselman's script suffers from the existence of Genet's play (which itself was sinuously filmed in 1974).

Genet soared far beyond the data of the story. He used the facts as a launchpad into a metaphysical agon, entailing aspects of reality and identity and morality. Kesselman's version is a reductive jolt, back to the data. Still, even if it had no work of genius to compete with, the screenplay of *Sister My Sister* would seem insufficient. A chronicle of disintegration is a long way from a drama of disintegration—such as, for instance, *A Streetcar Named Desire*. (I mention Williams's play, not to swat Kesselman with another work of genius, simply to illustrate the point.)

But whatever could be done with Kesselman's screenplay, Meckler and Richardson and May and all their colleagues have achieved it, with dedication and with art.

Carrington

DECEMBER 4, 1995 | Christopher Hampton is best known in this country for his dramatization, on stage and screen, of *Les Liaisons Dangereuses,* but he has been an eminent figure in the British theater for more than thirty years. For twenty of those years he has been interested in the story of Dora Carrington and Lytton Strachey and has been involved in several aborted attempts to film it. At last *Carrington* arrives, and in a way we can all be glad that it was delayed because Hampton became empowered to direct it, and his two leading actors wouldn't have been available twenty years ago.

These days a certain ridiculous risk is involved in making a film set in Britain before World War One: rote cries of "Masterpiece Theater" rend the air on cue. In this case, the cries, already audible, are especially dumb: the Carrington-Strachey affair is deployed before us for its depth of character. It would be silly, even ungrateful, to deny the benefits bestowed by Caroline Amies, the production designer, and Penny Rose, the costume designer. (I confess that I wondered how they made Strachey's tweed hat crinkle in just the right way.) But the appurtenances of class and of conscious bohemianism are integral to the characters themselves, not imposed as decor. Settings and story are unified.

That story will be familiar to those who have read Michael Holroyd's *Lytton Strachey* or Gretchen Holbrook Gerzina's *Carrington*. Hampton's screenplay is derived from the former. Dora Carrington, who disliked her first name and never used it, was born in 1893 to a middle-class family, and, sufficiently moneyed, devoted herself to a life of painting — amateur in the sense that she wasn't concerned with exhibiting and selling. Strachey, born in 1880, the son of a general, was educated at Cambridge, where he joined friends who later became what was called the Bloomsbury Group. Strachey, not very well off, wrote reviews mostly, without any strenuous ambition to get rich by writing. He and Carrington met in 1915 when he was well known in his circle as a homosexual, and Carrington was equally well known as a virgin. She soon changed her state, he never changed his, but the central fascination about them is that theirs is a love story.

Whether anything sexual ever happened between them, as may possibly have been the case, is not the point. They certainly had active sexual lives apart from each other. Yet they were mutually devoted, he in his designedly reticent yet airy way, constantly striving to translate experience into Wildean epigrams, she much more unguarded and frankly emotional, percipient and patient. Basically what is portrayed here is marital love without sex. Though each was active with other partners — Carrington even married someone else — their love was so strong that his death in 1932 became her own death sentence.

A cruel joke of fate, their situation? With Olympian detachment, we might say so; yet if Strachey had been heterosexual, he wouldn't have been the person he was, and it's the person he was that Carrington, knowing all about him early on, fell in love with and continued to love. Perhaps it wasn't a joke of fate, just a fate.

Still, it is that fate, settled early for both, that keeps this excellently executed film from being deeply moving. Once the pair fall in love, nothing fundamental changes for either. Each of them has multiple adventures: Strachey's biggest one is in becoming a best-selling author—first with *Eminent Victorians*—which disconcerts him a bit. The development in the film is in character, not in drama. That development has its rewards, of inflection and reflection, but they are not dramatic; and the finish of the story, for all its pathos, is relatively calm—a termination rather than a climax.

Paradoxically, none of this could be true if the two leading performances were not so fine, if these two characters were not worlds in themselves. Jonathan Pryce has already been garlanded for his Strachey with the Cannes Film Festival prize, and for a change that prize was something more than dim-witted obeisance to propaganda. Pryce, bearded and spindly, like a self-guided marionette, creates the anomaly of a physically weak man whose strength lies in flaunting that weakness. He has the advantage of speaking all the witty lines in the script; still, he himself creates a caustic charm.

Emma Thompson, who is Carrington, got no prize at Cannes, and my personal consolation is that no prize is good enough for her. Talk about the art that conceals art! Thompson never makes us feel that she is mastering a mood or responding tellingly or providing any other individuated touches. A soul, a spirit, a mind—this is not too strong—have been apprehended, and a body has been provided for them. By now we expect this of Thompson, from the spicy modern sex comedy of *The Tall Guy* through Shakespearean perfection in *Much Ado about Nothing* to the private-public, volatile yet well-bred Carrington. This film, for all its other brilliancies, would collapse without the central truth of her performance. Even Pryce's scintillation depends on her.

To which I must add mention of assistance she has had. The lighting of her face, in widely varied circumstances, by Denis Lenoir is marvelous. Lenoir doesn't prop up Thompson's acting the way cinematography must sometimes do, but he understands her face and what she needs. To which mention must be added the comfort of Michael Nyman's score, conceived in chamber music terms. I can't remember another film in which a string quartet accompanies sex scenes. Nyman's music bespeaks the world of these people.

Hampton directs with what can be called the courage of his convictions—about these characters. One archetypal instance is the first meeting of Carrington and Strachey. They are fellow-guests at a country house, and after they are introduced, they have nothing to say to each other. They're not much interested in each other. The camera holds them for, I'd guess, a full minute while they attempt to make comments, find few, and are both completely unembarrassed. After the film cuts to the next scene, we realize how tacitly funny that meeting scene was: we feel a tingle of anticipation that this picture is going to be handled intelligently. And it is.

Sense and Sensibility

JANUARY 8 & 15, 1996 | Lionel Trilling might have been pleased with at least one aspect of *Sense and Sensibility*. In his essay "Why We Read Jane Austen," he names her visual sense as one of her chief attributes, then says, "Notable among the elements of visuality . . . is that of *scale*, the relation in size between human beings and the components of their environment." Early in this film, soon after the death of his father, John Dashwood is riding in a carriage with his wife through the countryside, discussing the portion of his large inheritance that he ought to give to his stepmother and her daughters. (He had promised his dying father that he would help them.) Mrs. Dashwood keeps nipping at him to reduce the amount, and he is easy to convince. As his generosity shrinks, their mingy conversation is intercut with shots of the landscape they're traversing— pastoral, lovely, pure. This contrast dramatizes Trilling's view of scale. Every prospect pleases; only man and wife are vile.

The odd effect of this opening is charm. The sardonic point is certainly made, but the grace with which it is done, the chuckling justness of the perception, draw us into the film with added eagerness. No disappointments lie ahead. The director and the screenwriter truly understand the book's temper and tone. This fact is all the more gratifying considering who they are.

Ang Lee, the director, is Taiwanese, trained in theater and film in his own country and in New York. His best-known previous pictures are *The Wedding Banquet* and *Eat Drink Man Woman,* both of which are based in Taiwanese culture. Now here he is presumptuously understanding English culture at the end of the eighteenth century.

Scratch as hard as we like to disclose Asian influence in Lee's directing here, all we'll find is one more proof that a gifted director is something of an actor: with the right imagination, he can place himself at the center of perspectives far from his native ones. He can make his discoveries his domain. For instance, many of Lee's shots of interiors are framed by the doorways of the rooms in which people are sitting. This framing gently underscores that English age's passion for neatness, for containment—in furnishings, manners, outlook. Sometimes, with a tilt of the camera, he manages to suggest the serpentine wriggling of jealousies, in a sort of postscript to *The School for Scandal.* In any case, he shows both the sense and the sensibility of an artist.

Then there is the screenplay. More presumptuousness. Just because Emma Thompson has a degree in English from Cambridge, has co-written some of her theater and TV material, has proved in roles from Shakespeare through raunchy modern comedy that she is a magnificent acting talent, does that mean she has the right and ability to do a full-dress screenplay of a classic novel?

Headstrong as she is, she apparently didn't wait for an answer to that question: she simply plunged ahead. (The screenplay has just been published, along with Thompson's vivid, funny, gamy diaries of the shoot. Fifty photos, thirty-six in color.) The result can easily be chided by maniacally zealous Austenites, but such folk probably should not go to films of Austen unless they want to sneer. Of course Thompson has condensed; inevitably she had to add a line here and there to accommodate an action; and she has altered very slightly. For instance, Lucy Steele, the young woman secretly engaged to Elinor Dashwood's beloved, is made somewhat less vulgar here. When Elinor learns the happy truth about Edward Ferrars, she does not hurry from the room to "burst into tears of joy," she does it immediately, right in front of him.

Such adjustments—there are others—can hardly be counted grave losses. What is lost, what must be lost in the filming of any good novel, let alone a great one, is the prose. We've been told by some that the current wave of Austen adaptations shows that we hunger for a cosmos secured by good manners. For me, this film adaptation makes the matter more complex, almost contradictory. Shorn of the prose that in some measure fulfills the novel's theme, the action alone of this *Sense and Sensibility* adaptation becomes a somewhat pitiless exposé of a cruel society: young women whose sole function is to find proper husbands; young men whose sole function is to inherit money or to marry it. Thus, rather than extolling the allegedly enviable assurances of the past, the film implicitly admires the present for being in great degree different.

Yet, once again with an important novel, if something is lost or skewed through film transmutation, something is gained if the film is good—as it resoundingly is here. First, the actors. Absolutely every role is cast with the hand of a Cellini setting gems in a design. Here I can tender only a few actors a grateful bow. Alan Rickman, from his very first utterance, endows Colonel Brandon with gravity and secrets. Gemma Jones, as the mother of the heroines, worries with touching reserve. Greg Wise, as the devious Willoughby, has the immediate appeal he needs to make him dangerous. Harriet Walter gives the scheming Fanny Dashwood the profile of maneuver. And, surprise of surprises, Hugh Grant makes no faces. He acts. He really creates the harried Edward Ferrars—hobbled just a bit because Grant is the only one in the cast who seems uneasy in costume.

Then there are the two "title" characters. Miss Sensibility—or, as we might say, sensitivity—is a relative newcomer, Kate Winslet. At first she seems just one more English rose; but very rapidly she whirls into impulse and vulnerability and romantic intoxication with heart-aching verity. A captivating performance.

Miss Sense is played by the screenwriter, E. Thompson (who spent five years working intermittently on the script while she acted in seven films). As it happens, just after I saw *Carrington,* in which she plumbed the eccentric love of an upper-class Bloomsbury artist, I saw a videotape of *Look Back in Anger,* made some years ago, in which she played Alison, drowning poignantly in dreariness. Now her Elinor Dashwood arrives. Thompson's power of inner transformation is so acute as to be almost uncanny. She had a particular problem here. She is thirty-six and can't look a great deal younger on the screen. Elinor is—not only in age—a quite young woman. To help Thompson, her mother, who is forty in the novel, was cast older; so was her next-younger sister, Marianne, who is only seventeen in the novel. Still, Thompson's role, as conceived by Austen, is of a woman some fifteen years younger than herself. What's extraordinary is how Thompson (certainly with Ang Lee's help, as the diaries make clear) evokes the youthfulness without a touch of the coy.

Again, as with *Carrington,* let's disregard those who start yipping "Masterpiece Theater" whenever they see a period film; and let's admire the wonderfully suitable work by the production designer, Luciana Arrighi, and the costume designers Jenny Beavan and John Bright, all of whom worked on *Howards End* as well as on numerous period and modern films, plays and operas.

Patrick Doyle, who composed the excellent scores for both of Kenneth Branagh's Shakespeare films, did the music for this picture, grounding himself affectingly in Mozart slow movements. The cinematographer was Michael Coulter, a master of (seeming) candlelight and lamplight.

A last bow to Lindsay Doran and her producing colleagues, who were able to see in the director of *Eat Drink Man Woman* the director of *Sense and Sensibility.*

Fargo

MARCH 25, 1996 | The hot news about Joel and Ethan Coen is that they have made a tolerable film. Previously we were assaulted by the adolescent trickery and sententiousness of such numbers as *Barton Fink* and *The Hudsucker Proxy.* But in *Fargo* they have shucked the brightest-boys-in-film-school doodads and have, by and large, stuck to an organic story. The results are mixed, but at least they are not uniformly pretentious.

The story, said to be based on fact, begins in Fargo, North Dakota, and soon moves to Minneapolis. It's winter; everything is snowy. The whole picture seems to huddle in down jackets and to smell of damp wool. The nub of the plot is domestic kidnapping: a man hires thugs to kidnap his wife so that he can get ransom money out of his rich father-in-law. We know, naturally, that the plan is going to be stymied or there would be no picture. It ends with a number of killings and with almost a million dollars in cash lying buried in the snow that no one left alive is aware of.

The film's big trouble is that it wobbles badly in tone. The opening shot, eerily photographed by Roger Deakins, is of a car approaching through the snow, headlights on though it is day, while Carter Burwell's score prophesizes dark doings. But the doings that soon follow are much more farcical than grave. All through the film, Burwell's score seems to have been written for a different picture, and Deakins's camera seems to be searching for a Bergman subject.

The man who plots against his wife is played by William H. Macy, whom some directors continue to find interesting. One of the thugs is Steve Buscemi, who as usual—and entertainingly—acts in italics. His sidekick is done by Peter Stormare, the Swedish actor who has played Hamlet for Bergman as part of a long and varied career in his country's film and theater worlds. Here he is awesomely granitic.

The plum part went to Frances McDormand, who makes the most of it. She plays the police chief of a small town who happens to be seven months pregnant. At first she seems to be a female Dogberry, just a rube constable; but through her "Yups" and "Yeahs" we soon see a quiet intelligence at work. The Coen brothers wrote her role best. Much of the time they seem to have had *Pulp Fiction* in their ears—strings of incongruous banalities; but with this pregnant cop, they struck some gold of their own.

If only they had decided what kind of picture they wanted to make. The question is not academic nicety. Their jumbling of tones makes the grim parts harder to credit and makes the funny parts seem like old-fashioned comic relief. Still, *Fargo* is a great step forward for the brothers Coen.

Secrets and Lies

SEPTEMBER 30, 1996 | Aristotle was wrong: plot is not more important than character. Of course he was talking about tragedy, but that's no excuse. His dictum has become more and more questionable, especially in this century. Aristotle is challenged once again, in a small but unabashed way, by Mike Leigh's new film *Secrets & Lies.*

Leigh, deliberately or not, is an apt challenger because character is his prime interest. He is noted in English theater and film for his extensive work with actors long before the acting begins, leading them into ways of thinking and living that will help them to plumb their roles. The result, in such films as *High Hopes* and *Life Is Sweet,* is almost as if the actors came down from the screen and sat among us, so confident are they in their achieved new beings.

Leigh's last film, *Naked,* was a touch too mannered à la Godard to have his usual immediacy. But he's back in form with *Secrets and Lies.* The characters are pores-open vivid, so vivid that the gimmick of the plot and the feel-good ending don't distract much. (Take *that,* Mr. A.)

Hortense is a young black Londoner, an optometrist, practicing successfully and living intelligently. She was an adopted child, and her adoptive mother has just died. Hortense now wants to find her biological mother, and through a social agency she learns who it is. The agency advises her not to investigate further on her own, to let them handle it, but she disregards this caution and arranges to meet her mother, who, she has just learned, is white.

Cynthia, the mother, had given birth twenty-seven years ago when she was fifteen, doesn't even remember immediately having been with a black man, and had never seen the baby. The film proceeds through the effect that black Hortense has on Cynthia and on Cynthia's family—her other daughter, white and fully grown; Cynthia's brother and his wife: and the effect that this effect has on Hortense. Somewhat surprisingly, Hortense is accepted with relative ease. This is quite credible in the warm-hearted Cynthia and her equally warm-hearted brother, Maurice, who is a good man just to the edge of our belief; but it's not exactly foreseeable in the others, including the white daughter's white boyfriend.

Still, if disbelief isn't quite suspended, it becomes secondary because of the acting. It's excellent, all the way. The social worker in the agency at the start is played by Lesley Manville with such a subtle note of well-practiced friendliness, such a careful blend of professionalism and boredom, that our appetites are whetted for more acting at that level. And we get it.

Marianne Jean-Baptiste plays Hortense and makes us glad of it every moment. She gives the young woman pride and reticence and unhistrionic appeal. Brenda Blethyn, as her mother, triumphs in a particular way: she has to do a great deal of crying for several reasons, but it's never false or tedious, and she manages considerable variety in it, reflecting the different causes for the tears.

Timothy Spall is Maurice, owner of a neighborhood photography studio, who is a congenital force for goodness. Phyllis Logan is his chronically short-tempered wife, whose moods are eventually explained. Actors who play rebarbative parts often get inadequate recognition; so let's note Logan's skill and understanding. Claire Rushbrook, as Hortense's white half-sister, is even more short-tempered. She works as a street-cleaner, instead of going to college, as a sort of revenge on the world, an adult version of a childish tantrum. Rushbrook, too, presents a realized person.

Leigh certainly helped all these people to their performances and, knowing how good they had become, knew how to rely on them. For instance, at the first meeting of Hortense and Cynthia, they have tea in a drab little shop, otherwise empty. Leigh never cuts during this scene: his camera remains fixed on the two women sitting side by side. Implicitly he says to them: "The film is yours for six minutes. Please fulfill it." Which they do.

In quite different tempo, Leigh has compassionate fun with a long series of poses by Maurice's customers in his studio: anniversaries, engagements, solo shots, family groups—a fine series of acute vignettes. Leigh is sensitive, too, to the element of distance, which of course means the space included in a shot. He knows when a long shot will serve the moment best, and, with his reliance on his people, he never needs to use an immense close-up.

Leigh, the writer, ties up things somewhat neatly and is a touch homiletic. Leigh, the director of cast and camera, is masterly.

Topsy-Turvy

JANUARY 10, 2000 | Mike Leigh, both a writer and a director, is known for compassionate explorations of modern prole life such as *High Hopes* and *Secrets and Lies*. Now he presents *Topsy-Turvy*, which is, of all things, a biographical film about Gilbert and Sullivan.

To understand those two men, in fuller dimension than this picture itself provides, is to glimpse why the social-minded Leigh may have been drawn to them. In 1991 the English historian David Cannadine published an essay called "Three Who Made a Revolution": those three were Gilbert, Sullivan, and Richard D'Oyly Carte, the manager who was their advocate and who built a theater (the Savoy) to house their productions. Cannadine examines why those G & S pieces that are, for many Americans, remembered as school shows—*Iolanthe, The Yeomen of the Guard,* and so on—were irruptions in the complacency of the Victorian theater. Cannadine also notes that the expiration of copyrights in G & S works liberated them from musty "traditional" revivals and enabled fresh pertinent productions. He cites Wilford Leach's *The Pirates of Penzance* in New York in 1981 and Jonathan Miller's *The Mikado* for the British National Opera in 1986. (I would add Tyrone Guthrie's New York production of *H. M. S. Pinafore* in 1961.) We can infer that, whether or not Mike Leigh had read Cannadine, he was attracted to G & S because they were not mere Victorian confectioners, they were disturbers of the cultural peace.

No writer-composer team in the Anglophone world can match Gilbert and Sullivan. Ira and George Gershwin wrote enchanting songs, Rodgers and Hammerstein touched lots of common denominators, but who would think of their entire shows as *works?* (For the one exception, Gershwin's *Porgy and Bess,* DuBose Heyward was an important contributor.) A usual formulation is that G & S were "a genius." This cliché is much more needful for Sullivan than for Gilbert. Sullivan's other music—a grand opera, a symphony, oratorios, and more—has faded away, but Gilbert, on his own, wrote a gem of a play, a mordant social satire called *Engaged.* (He also wrote plays called *Topsy-Turveydom* and, anticipating Tom Stoppard, *Rosencrantz and Guildenstern.*) And the world would be poorer without his *Bab Ballads,* a collection of unsurpassed light verse, which he illustrated with his wickedly elfin drawings. If Gilbert had never met Sullivan (a clause that makes me shudder as I write it), he would still have a small place in literary history. Sullivan without Gilbert would now be remembered as the composer of "The Lost Chord" and "Onward, Christian Soldiers."

Leigh's film begins with the premiere of *Princess Ida* (1884) and ends with the premiere of *The Mikado* (1885). In between we get snatches of rehearsals, backstage difficulties, Gilbert's prowess as stage director (there is in fact a book on that subject), and the private lives of the two collaborators. What we do not get is any sense of the irruptive effect that Cannadine describes and that, I assume, was Leigh's initial interest. Some scenes of G & S activities, and of colleagues, are paraded past; then the first Yum Yum sings "The Sun Whose Rays," and the film stops. (Leigh doesn't even include the famous quarrel between G & S about a piece of carpet for the Savoy Theater, a quarrel that boiled into the law courts and separated the partners for three years. They reunited, but their last two collaborations were not successful.) The film just flicks the pages of an album. It's worse than inorganic: it teases us with the feeling that Leigh had a basic plan for the picture and never realized it.

Still worse, there are many scenes that add nothing. Why, for instance, do we see Gilbert's father imagining an attack by spirits? Such scenes as Gilbert being assailed by a ragged crone in a London alley or Sullivan's visit to a Paris brothel or drug use by one of the Savoy company may have been intended as rips in a prettified Victorian fabric, the "truth" about those days; but since there is no consistent program about that "truth," no full counterpoint of offstage reality to contrast with the onstage artifice, those scenes seem only afterthought apologies for dealing with this dainty subject.

Topsy-Turvy has some pleasures. First, obviously, are the numbers from G & S, solos, duets, choruses, which make us wonder again why some of the comic operas of Rossini and Donizetti are OK for the opera house but not *Iolanthe* and *Patience*. Then, Jim Broadbent's performance as Gilbert adds another warmth to his valuable career; Allan Corduner very nearly convinces as Sullivan; and Ron Cook is quietly winning as Carte. Lindy Hemming's costumes are exactly what they ought to be, and Dick Pope's cinematography has the right gaslight-lamplight feeling. Leigh directs smoothly in, for him, a new vein: not only in constructed scenes with the sorts of structure that he has never tolerated, but actual theater scenes, long shots of the stage intercut with close-ups of performers. Yet, the better that some of the picture's elements are, the more unsatisfying it is, the more we long for Leigh's realization of what was presumably his revisionist purpose.

Beyond the Clouds

OCTOBER 28, 1996 | The latest work by Michelangelo Antonioni, one of the premier artists in the world history of film, is *Beyond the Clouds*. The picture was shown at the recent New York Film Festival. As one who has severely questioned that festival, I must note that it has shown all three of Antonioni's films since *The Passenger* (1975). The two others were *The Mystery of Oberwald* (1980), adapted from a Cocteau play (one of only three films in Antonioni's career adapted from other people's material) and *Identifi-*

cation of a Woman (1982). None of the three most recent films has yet been released here. One doesn't have to believe that they are first-rank Antonioni in order to shudder at a system in which new works by a major artist are, so to speak, not acknowledged to exist.

Antonioni was eighty-three when he made *Beyond the Clouds* and, because of a stroke in 1985, paralyzed down his right side. He cannot speak. (I once had a ninety-minute conversation with him on PBS. When he was in New York in 1992, we shook hands—left hands—and he made some sounds in his throat.) How did he do a film?

First, the screenplay. It consists of four stories adapted from pieces in his book, *That Bowling Alley on the Tiber*. On this adaptation he had the help of his longtime collaborator Tonino Guerra and of Wim Wenders. Wenders directed the prologue and epilogue of the film and also served as standby director. (Wenders, eminent in his own right, has long been associated with the novelist-dramatist-filmmaker Peter Handke, whose work has distinct affinities with Antonioni.) The co-cinematographer, with Alfio Contini, was Robby Müller, a Wenders veteran.

Impressive though this team certainly is, its members emphasize that the whole project was closely under Antonioni's control. This becomes clear very early. The prologue done by Wenders is cinematically trite. We see the wing of an airliner above the clouds, then shots of the plane's interior and a man within it, then that of the man from the outside— as he looks through a window. (This shot, very familiar, always tickles me. From whose point of view? A passing angel's?) But, as soon as the first story begins, so does the real Antonioni. His ability to *see* is still overwhelming. We're in Ferrara (his hometown). A long perspective of a cloister-like walk with two modern young people in it strikes an Antonioni chord: people of the European present still embraced by the past, like it or not.

The man we met on the airplane is the *compère* for the film. He addresses us in English, sometimes on camera, sometimes on the soundtrack. He is a film director, the "I" of the *Tiber* book, thus Antonioni. (Whether this is true in the second story, where the man has an affair, is a bit more ambiguous.) John Malkovich plays this narrator-guide and is obviously meant to give the man depth. Malkovich has intelligence: even his worst performances convey it. But I don't find him, as is clearly intended, someone whom I immediately want to know more about.

For the first of the four stories Antonioni has found two young actors, Inès Sastre and Kim Rossi-Stuart, who are astonishingly beautiful. Lovers in Antonioni films are usually played by attractive people, sometimes more than that, but these two are remarkable. Antonioni seems to have departed from his usual practice in this instance to emphasize that their very difference from us, terrific though we of course all are, is emblematic.

The story (in Italian) is about a delayed encounter. The two meet by chance, then spend the night separately in different hotel rooms. Three years later they again meet accidentally, and this time they go to bed; but, after he has adored her exquisite body, he suddenly leaves, without actually making love. Nothing is said. We are meant to infer his thought that actual sex would be only a utilization of this perfect encounter, not its fulfillment. Tacitly, she perhaps agrees. If we can register the difference from the way we less beautiful persons might behave, the episode is, in two senses, platonic.

The three other stories are less resonant. In Portofino our cicerone meets a young woman who tells him in their first conversation (done in English) that she murdered her father, stabbed him twelve times. Since she was acquitted in her trial, the killing was apparently justified. (We don't learn why.) Her declaration doesn't discourage the man. They go to bed. Then he leaves, having said that he thinks twelve stabs were "domestic," fewer would have been murder. The woman's confession and its sexual effect on him have a certain pungency, but it quickly evaporates.

The third episode, set in Paris and done in French, is so neat that it's almost a satire on the neatness of French boulevard comedy. A wife leaves her husband because he won't stop an affair. She tries to rent the apartment of a man, she learns, whose wife has just left him for a lover. The two bereft ones get together.

The fourth episode, set in Aix-en-Provence and also done in French, is Gallic in a different way—a sort of Maupassant twist. A young man tries to pick up a young woman, even accompanying her to church. (Imagine a huge crucifix in the background of an Antonioni shot.) She is amiable, but she tells him that she is in love. As he walks her home, he asks what would happen if he fell in love with her. She says, "It would be like lighting a candle in a room full of light." When they part at her door, she tells him that the next day she will enter a convent.

There's also a witty little sketch, between the second and third episodes, apparently because Antonioni wanted a touch of lightness and a whiff of nostalgia. Marcello Mastroianni is a painter on a hill doing a landscape that Cézanne once painted, except that now there's a factory in the vista. Along comes Jeanne Moreau, who (in French) questions the worth of copying. He says that if he can at least repeat one gesture that Cézanne made, he will be gratified.

The chuckle is about more than painterly repetition. Moreau and Mastroianni were together in one of Antonioni's masterpieces, *La Notte* (1960).

None of these stories, except the first, incises deeply, but all of them are immersed in a sense of place, *riche* but not *nouveau riche,* no ostentation. Some old Antonioni elements and some new ones are used. We see a bit of a street carnival, as in *Blow-Up;* boats pass by just outside a window, as in *Red Desert;* the wind is a character in a scene, as in *Eclipse.* New elements are the cross-fades — I can't remember dissolves from one shot into another in previous Antonioni films — and the cuts to a black screen. But the most startling novelty is negative: the absence of his revolutionary attitude toward time. As Mark Rudman has said, "Antonioni is among the few directors who have had the courage to experiment with real time." (Remember the two lovers by the railroad track in *L'Avventura,* Vittoria at the airfield in *Eclipse.*) Not here. Time is used in conventional filmic ways. Apparently Antonioni felt that this material would not bear the weight of the virtual experience that he used so brilliantly in the past.

None of the performances is extraordinary, though all are adequate. The best-known actors, other than those already named, are Fanny Ardant, as the Parisian wife, and Irène Jacob as the nun-to-be.

Whatever we think of this film, we can all be glad that it was made. A collection of his writings and interviews, *The Architecture of Vision,* was published here recently. In one article he says:

There are moments when I seem to perceive, however confusedly, the *why* of certain things. When this happens, I become a combative optimist. . . . Am I not still here, making films (good ones, bad ones, whatever) which are always against something and someone? Isn't this obstinacy? And isn't this obstinacy itself a kind of optimism?

Perhaps the trouble with *Beyond the Clouds* is that it isn't "against" enough. But the obstinacy is inarguable.

Everyone Says I Love You

NOVEMBER 11, 1996 | Woody Allen's new film has charm. (I had to re-read that sentence. Yes, it's true.) *Everyone Says I Love You* is warm from its first moment, and, almost all the time thereafter, it glows. Why the difference from his past films? Look at this glittering roster of collaborators: Bert Kalmar and Harry Ruby, Walter Donaldson and Gus Kahn, Ray Henderson and Lew Brown and B. G. DeSylva, Richard Rodgers and Lorenz Hart, Cole Porter . . . others. They are some of the ace songwriters of the 1930s. Allen's new film is a musical, not with new songs but with rich old ones. To cap it, Allen's music director was Dick Hyman, whose arrangements are the best kind of Broadway pulsing and caressing. And right alongside Hyman's scoring is the choreography of Graciela Daniele, brisk, electric dance of the 1930s.

Let's not shortchange Allen's own contribution — besides originating the idea. Allen's directing career is a prime instance of on-the-job training: he began directing before he really knew how, but now he's so at ease that his films seem to have been born the way they are. The maker's hand is almost invisible.

Here's the beginning of this picture. The first shot looks streetward through one of the fountains in front of the Metropolitan Museum at a young couple. First reaction: this is going to be another one of Allen's odes to the New York that he loves. True, but there's something else: he has to establish that this is a musical. He does it just by *doing* it. The Boy turns to the Girl, and, instead of speaking, he starts to sing "Just You, Just Me." Right there in broad daylight on Fifth Avenue. It's Edward Norton singing, and it's Drew Barrymore responding. No dubbing of vocalists.

(One of Allen's happiest ideas. All the principals do their own singing, which makes the songs pleasant enough and — forgive the term — more real.)

The song continues. We move along the street. A black nurse and her aged white charge sing a couple of lines. Then a panhandler. Norton and Barrymore stroll past a high-fashion shop; three mannequins in the window dance to the tune . . . and so on. Ernst Lubitsch, thou should'st be living at this hour. Allen is a bright disciple.

When Norton goes to Harry Winston to buy an engagement ring, the salesman shows him some expensive ones. Norton suddenly bursts into song, telling us "My baby don't care for rings / Or other expensive things. / My baby just cares for me." The salesman joins him, as do other customers, along with some slick tap dancers from God knows where. (Graciela Daniele knows, too.) Norton then buys a ring, which gets interestingly lost.

And that's how the film goes, suddenly blossoming from time to time into song and dance, sometimes frenetic, sometimes poignant, always enjoyable. There are songs from Maurice Chevalier pictures and from Marx Brothers pictures. The film's title comes from a Marx Brothers number. The last sequence is a party in Paris at which everyone, male and female, wears a Groucho get-up, and we get "Hooray for Captain Spalding" in French.

This brings us to the story, or stories. They matter less than in most musicals. There's a glitch in the Boy-Girl relationship because of her brief excursion with a paroled convict brought into her life by her do-good mother, Goldie Hawn. (Who is also responsible for a surprise appearance of Itzhak Perlman and daughter.) Hawn's ex-husband is Allen, father of a daughter. Her present husband is Alan Alda, who brought along children of his own — including a politically conservative son who shocks his liberal father. (Ultimately the son is cured of his conservatism by surgery.) Also involved is an art historian played by Julia Roberts. (She sings "I'm a Dreamer, Aren't We All?") The plots exist only to provide rifts and reconciliations and changes of locale. Allen does plenty of New York adoration, but he also gives himself the chance to enjoy Venice and Paris. (He and Hawn do a dance on a Seine embankment that has some spiffy novelties.)

All the principals of the piece, except one, keep the film flying high —

especially Hawn. Now that she has abandoned her giggling "Laugh-in" persona, she has become a sturdy comedienne. The exception is Allen himself. The trouble isn't that he's always the same—Alan Alda is always the same—but Allen's sameness is uninviting; and it's dissonant. In his own ebullient picture, full of high spirits and high dudgeons, he snivels.

His performance doesn't even create self-parody. At one point in the picture, Julia Roberts has, for sufficient plot reasons, gone to bed with Allen and is in a semi-daze after his magnificent love-making. With a real comedian—say Robin Williams or Dustin Hoffman—this moment might be funny, a gorgeous woman reeling from an encounter with a shrimp. Here, however, all we can think of is that Allen, as director, is using his power to build himself up as a man.

Of course, *Everyone* doesn't really take place in the three cities of its settings, least so in New York. Musically, for instance. The whole cast knows and sings these golden oldies. We keep wondering about this, especially with the younger ones. Where's the rock, the rap? One brief scene in a disco gives us a funny slice of a rap singer's version of one of the oldies, but rap is there just to be put down vis-à-vis the "straight" oldies. Otherwise, all these characters exist in a rockless, rapless world. And virtually everyone in the picture is well-off. A musical doesn't have to plumb social strata: money is an enablement for plot freedom. But this vision of Manhattan society has the same relation to the facts as Allen's carefully selected views of Manhattan's loveliness.

What's most curious in Allen is his nostalgia. He keeps trying to remake New York into what he imagines it was like about the time that he was born (1935), with music drawn from the Broadway and Hollywood hits of that decade. *Radio Days* was an overt attempt to go back there; *Bullets over Broadway* was a grab at Damon Runyon. Through many of Allen's films, despite their freight of topical reference, there's a hint that things used to be better, especially the music. (Remember how Gershwin on the sound track supported the up-to-date *Manhattan*.) Allen, full of postwar frankness about neuroses, yearns for what he feels was a pre-war Eden.

How will these old songs fare today? At Joseph Papp's production of *The Pirates of Penzance* in 1980 I was surrounded by young people who had clearly never heard a word or note of Gilbert and Sullivan and were there chiefly (they said) because Linda Ronstadt was in the cast. As the performance rolled on, I could see how they were being captivated by the piece.

As they listened to the old, they were discovering, delighting in, something new. Maybe all those unfortunates who were born after World War Two will respond the same way to Allen's picture, to the Lubitsch *légèreté*, to those delectable old romantic songs. The opening line of *Twelfth Night*: "If music be the food of love, play on." What do you mean "if"?

Celebrity

DECEMBER 21, 1998 | Woody Allen's screenplay for *Celebrity* is an elaborated doodle. He seems to have lined up some reminiscences of past characters (a mixed-up writer, an unfulfilled woman) and of smart-set sterilities (parties, parties, parties), added a few jokes, not necessarily of the keenest (about a film critic: "He used to hate every movie; then he married a young woman with a big bosom and now he loves every movie"), seasoned with a few dabs of sex frankness, and then just switched the word processor on. This new picture looks as if Allen had tapped along hoping that the tapping would lead somewhere. It didn't, but he discovered that he had enough pages for a film anyway. (Including a few prestige-pumping quotes from Eliot and Tennessee Williams.)

This ad hokum script is the penalty that he and we must pay for his position. Allen is unique in American film, a writer-director who is in every creative sense independent and yet who in every industry sense is mainstream (glittery casts, first-rank technicians). Thus established, he can do virtually any project he conceives and can do it with top-notch colleagues — and his public will, in some measure, support him. (Especially abroad.) It would be easy to go through the Allen filmography and divide the list into those pictures that, whatever their defects, are memorable, and those that very probably would not have been made if they had originated with anyone else. High in this roster of non-existent yet existent films is *Celebrity*.

At least the leading male role, who is essentially the recently deconstructed Harry under another name, is not played by Allen himself. This is a plus, or anyway a helpful minus. But Allen has put Kenneth Branagh in the role. There's a difficulty here. The trouble is not that Branagh is a foreigner — his New York accent is passable. But the role is just a series of actions, mostly sexual, with no realized person behind them; and Branagh is not an actor of strong personality. His Henry V, his Benedick, his Hamlet were all clear-cut, but in those cases the author gave him a considerable head start. Branagh can fulfill what a good author gives him, but on his own, so to speak, he is pallid, almost transparent.

Branagh's wife here, from whom he separates at the start, is Judy Davis, an Australian who has played Americans before, for Allen and others. Davis is one of the best film actresses in the world, but it's discomfiting to see her in the female counterpart of Branagh's role—a series of sketches and incidents that pretend to delineate a human being. The woman had been a schoolteacher, and Allen contrives, not deftly, for her to become a TV personality under the auspices of a producer she meets who falls in love with her. She even takes a lesson in oral sex—from another woman and using two bananas—in order to please this new man more. (Allen, let's note, is not just being frantically up-to-date in sexual candor. He has been frank at least since *Everything You Always Wanted to Know about Sex* in 1972.)

Entwined with the adventures of the unyoked husband and wife are scenes in restaurants and at gallery openings and any other occasions that warrant the display of gorgeous women. A few of them Branagh pursues —in a manner apparently intended to suggest Allen's own jagged polygraph performing but that seems unattached to Branagh's body. Many of the scenes with women slog down into discussion, and the one point I really admired in the film was the fact that Allen dared to use a line that could be quoted against him. At one point a young woman says to Branagh, "Let's just stay in tonight and not over-analyze things." In this script, that was brave of Allen.

The Designated Mourner

MARCH 24, 1997 | Under the credits Kathleen Ferrier sings the haunting lament from Gluck's *Orfèo*. A man's voice says:

I have to tell you that a very special little world has died and I am the designated mourner. Oh, yes, you see, it's an important custom in many groups and tribes. Someone is assigned to grieve, to wail, and light the public ritual fire. Someone is assigned when there's no one else.

Thus begins Wallace Shawn's *The Designated Mourner.*

This is a film only because it was filmed. It must have been somewhat more comfortable as a play—it was presented last year at the National in London—if only because, at least since the early works of Peter Handke, this form of presentation has become familiar. *The Designated Mourner* is a piece for three speakers, who sit at a long table facing the audience and only occasionally acknowledge one another's presence. (This film was made with the original cast on weekends during the run of the play, at a studio outside London.) So the piece depends for its life on the quality of the writing and the speaking; and it achieves this life because the writing is insidiously excellent, and the speakers are always compelling.

The twin themes are harsh political tyranny and the waning of traditional culture. Shawn certainly doesn't gloss over the first theme, but he seems to have chosen it as a means of italicizing cultural decline. Unlike most works on these persistent subjects, Shawn's approach is oblique as well as direct, witty as well as horrified. The mourner he has designated is a lightweight who likes being a lightweight, a soufflé Spengler, dryly wistful rather than bumptiously tragic. This tone gives the work something more than novelty: we don't have to brace ourselves for an onslaught of woe, we are seduced into compassion.

The place is unnamed, but a tropical country is suggested. The three people are the mourner, Jack ("You can sum me up in about ten words: a former student of English literature who went downhill from there"); Judy, his sensitive wife; and her father, Howard, an intellectual celebrated for his contempt of the world. Of course there is more to each of them than these basics: the embroideries of their selves, which they provide in the film's ninety minutes, are, like most such embroideries, highly relevant.

The three are not viewed alike. Howard, played by David de Keyser, is more or less the crotchety old egotist we might expect. His daughter, played by Miranda Richardson, is vulnerable and passionate—again as we might expect. But Jack, in tenor and concern, is not what we might expect. Though he is caught in the same climate of oppression and is well aware of cultural withering, he talks about these things, and his love affairs and other troubles, with a detachment that seems to protect him. Shawn says that when he was writing Jack he was thinking of the man who plays him here, Mike Nichols. Perfect. (Doubly apt because at times Nichols even sounds like Shawn.)

Nichols makes his film acting debut here. He is known chiefly as a performer of theater satire and as a director of clever plays and films — clever, whether or not they were comic — and his very presence here confirms the timbre of Shawn's lone survivor. Jack is the only "inauthentic" one of the three, the only one who keeps on scrutinizing himself. At one point he says:

> Then I asked myself, Well, what about that noise I always hear, that intolerable noise which comes from somewhere inside my head? And I realized consciously for the first time that, rather like a singer who accompanies his own singing on the piano or guitar, I accompanied my life with a sort of endless inner tinkling, an endless noodling or murmuring — a sort of awful inner murmuring of reportage and opinions, idiotic arpeggios of self-approbation. . . .

And this is the man — slightly bored, slightly bored with himself, yet sufficiently concerned to see the gallows humor of his place as mourner — who tells us of the arbitrary five-year imprisonment of Howard and Judy by the brutal government, of their murder after their release. In their own ways, they themselves have recounted their harassment and suffering, but it is given to Jack to describe these matters fully in his own way. Late in the film he tells us that he was reading newspaper accounts of political executions, with photographs, and he saw that one of the victims was Judy. "I was lost," he says, immediately shifting to consideration of himself.

> Where was I? Blinded, you know, like a caught fish jumping about on the floor of a boat. And the funny thing was that aside from sweating and sort of panting — well, more or less exactly as people say when they speak about such moments, I didn't know what to do. I mean, *literally,* what to do — stand up, remain seated, stay in, go out?

So he reached for the porno magazines on the table next to him.

The film's director was David Hare, himself a dramatist and a film writer-director (at his best with *Wetherby*). Hare directed the National production of Shawn's piece, and here he does what he can to limber it into cinema. Most of the time he keeps us closer than the theater could bring us, with two-shots and close-ups and profile shots. He alters the lighting as he goes, and sometimes he cuts to different shots of the same face while that person is speaking. Richardson puts on sweaters; Nichols gets a different table, a café table, for the conclusion. But, wisely, Hare does not obtrude effects: he does just enough to tip his hat to the film medium without pretending that, generically, this is a film.

Wallace Shawn has been having two careers. As actor, he has been in numerous films, mostly in minor parts. His most notable work was in his own play/film, *My Dinner with André,* and his valiant struggle with the title role in *Vanya on 42nd Street.* As a dramatist, however, he has impressed from the start. I wasn't much taken by his version of Machiavelli's *Mandragola,* but his own plays — such as *Marie and Bruce, The Hotel Play* and *Aunt Dan and Lemon* (which has thematic links with this new work) — have been wonderfully disturbing. In all of them he has worked toward an idiosyncratic view of character and of form: toward distilled, pungent language. And in all these aspects *The Designated Mourner* is engrossing.

At the end Jack is in a park café. He eats a piece of pastry; then, as a "public ritual fire" for a lost culture, he burns the bit of paper that the pastry came in. "The bit of paper wasn't very big, but it burned rather slowly because of the cake crumbs," he says, sitting at the table, burning the paper as he tells us about it. Now he thinks he hears John Donne, who has been mentioned earlier in the film

> plummeting fast through the earth. . . . His name, once said by so many to be "immortal," would not be remembered, it turned out. The rememberers were gone, except for me, and I was forgetting, forgetting his name, forgetting him, and forgetting all the ones who remembered him.

Then, as Gluck returns to the soundtrack, Jack sits on a park bench, trying to make the most of what is left, in himself and the world. Again, he addresses us:

> What were we waiting for? The appearance of the Messiah? Was all this nothing? I was quite fed up with the search for perfection. And rather

amazed by all that I had—the lemonade stand with its lemonade, the café with its irritable customers and staff, the squirrels, the birds, the trees. . . . I sat on the bench for a very long time, lost—sunk deep—in the experience of unbelievable physical pleasure, maybe the greatest pleasure we can know on this earth—the sweet, ever-changing caress of an early evening breeze.

Thus ends this play/film—on a lyrical note of revised values, of consoling accommodation, with a civilization shrugged away.

Hamsun

MAY 19, 1997 | It would be something of an offense to say nothing about *Hamsun*—an offense to the artists involved and, in a way, to readers —simply because it hasn't yet found an American outlet. *Hamsun* was part of a Danish series shown at the Walter Reade in New York—Danish, though the director and leading actor are Swedish and the subject Norwegian. It was produced by a consortium of Scandinavian groups and is accounted Danish because of its distributor.

The director was Jan Troell, little heard from since his Hollywood misadventures in the 1970s. He is the fine artist who made *The Emigrants* (1970) and *The New Land* (1972), a two-part work about Swedish immigration to this country in the nineteenth century, films epic in scope and beautiful in texture. (Troell, who began as a cinematographer, also shot both of those films and much of *Hamsun*.) The leading actor in those two films was Max von Sydow, and von Sydow plays Hamsun.

First, a reminder about Knut Hamsun. He won the Nobel Prize for literature in 1920, and by the time this film begins, in 1935, he was seventy-six years old and world famous. Among his many works *Growth of the Soil* is probably best known, but my own favorite is *Hunger*. (It was filmed in 1966 with Per Oscarsson ablaze in the autobiographical leading role.)

At the start of the film Hamsun fervently approves of Hitler. As war nears and Norway is subsequently invaded by Germany, Hamsun's support is unflinching. He disapproves of certain actions by the Germans and by Norwegian Nazis, but he never wavers fundamentally in support of a program that he thinks will give Norway a rightful place among nations.

When the war ends, he is a public embarrassment to the restored democratic government. They try to treat his politics as a dotard's wanderings; he goes through mental examinations, hospital, prison, trial, but he comes out of it all still firm in his beliefs. His last book, a memoir called *On Overgrown Paths,* is proof that his mind was clear.

The subject is interesting and difficult. How does one deal with the steadfastness of a man whose views are loathsome? (Hamsun claimed, probably with truth, that he never knew about the camps, but he certainly knew about the executions going on around him.) For a start, we need to learn how he came to his beliefs. In 1973 the German playwright Tankred Dorst wrote about Hamsun in *Ice Age* and, as I recall, dealt with the source of Hamsun's views; but this film, though two and a half hours long, does not.

The screenplay by Per Olof Enquist, based on a book by Thorkild Hansen, omits any reference to the fact that in his youth Hamsun emigrated to America *twice,* failed to establish himself here, and went home thoroughly disliking America. Along the way, he also acquired a loathing for British imperialism and, as *Hunger* indicates, an admiration for physical endurance and dedication—the sorts of qualities apostrophized in Leni Riefenstahl's Alpine films.

None of the above can begin to justify Hamsun's Nazi beliefs, but it does help to explain them. Without a basis, his actions in the film seem to float in midair. Many of the sequences are excellent, particularly one at Berchtesgaden, where Hitler receives the old man reverently and soon loses his temper because Hamsun keeps pressing questions about the Norway *Gauleiter.* I wish the film clarified the source of Hamsun's politics as well as it dramatizes the convolutions of his character.

Still, whatever its faults, *Hamsun* is a treasure because of von Sydow's performance. This great actor, in Bergman's films and in some others, has enriched our film legacy with his art. One proof of his greatness is that his Hamsun can't be called his best work: it joins the wonders in his past—for just one instance, the grim weathered peasant in Bille August's *Pelle the Conqueror.*

Others in the *Hamsun* cast are excellent, notably Ghita Norby as his wife. But the center, something more than the center, is von Sydow's Hamsun, a towering tree at the start that is shaken but does not break. It was daring to make a film about this man because it doesn't end with contrition, but Troell's security was von Sydow, who can never have our sympathy yet does have our frightened fascination.

La Promesse

MAY 26, 1997 | Liège, in Belgium, is a heavily industrialized city. Seraing is a suburb, populated largely by Liège workers and—nowadays—ex-workers. Unemployment is high. As in other European industrial cities, many in that workforce are immigrants from all over the world. Also, as elsewhere, many of those immigrant workers were smuggled into the country and have no papers or, if they once were legal, have overstayed their permits. Thus they are easy pickings for local people who rip them off for lodging and various kinds of help.

This is the subject of *La Promesse*. Rather, this is the setting: the film concentrates intensely on a few people in that setting. *La Promesse,* though generated by social and economic conditions, is not a socioeconomic report: it's a moral drama, simple and deep. There's a familiar paradox: by concentrating realistically on people in a certain context, the film goes past the realistic into the thematic, the abstract.

This wonderful picture was made by two brothers, Luc and Jean-Pierre Dardenne, born in Seraing and now in their forties, who have spent most of their twenty-year filmmaking career doing documentaries for European television. They have made two fiction features, unseen here; and with this third feature they step into the front rank of contemporary directors with social concerns, alongside Ken Loach and Mike Leigh.

The film begins with one person and follows him into a complex environment. Under the credits we hear the thrum of a machine—no music. We see Igor, a nice-looking if impassive fifteen-year-old, pumping gas at a garage. An old woman drives up, and Igor fixes something under the hood of her car. She gets out to look at it, and he gets in to start the motor. He sees her wallet on the seat next to him and snatches it. When she notices that it's missing, she is especially upset because she has just picked up her pension. Igor advises her to go back and look in the parking lot—there are a lot of thieves about, he says.

Igor goes through the garage to the backyard where he takes out the money, then buries the wallet. In the garage his boss is about to teach him something about soldering when a car hoots outside. It's Igor's father calling for him early. The boss is vexed, but Igor leaves.

This brief sequence is like an overture to the whole film. Igor is brisk but polite, with the old woman, with his boss. His entire conduct, including his thievery and his composure at taking the old woman's pension, is serious, merely part of his behavior pattern. We have been given a quick but graphic sketch of Igor's mind and bearing—and more. This opening sets the Dardenne camera style. Urgent. Close. Igor moves quickly, and the camera follows him: his kinesis is the film's. No time is wasted on establishing shots or vistas. To be with Igor is to be in his tempo.

We now see where he got it: from his father, who is also the source of his ethics. Roger is a jowly, bespectacled working-class man, always driving or moving hurriedly. He owns and runs an old building split up into tiny apartments where immigrant workers live at high rents. Roger also does some transporting, some document-forging, other scams. His attitude is business-like, not consciously criminal: serious, brutal if necessary, but generally matter-of-fact. Igor clearly accepts this hustle—wed to the camera's hustle—as the order of the universe.

Then a young African woman, Assita, arrives from Burkina Faso with her infant son. She is there to join her husband, Hamidou, already resident in Roger's flophouse. She is tall, dignified, assured. As soon as she is with Hamidou, she gives their baby a ritual bath to protect him from the evil spirits in this place.

A few days later Hamidou is working on a scaffold on the building next door when the police arrive unexpectedly. Roger sends Igor to warn Hamidou to hide because the African's papers are no longer good. In his hurry Hamidou falls from the scaffold. He thinks he is dying. Igor finds him; and Hamidou makes him promise to take care of Assita and the child. That is the promise of the title.

Hamidou need not have died. Igor tries to halt the bleeding and get him to a hospital, but Roger comes along, stops the first aid, and refuses to take Hamidou to a hospital because of the legal trouble that would follow. He orders Igor to help him hide the African under some canvas. Later, he and Igor bury the corpse in cement. When Assita asks about Hamidou, Roger tells her that he has gone off for a while. Roger hatches a scheme to get her to return to Burkina Faso without Hamidou, but she refuses to leave. Igor begins to take steps to protect and help her. The gravamen of the picture is what happens to Igor because of his promise.

Why, suddenly, in this speedy, money-focused life, did this particular promise hold him? First, the shock of death. Second, Roger's behavior, which Igor understands—Roger is protecting himself and *his* family—but which nonetheless shocks him. Third, most important, Assita herself. This grave, composed woman refuses to waver in her duty; she will wait for her husband, no matter how harassed she is. She relies on magic and juju—she consults an African seer to find out about Hamidou; she splits a live chicken to read its entrails—but rather than seeming barbaric, she appears to Igor to be in touch with larger matters than the daily frantic grubbings of himself and his father.

It is through her clarity that he first glimpses virtue. It is through her loyalty that he first understands selflessness. None of this is preached: it happens. Just as Igor snatched the wallet at the start without thinking it exceptional, so Assita cares for her son and is devoted to Hamidou—it is the order of things. The film ends with Igor touched more profoundly—too profoundly for surface emotion—than he suspected was possible for him.

Olivier Gourmet plays Roger with a dispatch that implies thought and resolve. Jérémie Renier as Igor is, because much younger, more remarkable. Helped by the brothers Dardenne, he metamorphoses from his father's son into a daring, somewhat frightened but courageous individual. The catalyst is Assita, played by Assita Ouedraogo. She is a schoolteacher in Burkina Faso and is not related to the filmmaker Idrissa Ouedraogo, though she has appeared in three of that master's films. She seems to assume nothing in her role: she simply endows the film with her beautiful presence.

The Dardenne brothers, as shown by their empathic casting, their very choice of theme, have confessed to a burden. They believe in hope. They insist that under the frenzy of our world, physical and moral, there is quiet. And that the quiet in one person, born to it in a remote place, can speak to the quiet that is buried in a native of noise. They insist with such subtle fervor that they induce us, too, to share that burden of hope.

Chronicle of a Disappearance

JUNE 30, 1997 | It is set in Israel—Nazareth and Jerusalem. Almost all the characters are Palestinian. Here are some of the scenes, at random:

The opening shot, before credits, is a huge mass, dimly lit, unrecognizable. The camera moves around it, the light grows, and it becomes an immense closeup of a man's head resting on his hand, sleeping.

First scene after the credits: an elderly woman comes into a living room, sits on a sofa facing us, and complains at length about the behavior of a relative. Then another elderly woman comes in, says nothing, and the two go out together.

Two men sit outside their gift and postcard shop in the sun. A group of Japanese tourists pass between them and us. One of the tourists stops to take a picture of the two men, then leaves.

A group of elderly women sit around a kitchen table, working. They discuss the peeling of garlic.

A man sits at a kitchen table working on something with small tools. From time to time he glances at a tennis match on TV, which we hear but do not see.

In a long shot a car pulls up in front of a country store. Two men get out and start to fight fiercely. Men come out of the store and separate them. The two men get back in the car and drive off.

Later, same long shot, another car stops in front of that store; two men get out and fight. Men run out of the store and stop them, reproving a father for hitting his son. The father and son get back in the car and drive off.

Still later, same long shot, another car pulls up in front of the store. Two men get out, simply change places in the front seat, and drive off.

An Orthodox priest on the shore of the Sea of Galilee, speaking Russian (I think)—all others speak Arabic—says that this is the water on which Christ walked. Now, he says, the sea is so full of the excrement of German and American tourists that anyone could walk on it.

The film is called *Chronicle of a Disappearance,* a first feature by Elie Suleiman, a Palestinian who was born in 1960 in Nazareth. Suleiman spent a dozen years in New York, studying film and making a few shorts, then returned to Nazareth. In 1994, he moved to Jerusalem and took a post at

Bir Zeit University. The scenes sketched above, a few out of many, take place in Nazareth; here are a few set in Jerusalem:

In a conference room Suleiman himself is announced to speak about his aesthetic criteria. When he steps to the microphone, the p.a. system yowls with feedback. Repeated attempts to correct the trouble don't help. He never speaks. A young Palestinian woman called Adan, very mod-looking, who lives in East Jerusalem, makes telephone calls trying to find an apartment in another part of the city. She mentions that she's Arab, and people hang up; or they hear that she speaks Hebrew with a foreign accent and they hang up.

Adan, with a walkie-talkie, sends a lot of phony commands to police patrol cars. A hopeless mix-up results.

Suleiman is sitting quietly at home when two members of an Israeli SWAT team break in and begin to search the apartment. Suleiman, un-frightened, silent, courteous, allows them to proceed. They pass through the apartment and leave.

Adan is arrested and taken off. She and her captors are silent and calm, as if they were all doing a rehearsed scene.

We see a swimming pool with a large head of Arafat on the wall behind it. A swimmer is doing laps in the pool.

Back in Nazareth (I think) we are in a living-room, watching from be-hind an elderly couple who face a TV set. The announcer says that the day's programs are finished. On the screen appears a rippling Israeli flag, and a band plays "Hatikvah" all the way through. The couple sit there; then the camera comes around, and we see that they are both asleep.

After almost every scene in both cities, an inter-title appears: "A Day Later." The words are especially pungent in Nazareth, where it's hard to tell whether it's a day later or a day earlier or a week ago or a year later. In Jerusalem, the intertitle has a bit more point, except that the dead-pan conduct in almost every scene works, quite intentionally, against any sense of dramatic swell.

From the gabby old woman at the start, and almost unbrokenly throughout, what sustains this film is Suleiman's intelligent, taciturn wit. This is especially incisive considering the touchiness of his subjects. He has a real talent for astringent implication, thus depending on the kind of viewers who want to play his delicate game—and respond to its purpose. Instead of one more passage through materials that are all too grimly familiar, he presents them for viewers who know the facts but who will appreciate a fresh aspect. (I was cheered to note that among the many sponsors of the film listed at the end were the Israeli Ministry of Culture and the American National Endowment for the Arts.)

Chronicle of a Disappearance is a film of the Absurd. If Ionesco had been a Palestinian and a filmmaker, he might have made it. By treating these subjects almost in the abstract, by working every scene against conventional expectations of growth and cumulation, by refusing to blink at the touch of the ridiculous in all tragedy, Suleiman refreshes us. He mocks nothing, but, like all good Absurdists, he looks at things bifocally: from the point of view of a fly on the wall and under the eye of eternity.

In the Company of Men

SEPTEMBER 1, 1997 | Here is yet another new, true talent. In the past few months we've seen the arrival of some extraordinary director-writers, Elie Suleiman (*Chronicle of a Disappearance*) and the Dardenne brothers (*La Promesse*). Now a first film by Neil LaBute, *In the Company of Men,* certainly ranks him with those others.

LaBute, an American, is and continues to be a playwright as well as screenwriter, so let's look first at his screenplay. *In the Company of Men* concerns a cruel male prank played on a woman. Chad and Howard are young executives of a huge corporation. They were college friends: Howard outranks Chad at the office. Both men have had multiple dealings with women, and both have had troubles therein. They are now being sent, for a six-week project, to an office of their company in another city, and Chad proposes a scheme. Howard soon agrees. In that other city each will woo the same young woman, yet unknown, and will persuade her of his seriousness. Then they will simply leave at the end of six weeks—"pull the rug from under her" is their phrase—and have her misery to chortle over for the rest of their lives.

Of course we know from the start that, just because the scheme has been hatched, it will not turn out as planned. But this surety on our parts becomes part of the subtext of the picture, whose main text is the exercise of power, ruthlessly. Two males, Chad who schemes, Howard who not-too-reluctantly complies, are having their revenge on women in what may be the dwindling days of male dominance. All through history, despite that dominance and allowing for exceptions, men have been the suppliants, women the grantors, and these two males are out for revenge — possibly before it is too late.

A particularly poignant touch, which broadens rather than narrows the film, is that the girl they choose in that other city is deaf. A highly competent typist in the large office, attractive, bright, winning, Christine is stone deaf. This increases the delight particularly of Chad because, as he thinks, it makes her more vulnerable. But for us she becomes more complex, more versed in ways she must handle every experience. In the end the rug is pulled from under her, as planned. But another rug is also pulled, which was not planned — involving Howard's involvement with Christine.

And there's still a third rug. What insidiously complicates this sexual-power prank is its intertwining with business-power maneuvers on Chad's part. Chad, as we soon see, is not only out for sex revenge but business revenge, a resentment, cloaked under heavy palship, of Howard's position in the firm. This resentment works its way out through various dealings, but the most errant and brutal display of office power occurs in a scene with an ambitious black junior of Chad's, as Chad humiliates him in the guise of testing his stamina.

The dialogue crackles forward at a level that has been set in recent American films by such director-writers as David O. Russell (*Spanking the Monkey*), Hal Hartley (*Simple Men*), Whit Stillman (*Barcelona*). It's insufficiently acknowledged that the writing — the sheer writing — of some younger American filmmakers is at least at the level of some of their contemporaries who write only for the theater. No one or two lines would adequately convey the feral vitality of LaBute's writing, the slashing-and-biting as dynamics. He writes with that razor-keen edge that keeps the dialogue moving just past what we expect, without seeming freakish or fake. His two men speak like people who are tired of conventional movie dialogue yet often find themselves in movie situations and who itch to freshen up what they say.

LaBute has disclosed that the inspiration for his film came from Restoration comedy, and surely the patterned vices of Congreve, Vanbrugh and Company streak the air around this picture. But, early on, I began to think of a play from another time and place, Musset's *No Trifling with Love*.

This seemingly light, bitter, ultimately terrible play crystallizes the unforeseen results of games with human feelings in something of the same mode as LaBute's piece.

An unusually fine screenplay, then, yet LaBute's accomplishment goes further. He has envisioned a cinematic style for his film that harmonizes exactly with its theme and mood. Excepting the work of Miklos Jancsó, I have rarely seen a film in which there was so little editing. Scene after scene, particularly the shorter ones, is set before us, in a complementary frame, then played in one steady shot. In the longer scenes LaBute edits, sparingly. Mostly he puts an audio-visual plaque before us, its cool presentation a perfect match for what is going on. Tony Hettinger, the cinematographer, understands exactly what is wanted, and he renders the interiors of airports and corporate beehives as frigid testing grounds for the spirits of the people within.

Some secondary characters fill out the design, but in principle this is a three-character film. Stacy Edwards, lovely, plays Christine with dignity and warmth. The hollow voice that Edwards uses soon becomes nothing more or less than the deaf Christine's voice. We expect her to speak this way, that's all, and she is so taking that we want to hear what she has to say.

Matt Molloy plays Howard, giving unexpected strength—therefore interest—to a character who seems at first to be something of a stooge for Chad even though he outranks the other man. The metamorphosis that comes Howard's way is genuinely moving.

Chad, the key player in the enterprise, is done by Aaron Eckhart, who might be called a young Charlton Heston except that he is much more supple in every way. Chad—the character as such—does considerable acting in the film, and Eckhart handles the two tracks of the man with utter conviction. At the end, in circumstances we have not foreseen, Chad says smugly that he can sell anything. This seems to be true; and Eckhart presents it so that we know that Chad doesn't know how much he is saying.

In LaBute's delicately savage film, evil goes unpunished. What a relief. We are flooded, in films and plays and novels, with so-called "affirmation of the human spirit," which means that good triumphs and/or virtue is rewarded. As if that were all of the human spirit. Some of us have noted other aspects of that spirit. Sometimes, not infrequently, virtue is defeated or ignored and other qualities triumph. LaBute is affirming the human spirit, all right—just a somewhat neglected area of it.

Your Friends and Neighbors

AUGUST 31, 1998 | A young man lying in bed is caressing the breast of a young woman lying next to him. "How does that feel?" he asks. End of the film.

It's the perfect finish. This quasi-clinical tone, this sense of sex as physical therapy, dominates the whole picture. It opens with that same young man practicing the moves of intercourse, not masturbating, and it progresses in that gymnastic mode right to the breast-fondling finish. *Your Friends and Neighbors,* written and directed by Neil LaBute, continues the exploration of contemporary sexual attitudes that he began last year with his extraordinary *In the Company of Men.* Now LaBute takes the inquiry further, into almost laboratory-controlled coolness.

It's possibly inaccurate to talk flatly of LaBute's first and second films because we're told that he wrote both screenplays at about the same time. But the one that he made first is a contrast with the new one. *In the Company of Men* concerned the figurative revenge that two young men wreak on women by wooing a young woman individually and abandoning her together. The vindictive prank is spoiled by the inception of deep feeling in the young woman and in one of the young men.

Not in *Your Friends and Neighbors.* No feeling irrupts here except sexual desire. LaBute said that his first film was inspired by Restoration comedy; now LaBute takes that Congreve-Vanbrugh view even further—people who think themselves masters of the universe without realizing how constricted that universe is. This time we go to frigid extremes.

A sort of gavotte, then, mostly horizontal, involving two young married couples, along with a young man and a young woman, in which partners are changed. The plot doesn't need sketching. Let's just say that the setting is urban and that each of the two couples has dissatisfactions and itches, and that each individual in the quartet is in some measure emotionally slothful while sexually vain and demanding. The two single people act as variant partners, including a lesbian interlude for one of the wives.

Your Friends and Neighbors is about ego and gratification. Our era was called the age of narcissism by Christopher Lasch; LaBute proposes the age of hedonism. Instead of the infant bawling for his toy, with pleasure as his sole standard, we have adults crying for sex, with pleasure as their prime standard. The net effect of the film is rather frightening, predictive of an emotionally arid world.

LaBute's directing here is somewhat different from his first film. He now uses more editing, more intercutting within a scene, less crystallizing of a scene in one continuous shot. He likes recurrent visual themes. For instance, the single woman works in an art gallery, and every one of her encounters with people in the cast takes place in that gallery in the same shot, the same framing. LaBute's dialogue reminds us that, along with that of such others as Hal Hartley and Jim Jarmusch and Whit Stillman, the sheer writing, these days, of some American films is remarkably fine.

LaBute has cast his film to match, with people who can handle his dialogue neatly. As one of the husbands, here is Ben Stiller again, selling his gently aggressive urbanity. Aaron Eckart, who was the nastier of the two men in LaBute's first film, is softer here as the other husband. Jason Patric is suitably dangerous and repellent as a freelance stallion. Nastassja Kinski, her being seemingly refreshed, is supple as the art-gallery woman. Amy Brenneman is sufficiently uneasy as one of the wives. A special bow to Catherine Keener, the other wife. In *Walking and Talking* and *Living in Oblivion,* among other films, she showed a unique quality, an ability to treat candid material with almost surgical precision, cool but fundamentally comic. That quality flowers here.

Titanic

JANUARY 5 & 12, 1998 | Reasons for the interest in *Titanic* are not obscure. The luxurious *Titanic* was called unsinkable, the safest ship ever built; and it went down on its maiden voyage in April 1912, four days after it had sailed from Southampton for New York. Within a few hours of hitting an iceberg, dabs of caviar on special dinnerware had given way to life jackets in the freezing Atlantic. The contrast is hypnotic, especially when we know, as the passengers did not, what is going to happen—from the golden salons down to the crowded steerage. The whole story is a relentless reminder that death is always there pawing at the portholes, and that it takes very little—one miscalculation in this case—to render the most resplendent order into primal chaos, then into nullity.

And there's something else. The twentieth century dawned as the peak of all centuries: the Western world was confident, accomplished, bound for a future of unlimited glory. The *Titanic* was as good a symbol as any of the century's early afflatus, and it had no sooner appeared than it was destroyed by human error. The disaster can be seen as an instance of the gods reproving hubris or, if you prefer, of the self-deceptions of ego. The pride and the smugness that created the *Titanic* and its fate seem to me not completely disparate from the larger prides and smugnesses that brought about World War I two years later.

In order to make this film, a story had to be invented. James Cameron, the writer-director, has used an old formula with a new twist. In the ocean-bottom wreckage of the ship—I assume the year is post-1985, when the salvage crews descended—a drawing is found of a nude young woman wearing a diamond pendant. The drawing is published in newspapers. A very old woman telephones the salvage ship to say that she is the girl in the drawing. She is flown to the ship and tells the crew her story.

She is played by Gloria Stuart, an American screen beauty of the 1930s, now completely winning. Her account is the film, through flashback, a tale of the girl's engagement, arranged by her mother, to a very rich man whom she doesn't greatly like, and of her encounter with a dashing young artist in steerage. The resulting triangle is collapsed by the iceberg, and eventually the mystery of the diamond pendant is resolved.

The dialogue and characters of the main story are completely predictable, presented as if we would want a predictable story because our interest is elsewhere—which it certainly is. We just need enough actors and plot to make the film possible. Kate Winslet as the young woman is so heavily made-up that her face seems lacquered into place. Leonardo DiCaprio as the artist is insubstantial, lightweight in every regard. Billy Zane, as the rich fiancé, at least gives some color to the slightly sadistic millionaire.

But with the ship, with its totality of people, Cameron is wizardly, creating an entire society threading through the various strata of a world that has been set afloat from the rest of the world. The editors, headed by Conrad Buff, are dextrous past dexterity, acute to pace and necessity in this long film. The really crucial element *is* an element—the sea, especially when it savagely invades the ship. Bursting through gaps in the hull, rushing down corridors, licking at rooms, triumphing over great ballrooms and tiny closets, down stairways and into elevators, the sea, in the hands of Cameron and his technical associates, becomes hungry, vindictive. The Atlantic seems enraged by the word "unsinkable."

Wag the Dog

FEBRUARY 2, 1998 | Political satire makes us feel good. Ever since it began in dramatized form — 2,400 years ago with Aristophanes — it has been a means by which an audience of the powerless could enjoy criticism of the powerful. Curiously, however, in modern times the critical function has been at least matched by another function that had always lurked below and has now grown: vengeance.

The arrival of mass media brought with it a paradox. The constant drizzle of governmental propaganda on us swelled through this century to a flood, but the more invasive the means of communication became, the less we in the public felt that we communicated — with those who govern our lives. Occasional attempts are made to close this gap, or to seem so: Jimmy Carter's phone-ins at the White House, Clinton's "town meetings." Still, the most telling effect that the public has on governmental behavior these days is not through elections, which at every level have become slugging matches between rival campaign funds, but through popularity polls, as crude a means of political criticism as could be imagined. (Personal behavior of presidents, for instance, affects polls no less than grave policy decisions.)

The only gratifying revenge we can have on the powerful, not only for their actions but for *being* powerful, is through satire. It has not resulted in much change in America, and now it may result in even less, but, oh, does it make us feel better. Will *Wag the Dog* deter another Panama or Grenada adventure? We can doubt it. But at least the film demonstrates, with wit, that we are not unwitting. Our laughter at the film is our moment of absolute equality with our governors.

The screenplay is by Hilary Henkin and David Mamet. (*Variety* reports that Barry Levinson, the director of the picture, is unhappy with the Writers' Guild decision about those credits: Levinson thinks that Mamet should have had first or sole credit.) It's adapted from a novel by Larry Beinhart, but the dialogue stings like Mamet. The film's style is, inevitably, cartoon: characteristics of familiar public figures are exaggerated, as are familiar political ploys. And, almost consistently, it sizzles.

The president, never named or shown, is running for re-election. Eleven days before Election Day, he is charged with sexually molesting a Girl Scout who was on a visit to the Oval Office. A White House staffer, played by Anne Heche, turns for help to an experienced spin doctor, Robert De Niro. The spinmeister quickly resolves that only a war can save the president: a war will distract attention from the sex story and unite the country behind the president. The war, De Niro decides, should be with Albania. He then flies to the coast to engage a Hollywood biggie, Dustin Hoffman, to "produce" the war.

The plot snowballs quickly, getting so large as it rolls that it's harder to control. The brisk dialogue whips it along, but eventually the story bulges through its own conventions. A Hollywood model is hired to enact a horror scene from Albania for a phony TV news clip. Can we believe that no one would recognize her? Absolute secrecy about the war scheme is enforced under pain of death, yet a lot of people along the way unavoidably learn that it's just a scheme—plane pilots, a filling-station operator, and others. How are the schemers assured that beans will not be spilled?

Nonetheless, the film provides a two-hour high, a pleasant delusion of standing toe-to-toe with those who stand above us. (It's notable that political satire is becoming a Hollywood staple. Among other relatively recent examples, *Bob Roberts*). The lift of the picture comes, after the screenplay, from Barry Levinson's bustling direction and from the editing of Stu Linder. Many of the jokes depend on timing, not by the actors but by cutting from one face to another and back again, all done deftly. Levinson has wound up his two principal actors and set them off. De Niro hits the ground running (a relief from his lethargic role in *Jackie Brown*) and slices through the picture like Machiavelli gone electronic. Hoffman gives us an ego almost extracted from the body like a live, wriggling nerve. His gift for comedy was evident thirty years ago in a play called *Eh?;* that gift has lain dormant for long stretches in his career, but here it sparkles. Anne Heche does competently what is asked of her.

At one point Heche says that television has destroyed the electoral process. Oversimple, yes, but not false. In a way, a weird way, it would be reassuring to hear a real White House staffer make that comment some day.

Bulworth

JUNE 8, 1998 | Hollywood and politics have been going together for a long time. Kevin Brownlow showed in *Behind the Mask of Innocence* that political comment in American films began much earlier than is generally thought. But Hollywood figures as political activists themselves—that phenomenon began, I'd guess, in the 1930s. One of my fond memories: in the 1936 presidential campaign James Cagney and Robert Montgomery on a pro-Roosevelt radio show singing, to the tune of "The Old Gray Mare," a duet that went "The old red scare, it ain't what it used to be." (Years later both of them became famously conservative.)

Since World War II few stars have been more politically active than Warren Beatty, always on the liberal side. Until now, however, this actor-writer-director-producer has made only one film with overt political content, *Reds,* and for all its revolutionary ambiance, the emphasis there was more on the lives of the principals than on their ideas. Now Beatty presents *Bulworth,* in which the politics is more important than the people.

Beatty wrote the original story and co-wrote the screenplay with Jeremy Pikser. The time is 1996. At the start of this comedy-drama, Senator Bulworth of California is running for reelection. But he is depressed and suicidal. He engages a hit man to knock him off during the campaign, after arranging for a $10 million life insurance policy payable to his family (though relations with his wife are cool). The policy is payola for a favor to a big insurance company.

While campaigning, Bulworth suddenly becomes a new man. Unexpectedly he begins telling the truth, instead of pumping bilge, and he tells it in sulfurous terms, confessing to poor blacks that they have been betrayed and to rich Jews that they have been fawned on. At a black church he spots a beautiful young woman, Nina, who spots him. An affinity develops between them even as he rushes on in his revisionist campaign.

Partly because of this affinity but mostly because of his liberated conscience, he becomes a white Negro. (This Norman Mailer term was recently the title of a Henry Louis Gates Jr. article about *Bulworth.*) He begins to speak in rap rhymes. He dresses as a young black man, with a ski cap on his head. Instead of ruining his electoral chances, these changes spark his campaign and make him a national celebrity. Enlivened, inspirited, he tries desperately to call off the hit he has arranged.

He gets somewhat involved in Nina's family's troubles. All the while he keeps blazing along the campaign trail, rhyming out facts about conditions for American blacks, trying harder and harder to become black. Very near the end, when he tells Nina in the middle of a crowd that they will have difficulty together because of their race difference, she says, "You're my nigger," and they kiss passionately. This, however, is not the end of the picture.

Two recent political films, *Wag the Dog* and *Primary Colors,* were not really about issues but maneuvers. *Bulworth* steps right into a major issue, and the central metamorphosis is a keen, bitterly comic idea. But the screenplay, for all the care that has obviously gone into it, seems like a first draft. At the main moments of transition in the story, we can almost hear Beatty and friends saying, "We'll fix this later." At the beginning, for instance, Bulworth is sitting in his Washington office, looking at pabulum TV spots of his, apparently a successful, powerful man arranging deals. He does have one brief crying jag, unexplained, but it's hardly enough to explain his wish for assisted suicide. The hit arrangement creaks with unpreparedness. (And, a bit of bad luck for Beatty, a recent Ukrainian film, *A Friend of the Deceased,* uses the same plot device: a man arranges for a hit man to kill him, then tries to call off the deal. In 1990, the device was used in a Finnish film called *I Hired a Contract Killer.*)

Mrs. Bulworth's behavior in public and private is hard to believe. Candidates' wives don't often upbraid their husbands in front of others for being late. And the likelihood seems dim that such a wife, in the middle of a campaign, would have an affair, in these days when investigative reporters are drooling with rapacity.

Then there is Bulworth's transformation. It is simply not adequately motivated. When it happens, it seems quite arbitrary, making us aware of plot mechanics instead of filling us with admiration. It is just as contrived as the contract on his life.

What's even worse is the way his transformation is received. When it happens, his aides are naturally appalled; but the media and the public respond with huzzahs. This is sheer farce carpentry, on a different plane from the gravity of Bulworth's utterances, especially since his language on TV is laced with words that no network would, as yet, carry.

All these structural gaffes are doubly regrettable: they could have been fixed, and they seriously hurt a film of admirable purpose. Beatty wants to blast us with some facts about race in this country: despite the black sports stars and mayors and professors and lawyers that we know about, most African Americans live *outside*. Rap music is anger music, hate music. Social and political programs can help, have helped, but the real program has to be internal—within white people. Bulworth, slightly crazed, is trying to dramatize this basic truth in his very being. But his story's structure impedes him.

Christine Baranski, as Mrs. Bulworth, is her usual valuable self, pungent and unique. Nina is the exquisite Halle Berry, every bit as persuasive as she needs to be. Jack Warden as an old pol, Paul Sorvino as a tycoon lobbyist, Oliver Platt as Bulworth's right hand, are all reliable craftsmen, always welcome. In *Reds* Beatty used a well-known author, Jerzy Kosinski, to play Zinoviev; here he uses a well-known author, Amiri Baraka, to play a ragged homeless man who recurs like the soothsayer in *Julius Caesar*. (Baraka has the last line of the film, something cloudy about being a spirit, not a ghost.)

Beatty himself is high wattage, revved up, sharp in his comic timing, gleaming with eagerness to put his film across. As director, he carries on from where he left off in *Reds;* he is sure and fluent, and occasionally he tips his hat to the past. In *Reds* he paid his respects to Eisenstein; here it's to Capra. In the middle of one of Bulworth's revolutionary talks, the electric power is suddenly switched off to isolate him, which is what happened to Gary Cooper in *Meet John Doe*. (Capra's grandson was a co-producer on *Bulworth* and doubtless appreciated the homage.)

A pity that the contrivances of the structure nag at the truths in the film. It is especially painful because this is clearly a crux in Beatty's life. *Bulworth* is to Beatty very much what Bulworth's conversion is to him, a chance to revitalize his career. Beatty has faded in the last decade, partly because of inactivity, partly because of his last film, *Love Affair,* a remake of a 1939 weepie that even I couldn't drive myself to see. *Bulworth* could have gone far to reestablish him. Well, it may go far, anyway, because a good deal of it is politically sound and theatrically glittering.

JUNE 29, 1998 | Samuel Beckett's short film called *Film* is about a person's being perceived. *Esse est percipi* is the picture's motto; to be is to be perceived. *Film* shows us a man, played by Buster Keaton, trying to avoid being looked at, fleeing it, and finally discovering, to his horror, that it is impossible to escape being seen. Beckett's work, then, is a small agon of the entanglements of living and a sly dig into the metaphysics of film itself.

We know, and we relish the knowledge, that a film character is not alone even when he may glory in solitude. He wouldn't be there except so that we can see him. This large encircling paradox often tempts us to consider how the character (not, of course, the actor) would react if he knew he were being watched. His horror might at least be the equal of Keaton's.

The Truman Show is a reminder of the Beckett theme. The screenplay by Andrew Niccol starts from something like Beckett's abstraction and reifies it with details of contemporary culture, then moves on into fantasy.

The basis is simple and sickening. Truman Burbank is a thirty-year-old insurance salesman who lives on a street of tract houses with his magazine-ad wife and neighbors. This good-sized community is on a big island. There's one point of marital disagreement early on. Truman's wife wants a baby; Truman wants to travel, and he dreams of Fiji.

The audience is warned from the start that Truman's cookie-cutter life is in some way extraordinary; the very first shot is of a TV director, played by Ed Harris, commenting on what we are about to see. At first this is a bit puzzling, but gradually we understand, helped by the fact that many shots of daily doings in Truman's life are framed as if on a TV screen. It becomes clear that absolutely every moment of every day of Truman's life is being watched by hidden TV cameras and is being broadcast on "The Truman Show," which is an international hit. What's more, the film begins on Day 10,909 of the show. It has been going on since his birth.

Truman himself knows nothing about the show. Nothing. Every other person whom we see, except one, is rehearsed and programmed for TV, including his lovey-dovey wife. Every person in the street or in his office is, knowingly, part of "The Truman Show." (So, though he is unaware of it, Truman isn't really living a real life.) When he eventually finds out about all this, his reaction is like Keaton's, except that his horror moves him to action.

Truman hasn't known about his TV show because apparently it isn't broadcast on this island. He sees only the local paper. He isn't aware of the Truman T-shirts or the Truman bars where people gather to watch his show. A graphic reason is supplied why he never leaves the island.

We understand why Truman's new itch to travel is opposed: it would take him off the huge TV stage, and it would inform him about the show itself. But he begins to suspect, anyway. A theater-lighting fixture falls from the sky into the street in front of his house. In a storm at the beach, a shaft of rain hits him like the beam of an overhead spotlight, and when he moves, the beam moves with him. More clues to his TV existence soon follow. (The TV director's control of the elements is godlike. My favorite line in the script comes when, in the gigantic spherical TV control room, the director barks at an assistant, "Cue the sun!"—and the sun comes up on Truman's island. Note that the name of the TV director is Christof.)

Most of our questions about the plot are answered as the film proceeds, but we shrug them off anyway, answered or not. We don't want the fantasy interfered with because it keeps striking home ferociously. It doesn't take long to see the dark underside of the film's theme: the captive of TV isn't Truman, it's the audience. Us. And our love of that captivity, the gobbling of shows—fictional drama or news or sports or politics, but always *shows*—engulfs us. We used to go to theaters and films; now, more seductively than radio, TV comes to our homes, entwines us. (And is paid for, in "The Truman Show," not by commercials but by "product placement." We see the brand name on a six-pack, etc.) The shows don't have to be dramatic, as "The Truman Show" and most TV attests. They need only be shows, life outside transmitted to the TV screen inside.

Toward the end, after Truman discovers that his entire life is a show, Christof is at first not worried because he thinks that the imprisoned protagonist likes his "cell." When Christof learns otherwise, he warns Truman that if he leaves he'll discover that life outside the enormous TV stage is no more real than within. (Discomfiting, when we see how the office chat on the TV show resembles the chat rituals of all offices.) But Truman, something like Keaton, would rather not be perceived; and his urge is seconded by the one non-TV person among the principals, a young woman who truly loves him, who has been watching the show and hoping.

Despite its grim reminder of our media slavery, *The Truman Show* refreshes. Besides its novelty of subject (although I'm sure science-fiction experts could cite antecedents), it has dash and daring. The director—of the *whole* film—was Peter Weir, the Australian whose career has ranged from *Gallipoli* to *Witness* to *Dead Poets Society,* and who is adroit here in letting the TV presence in Truman's life seep into our awareness. We learn that 5,000 small hidden TV cameras are watching Truman everywhere, always, so we can appreciate some of the queer shots we have seen—like, for instance, one through the digital clock on the dashboard of Truman's car.

A lot of blather has erupted about Jim Carrey's performance as Truman. My own view of it is, in a sense, negative: at least Carrey has omitted almost all the muggings and cavortings by which he prospered. Weir has sheared off most of Carrey's high-school exhibitionism, and, in any case, the script itself helped to keep him from being unbearable. Whether this new-found restraint proves that he has undiscovered depths and possibilities is a question. But of course we can hope.

Laura Linney, as Truman's wife, supplies the requisite steel under the chickabiddy surface. Natascha McElhone, as the true young woman, endows the film with its one soft touch, a scent of romance. The cinematographer, Peter Biziou, veteran of such eccentric numbers as *Bugsy Malone* and *Life of Brian* and *Time Bandits,* suggests subtly from the start that all this world's a stage.

The Thief

AUGUST 10, 1998 | An attractive young widow and her six-year-old son are traveling on a crowded train. It's the Soviet Union, 1952, and she is hoping to find a job somewhere. A good-looking army captain enters the compartment, impresses her, and relatively soon, while the boy sleeps, gets her into a corner of the train where they make love.

Subsequently, all three leave the train together at whatever town it happens to be and find a room. In the course of time she learns that the captain's uniform is a masquerade, that he is really a thief. After he gathers up a sackful of pilfered saleable goods, they move to another town where the game is repeated. And on to other towns.

She protests his thievery, but she is so besotted with him that, though they quarrel, he always wins. At last she breaks free, but with sad consequences. Then there's an epilogue eight or nine years later, when the boy is an adolescent. (Throughout the film his mature voice is on the soundtrack, recalling, unifying the story elements.) Accidentally he meets the spurious captain and settles accounts for his mother's sake.

The film is *The Thief,* and its story as sketched above makes a pleasant romantic drama. But that romantic drama is as much a disguise as the captain's uniform. Basically, the film is a political allegory. On the captain's chest is tattooed the face of Stalin, and at various gatherings he proposes a toast to Stalin. He symbolizes Stalin himself, a thief who has seduced the boy's mother, Mother Russia. The boy himself is the new generation that rids its country of Stalin.

After the death of Stalin in 1953, and the passing of Stalinoid leaders in other countries, Eastern Europe sent us films about the evils of the old Communism while the new Communism was still in place. (E.g., *Love* and *Angi Vera* from Hungary.) It's interesting that, with the new order now also passé, an anti-Stalin film is made in suggestive rather than direct form. All to the good, however. Pavel Chukhrai, who wrote and directed, makes the slyness of the film's method resonate the deviousness of the thief himself.

Chukhrai is helped immensely by the three leading performances. The six-year-old, Misha Philipchuk, is one more of those marvelous puzzles: a child giving a complex performance. Obviously he had a good director, but that obvious fact doesn't explain how he, like other marvelous children, understood what the director was saying. Ekaterina Rednikova, as the widow, has vulnerability and strength and a soft bloom of sex. Vladimir Mashkov, the captain-thief, is a real find. Magnetic without being depressingly handsome, flexed and agile in his acting, with a voice that reinforces his appeal, Mashkov could have a considerable career. He made me think of the young Jean Gabin.

Along the way, Chukhrai evokes a sense of national restlessness in postwar Russia, and he etches numerous small portraits. European films, not least Russian ones, have always been bounteous with small character sketches; directors have made the most of intriguing types to be found in odd places, along with a large complement of capable actors willing to take minor roles. Chukhrai makes the most of his good luck in both regards.

There's Something about Mary

AUGUST 17 & 24, 1998 | If a time capsule is being prepared to be opened 100 years from now, make room in it for *There's Something about Mary*. When the people of 2098 see it, they will get a clear idea of the taboos of our time, because this raggedy farce makes a point of violating as many taboos as it can.

It's as if the writers, Ed Decter & John J. Strauss and Peter Farrelly & Bobby Farrelly, began by making a list. (The last two also directed.) What, the quartet presumably asked, are the subjects about which one is not permitted to joke? Then they proceeded to make jokes about them — cruelty to animals, people with braces on their legs, gay men, and, in gross detail, masturbation. These and many more are packed — nay, pummeled — into the screenplay. Woven around them is a story of sorts, purposely porous to allow easy entry for gags. And, to underline the casualness, a pair of minstrels wanders through the film, singing appropriate numbers, which is a device I can't remember since *Cat Ballou* (1965).

Ted, a Rhode Island high school boy in the 1960s, with braces on his teeth, is miraculously asked by the prettiest girl in class, Mary, to escort her to the senior prom. When he calls for her, he visits the bathroom in her house, gets his equipment caught in his zipper, and has to be taken to the hospital. (Even before this the film has announced its laugh level.)

Years later, now a successful man, Ted cannot forget Mary. He hires a seedy private eye, Healy, to find her, which the eye does. She is now a physician in Miami. But Healy himself falls for her, lies to Ted about her present situation, and woos Mary. Many, many gags follow, some of them laugh-provoking, all of them vulgar.

Bernard Shaw said:

> I go to the theatre to be moved to laughter, not to be tickled or bustled into it, and that is why, though I laugh as much as anybody at a farcical

comedy, I am out of spirits before the end of the second act, and out of temper before the end of the third, my miserable mechanical laughter intensifying these symptoms at every outburst.

Thus with this film and me.

Ben Stiller, who plays Ted, is a phenomenon of sorts. He is short, bow-legged, a model of misproportion; but when the camera stays fairly close to his face, he is the quintessence of latter-day TV-comedy playing: with broken sentences, repetitive phrases, choked utterances, all served up in an omelet of tacit feelings. Matt Dillon, as Healy, finds the right exaggeration to take his performance just over the border into burlesque sketch-playing. The sparkler in this rag pile is Cameron Diaz as Mary: quick, witty, pretty, warm. There *is* something about Mary.

Lolita

OCTOBER 5, 1998 | Bill Clinton influences the film world. The missile attacks that he recently ordered have revived interest in *Wag the Dog*. His personal behavior has extended permissiveness in public discussion; so it has, in some degree, affected the atmosphere in which *Lolita* arrives. Candor passed a milestone in this country with a comment by a man interviewed on a news program last month: "I never thought I'd have to explain oral sex to my eleven-year-old daughter." And this is only one of the fractures of reticence that have lately been crackling all around us.

Clinton is not into pedophilia like Nabokov's Humbert Humbert. Still, his sexual activities and the publicity about them have made a difference, I'd guess, in the possible shock quotient of this film. No one in his right mind, or even a fragment of it, would make light of pedophilia; but a work of art on that subject cannot now be as completely—or merely—shocking today as it once was. "Once" means a year ago.

The film coils and uncoils like a snake in the sun, sinuous, alluring. In essence, even though essence is not really enough, it is much closer to the novel than the 1962 version, nominally adapted by Nabokov himself. He later said that Stanley Kubrick's film was "first-rate, but it is not what I wrote." Stephen Schiff made the present adaptation, which is published by Applause. (He notes that he retained a few lines from an earlier, discarded version that Harold Pinter wrote for this production.) Schiff calls *Lolita* "the greatest American novel of the postwar era." Even while gurgling some dissent about "American" and the implied slaps at Bellow and Pynchon, we can admit that Schiff has honored his high opinion with a screenplay that, in sum, does about as well with the novel as a screenplay could.

The director, Adrian Lyne, who has specialized in suave renditions of such steamy material as *Fatal Attraction* and *Indecent Proposal,* keeps this new film gliding. He repeats visual effects — too often he frames shots with an irrelevant object large in the foreground, just to surprise us — but he has a gleeful sense of the physical. In the flashback sequence of Humbert Humbert at thirteen, with a girl of twelve, we can almost scent the warmth. Later, with Lolita herself, Lyne suffuses us with the feel of her clothes, the silk of her skin. In the novel Humbert calls her "my hot downy darling," and so Lyne renders her. A few of Lyne's touches are lumpy, like the symbolic shot of flies caught on flypaper, but, during the cross-country trek of Humbert and Lolita, Lyne dabs in enough earnest/ludicrous American topography (a motel that consists of wigwams) to underscore how far afield this European intellectual has been led by his glands.

Humbert is now Jeremy Irons. Not long ago I saw the Kubrick film again and was again convinced that, thin though the screenplay is, James Mason is the ideal Humbert. He gives us a doomed man, conscious of it, accepting it. Mason once predicted that *Lolita* would be filmed again; and here is Irons in the role, giving it his customary vestments of intelligence and sensitive reticence, but at his deepest he is no more than melancholy. Mason suggested a tragic fall.

Dominique Swain seems both younger and older than the first Lolita, Sue Lyon. Literally Swain is younger than Lyon was; but she deals more cannily than Lyon with the power bestowed on her by the development of her body. Swain combines a child's delight at a new toy, sexual attraction, with a woman's knowing use of it. She blends her liking for comic books and jawbreakers with her precocity in bed. The film is careful never to display her breasts, but her body is still the real site of the drama.

As Lolita's mother, Melanie Griffith at last finds a role that her squeaky voice fits suitably. She lacks the pressing yet pitiful vulgarity that Shelley Winters gave the woman, but she is pathetic enough. Once again, Quilty is a problem. The earlier version had a bit too much of Peter Sellers, as chameleon star; this new Quilty has a converse problem. As the demonic nemesis, Frank Langella has too little flavor, and he is tenuously attached to the story. In character terms it's the chief weakness in the adaptation: the role is treated almost as if the audience has read the novel and will know who and why Quilty is.

But Quilty is not the basic trouble—and unfortunately there *is* one. Though this film is fuller than Kubrick's, it too fails the novel. Probably any film must fail, because *Lolita* cannot truly exist outside the novel. Nabokov gives us the chronicle of Humbert's perversion in coruscating prose; and that prose is where the story lives, as porpoises live in the sea.

Nabokov said of his upbringing: "I was a perfectly normal trilingual child," but because of circumstances, "I had to abandon my untrammeled, rich and infinitely docile Russian tongue for a second-rate brand of English." Even if this is only a coy way of drawing attention to his latter-day mastery, it still is mastery. Humbert Humbert's saga is spun in gorgeous language that is outside the domain of film.

Of course it's common to sigh about a picture made from a superior novel that, however good, it cannot compensate for the loss of the medium in which the work was conceived. But with *Lolita* this is much more true, not only because of the quality of the prose but because that prose is used to recount a story of deviance. True, as Alfred Appel, Jr. points out in *The Annotated Lolita*, Humbert eventually comes to a "declaration of genuine love and, finally, to a realization of the loss suffered not by him but by Lolita"; but these passages seem last-minute attempts to balance the book—in which Humbert has called himself a pervert, a victim of pederosis. Additionally, Nabokov uses a foreword by a fictitious Ph.D. to weigh in on the "respectable" side, and he uses *mors ex machina* to deliver both his principals from the long-range results of their behavior.

Still, Nabokov wrote a flaming rhapsody about the love affair of a mature man and a twelve-year-old girl. He tempered the story slightly with small apologetics, but for the most part the book exults in ecstasy, like the work of Sade or Huysmans or Choderlos de Laclos. *Lolita*, through its very beauty, touches taboo depths in us just as those other authors do; and it seems to me both ridiculous and offensive to a major artist to say that this book is anything other than a soaring canticle of socially unacceptable erotica. The Clinton era makes the action of the novel, adapted to the screen, less egregious, but the action as such is only a synopsis of the work. Shorn of Nabokov's language, as it must be, any film of *Lolita,* even one as adequately made as Lyne's, must seem somewhat gaunt.

Happiness

NOVEMBER 9, 1998 | It's a mite early to be summing up the twentieth century, but *Happiness* is so up-to-date that it deploys the past behind it. Todd Solondz's film wriggles and smirks and suffers and chuckles on a base of assumptions—about us. It seems to say: "Well, people of the nineties, see what this century has led to in love and desire and loneliness. And see what you're now willing to accept in a film about such things."

I missed Solondz's first film, *Welcome to the Dollhouse,* but *Happiness* very quickly displays finesse and control, colored by a nearly exultant glee. The title is self-evidently ironic. Who today would expect the picture to be about happy people? Three sisters are at the hub of things, one of whom is not yet unhappy. The sunny one, Trish, is a New Jersey housewife with a psychiatrist husband, Bill, and three children, notably eleven-year-old Billy. Helen, unmarried, is a melancholy, self-dramatizing poet in Manhattan, inventing traumas in her past to feed her poems. Joy, who works in Manhattan and lives in New Jersey, also unmarried and hungry for love, is beating at the iron door of life with tiny fists. Two of the three sisters, Helen and Joy, are central to their stories. For Trish, the colors of her life change, as husband Bill moves center in her strand.

Helen gets involved, via telephone, with a man who (unknown to her) lives in the next apartment. Joy, who teaches adult immigrants, gets involved with a Russian taxi-driver, so tightly that his Russian girlfriend comes around to assault her. As Trish fades into the background of her story, Bill's problems take over. Successful professional though he is, he only now begins to face his homosexual leanings—pedophile, moreover—and begins to act on them.

Helen's neighbor is Allen, employed in a brokerage house, who comes home at night and drinks, makes obscene calls, masturbates; vulnerable, he succumbs to a plump woman across the hall who is even more desperate than he is. The parents of the three sisters, Lenny and Mona, live in Florida and are having their own emotional problems, as Lenny dallies with a middle-aged woman who lives nearby and is on the prowl.

Solondz does well with his cast, all of whom fill their roles to the brim. They breathe with some of the same sense of integration that Mike Leigh gets from his comparable London films, yet Solondz, as far as I know, doesn't put his cast through Leigh's long periods of character saturation before shooting. Jane Adams (Joy), Lara Flynn Boyle (Helen), Cynthia Stevenson (Trish), Ben Gazzara and Louise Lasser as their parents, Rufus Read (Billy), and Phillip Seymour Hoffman (Allen) all deserve more praise than I am giving them. I cite only two of the cast specially: Jared Harris (son of Richard) shows unexpected solidity and strength as the Russian. Dylan Baker does a grave, contemplative balancing act — or unbalancing act — as the psychiatrist who knows he may be wrecking his life and can't stop.

However, this catalog of desperations disserves the film in one way: it doesn't make clear that *Happiness* is a comedy, certainly black but nonetheless comic. Every one of these accounts of loneliness and frustration is tinged before or during or after with a hint of the author's amusement. Take the opening scene. The film begins with an immense close-up of Joy at a restaurant table, then a close-up of her escort (Jon Lovitz); and we then get dialogue of the subcutaneous, nerve-twisting, present-day comic kind in which Joy tells the man that she doesn't want to see him anymore. The scene is a neatly shaped verbal ballet of satire. But later we learn of the ghastly aftermath.

The comic texture of the scene and its ultimate shock typify the view that Solondz has of his film — and of his people: pitiable yet risible or, in this first episode, the other way around. There's a scent of Woody Allen in the air, but Solondz burrows through to bleak consequences more thoroughly than Allen.

This view that Solondz has of his characters makes us look at the film as a marker on the road. Emotional frustration is hardly a novel topic, but Solondz's cool, wry view of his people fits the postmodern temper snugly. And it's remarkable that a recent documentary confirms the tone of his fiction. In *Unmade Beds* people talk about themselves in terms quite like *Happiness*. The love lives of four New Yorkers, male and female, have been chronicled by Nicholas Barker who, through some wizardry, has induced these people to speak candidly; and it all comes out as a corollary to Solondz's film. The simultaneous appearance of these two pictures, made quite independently of each other, is eerily fascinating.

Solondz provides yet another ending-of-the-century marker: the sexual details. Curiously, the reviews of *Happiness* that I've read, all favorable, euphemize the frankest elements in it. This is to diminish its relevance, I think, but—a societal paradox—some reviewers can accept daring elements in a film and recommend that film to their readers although they are not permitted to specify those elements in their publications.

Examples. Bill asks his son Billy, who is becoming sexually itchy, if he knows how to masturbate and, if not, offers to instruct him. Billy declines. (In the film world this is the Year of Masturbation. A chief gag in *There's Something about Mary* derives from it.) Bill subsequently drugs his whole family and Billy's sleepover friend so that he can sodomize the visiting boy. When the sodomy is discovered by that boy's physician and Bill is accused, Billy asks him if it's true. When Bill admits it, Billy asks wistfully if Bill will do it to him. (Bill, drawing the line, says no.)

Because of the scandal, Trish leaves Bill and takes her children down to her folks in Florida. Billy is on the balcony of the Florida apartment, sees a shapely young woman in a bikini below, masturbates, and, for the first time, ejaculates. (Thus, Solondz implies, taking his first step toward the ranks of love-and-sex frustrations.) Billy goes in to report his achievement proudly to his family at the dinner table. Meanwhile, the family dog licks Billy's semen from the balcony rail, then goes in and licks Trish's face.

What's most important about these franknesses, I'd say, is Solondz's belief that the audience would accept them and the fact that he has been proved absolutely right. (The first potential distributor declined the film; nevertheless it's launched.) That acceptance is at the very least a drum-beat in the march of time, as the century winds down.

Supervening all these matters is the fact that Solondz is gifted. *Happiness* is not schlock by a crass sensationalist. It is the work of a talented man who knows his characters and his audience and, with more drollery than compassion, confronts one with the other.

Dancing at Lughnasa

NOVEMBER 30, 1998 | Here is Meryl Streep again. (And, I hope, again and again.) Now she joins a group of mostly foreign actors and performs as one of them. In *Dancing at Lughnasa* she is one of five Irish sisters, and Streep—a New Jersey lass—comes off as truly Donegal as any of the native Irish performers.

Of course she has always cherished accents as chances for virtuosity—Polish in *Sophie's Choice,* Dixie in *Silkwood,* high British in *The French Lieutenant's Woman*—but in few of the past films was she closely surrounded by a cluster of native speakers. Two of the prominent men in the *Lughnasa* cast are also non-Irish—Michael Gambon, playing the priest who is the sisters' brother, is English, and Rhys Ifans, the lover of one of the sisters, is Welsh—and they do well, but they do not need to belong to a tight nuclear group as Streep must and as she flawlessly succeeds in doing. I couldn't help wondering what the Irish women in the cast thought of their American sibling. It's easy to imagine an initial resentment as, for commercial reasons, a Yank film star took the dominant woman's role from an Irish actress; still, it's even easier to imagine how Streep's authenticity won them over. Anyway, imaginings aside, the result is marvelously homogeneous. For the 94 minutes of this film, Streep was born in Ballybeg in Donegal just as surely as her sisters were. Once more in a Streep transmutation, accent is almost the least of it, just one aspect of a created character in every shade of mind and soul.

Pat O'Connor, who directed *Circle of Friends* with warmth and flavor, treats *Dancing at Lughnasa* almost as the product of the Donegal countryside. For O'Connor, the rigor of the story, its rootedness and its attempts to break loose, seem the harvest of the landscape where it happens. (The year is 1936.) Frank McGuinness made the screenplay from Brian Friel's play—the same McGuinness who did the version of *A Doll House* that was on Broadway a few seasons back—and has eased it into its new form with no more "opening up" than is helpful.

Which brings us to Friel's play itself. First, the title. Lugh, pronounced Loo, was the Celtic god of the harvest. Lá Lughnasa, pronounced Loonasa, was the god's feast day and, sixty years ago anyway—which may be one reason why the piece is set back in 1936—was still celebrated in some parts of rural Ireland with bonfires and dancing. Friel's play is not about the survival of paganism, however—not in any deistic sense. It deals with the suppression of earthy instincts and their inevitable explosion, and those instincts are here linked with primitivism. To be natural, the play implies, is to burrow beneath the strictures of our civilization. This theme is signaled at the very start: around the opening credits of this picture about Donegal folk we see African masks and sculptures. The film's license for the African objects comes from Jack, the brother of the five Mundy sisters, a priest who has spent many years in Uganda and, returned to this Donegal cottage somewhat muzzy in his mind, often adverts to his experience of Ugandan rituals.

The Mundy sisters range in age from the twenties well up into the forties, or beyond. Four of them are, presumably, virgins; one of them has a "love child," a boy, but no lover. In fact, during the play the boy's father comes to tell the boy's mother that he's off to fight against Franco in the Spanish Civil War. The youngest sister, who is simple-minded, has a married man tagging after her to console him for his departed wife; she is willing, but her sisters interfere for her own good.

Into this small house of large congested feelings comes the family's first radio. It breaks down, and its repair coincides with a crisis in both the finances of the Mundys and the writhings of buried sexual feelings — along with, in Friel's somewhat patent design, the arrival of Lughnasa. As the radio feeds music into the cottage, one by one the sisters begin to dance, and the climax of the film is this uncharacteristic outburst of near-wild physicality — their own private Lughnasa. The film is able, aptly, to take that dancing outdoors so that they dance on the earth itself. What happens afterward is merely the subsiding of this brief ecstasy: the five sisters settle into lives that differ — but only in kinds of drabness — from their previous lives, as described for us by a voice-over.

This material could have made a solid one-act play, like Synge's *Riders to the Sea* or Frank O'Connor's *In the Train,* but Friel has drawn it out into a full-length work which, for all the crinkle and lilt in some of the dialogue, sags in the middle. Once we know the tension, the unsatisfied hungers among the sisters, we sit around waiting for the explosion. Very little organic drama grows between the exposition and the explosion. Friel fills in the interim with exploration of characters who are not, as he draws them, deeply explorable. (For instance, he plunks in several minutes with the sisters grouped around a table leafing through an old photo album, just to add body to the piece.) Then, after the outburst of dancing, the film is tied off hastily with that most glib of devices, the voice-over.

And that voice-over itself is strange. It is spoken by a man who was the boy of the story, looking back years later on this summer of 1936. A curious retrospect. We have seen a drama of bitterness, frustration, disintegration; but his memory of that summer, he says, "owes nothing to fact." He remembers it as a time when everyone was "floating on sweet sounds." Either Friel is trying to paint a golden glow on his dark story as it fades away or else he is trying to show us how memory, especially that of childhood, can shape the past the way we wish it had been. But if this latter is really what Friel intended, it makes the body of the play seem all the more attenuated—the lengthy posing of some grimness just so that a man, who was a boy then, can remember it otherwise.

But, Friel apart, the making of the film is impressive. In addition to Streep, her sisters are as vital as the script allows—even a bit more so: Catherine McCormack, Kathy Burke, Sophie Thompson, and (from the play's original cast) Brid Brennan. Michael Gambon, by now a welcome figure, generates a kind of awesome pathos as the priest-brother who comes home dazed by Africa.

Hilary and Jackie

DECEMBER 28, 1998 | *Hilary and Jackie* is an English film and does not of course concern two American First Ladies. The two women of the title are the (factual) Du Pré sisters, the first of whom was a flautist who retired early into happy domesticity, the second of whom was Jacqueline, the famous and beloved cellist who died in 1987 of multiple sclerosis at the age of forty-two.

The screenplay by Frank Cottrell Boyce, based on a book by Hilary and Piers Du Pré, treats the story of the two sisters as a lyric—a song of sisterly love, nourishing yet difficult, as deep love between siblings often is, further complicated by Jackie's solipsism, which increases as her fame grows. Eventually it even intrudes into Hilary's marriage. Annand Tucker, the director, who makes his feature debut here after much work with the BBC, concentrates on the swell and surge of Boyce's script and succeeds in giving the film a touch of other-worldliness from start to finish. Tucker is over-fond of 360-degree shots—he circles the two sisters when they are children on a beach, he circles Jackie when she is playing—but he convinces us that we are dealing with extraordinary people, even when they are sitting in an ordinary kitchen having breakfast.

On that beach at the start the two very young girls see a mysterious woman. Jackie goes over to speak to her, then whispers to Hilary what the woman has said. We don't hear it. At the end, in a dream sequence, we see that scene again, and this time we learn who the woman is and what she says to Jackie. This prologue and epilogue, the only mystical elements in the film, do not help.

But aside from this mystical lapse, the film takes the two girls—realistically, endearingly—into adolescence and first maturity with glow and excitement and hurt and welcome touches of silliness. Hilary manages to recover from the discovery of Jackie's musical superiority—Hilary is greatly helped by a devoted young man—and Jackie never commits the barbarism of trying to console Hilary in this matter.

Jackie meets Daniel Barenboim, converts to Judaism, and marries him. The marriage, happy enough in some regards, does not completely prosper. Depressed and nervous, Jackie goes to stay for a while in the country with Hilary and Kiffer, her husband, and their children; and Jackie suggests that she share Kiffer's marital attentions. After some reluctance and disagreement, this happens—we're not sure how often—and it restores Jackie's spirits. Barenboim visits; but, though sympathetic, is willing to leave Jackie there.

In time Jackie resumes her career, international and garlanded, until the disease starts to encroach in 1973, when she is twenty-eight. (The film omits the fact that she continued to work—as a teacher, including TV classes.) We are given just enough of her physical decline to see that a winged spirit is being more and more completely immured in torment.

Emily Watson, familiar from *Breaking the Waves* and *The Boxer,* plays Jackie and is generous with the young genius's "genius-ness." Watson has an instinct for naked, electric emotion, for lightning response, but once in a while Tucker asked for, or permitted, a touch of the consciously fey that won such plaudits in *Breaking the Waves.* As Hilary, Rachel Griffiths is absolutely lovely and lovable; so is Celia Imrie as the mother. Charles Dance, a distinctive actor, is wasted in the nondescript role of the father; but David Morrissey tumbles in winningly as Kiffer. James Frain has the peculiar job of being the young Daniel Barenboim. I assume that the real Barenboim saw and approved, which doesn't make it less peculiar. (A few years ago I went to a Barenboim piano recital, was enchanted by his playing, and was struck by the contrast between his music and his completely impassive demeanor. This film, concerned with the much younger man, only underscores that contrast.)

Shakespeare in Love

JANUARY 4, 1999 | In *The Genius of Shakespeare* Jonathan Bate says that, contrary to the general impression, "We know a great deal more about Shakespeare's life than we do about the lives of his fellow-dramatists and fellow-actors." We know it from official documents, says Bate. "But . . . we do not learn very much from them about his character as it affects what we are interested in: his plays." Luckily for the gaiety of nations, this point hasn't hindered Marc Norman and Tom Stoppard, co-authors of *Shakespeare in Love.*

Stoppard said recently on TV that Norman, an American who had written such items as *Cutthroat Island* and *Waterworld,* did the first draft of this screenplay; then he was called in. Who wrote this or that scene in the final version is of course indecipherable to us, but the result is clearly the work of people who know a good deal about the Elizabethan era and theater, so much so that they can play games with the material. This picture plays some diverting ones. With most historical films the informed viewer scrutinizes in order to cluck at errors. (There are books full of such cluckings.) With *Shakespeare in Love* the more one knows, the more one can enjoy the liberties taken.

John Madden, the director, aided by Martin Childs, the production designer, and Sandy Powell, who did the costumes, crams the London of 1593 with the hubbub and bustle and squalor and panoply that history justifies, and it's all centered on a Bankside theater, the Rose, owned by the hard-pressed Philip Henslowe. This is factual: then comes the fantasy. Young Shakespeare, actor and playwright attached to the Rose, is trying to write a play for his company, and so far he has little but the title, *Romeo and Ethel, The Pirate's Daughter.* No Elizabethan or Jacobean play's title has that sort of formulation; thus, all that remains is to find out how we get to *Romeo and Juliet.*

To begin with, Shakespeare gets advice from his coeval and rival,

Christopher Marlowe (a brief, incisive appearance by Rupert Everett). But the true inspiration for the plot of his play, even for scene structure, comes from the happenstance that Shakespeare falls in love—with the daughter of a wealthy family. The fact that he has a wife and children back in Stratford doesn't hobble his passion, and the young lady, who hasn't yet learned about his family, responds. Her name is Viola, another Shakespearean promise. (Her last name is de Lesseps. Is it some sort of private joke that the authors chose the family name of the man who, three hundred years later, built the Suez Canal and attempted one in Panama?)

Materials for the play, as Shakespeare keeps trying to meet his deadline, come from his experiences with Viola: her father's objection, her aristocratic fiancé, duels, a balcony scene complete with nurse, and more. I haven't seen such close correspondence between experience and art since a play about Wagner, in the 1930s, in which he is struggling to compose *Tristan,* embraces a new mistress one evening, cries "I have it!", then rushes to his piano and whams out the *Liebestod.* I was too young then to be anything but outraged; in *Shakespeare,* I thought it was an entertaining parody of the creative process, all the more entertaining because of its heat.

The screenplay also uses, with a swirling hand, a familiar Shakespearean device, the woman disguised as a man. Viola, mad for the poet, uninterested in the fiancé who has been arranged for her, transvests to become an actor in Shakespeare's theater (women of course being prohibited on the stage). This leads to a device that asks for our generosity. When we first see Viola, she has flowing blonde hair. When she appears in the theater, she has close-cropped brown hair, and we think that she has had herself shorn and dyed. But then we see her back home with the honey locks again. This back-and-forth hair-changing goes puzzlingly on. Oh, well, a fig for explanations. It's so incredible that, like Shakespeare's writing of his play (which is eventually called by its familiar name), we shrug because what's happening generally is so pleasant.

Other plot strands counterpoint the central story—Henslowe's woes with his creditors, the harrying of the theater by the Master of the Revels, the news of Marlowe's death and its effect, the presence of a twelve-year-old gamin named John Webster who hangs around the theater teasing people with live mice (a hint of the man who would write *The White Devil* and *The Duchess of Malfi*). Queen Elizabeth herself is the *dea ex machina,* solving all problems at the end insofar as they can be solved. Her last line is a request to Master Shakespeare for a comedy, perhaps a play for Twelfth Night. He sets right to work; he already knows the name of the heroine.

John Madden's last film was *Mrs. Brown,* in which he deployed the relationship of Queen Victoria and John Brown with stateliness and wit. Here he has seemingly swilled some of Falstaff's sack and has had robustious, fiery fun. Judi Dench, who was his Victoria, is Elizabeth here, and no one else could be tolerated in the part. Madden's most impressive achievement, amid all the hurly-burly, is an intimate, almost internal one. He gets a full, feeling performance from Gwyneth Paltrow as Viola. Up to now I've never seen Paltrow do anything but present the shape and exterior of roles, from Jane Austen's *Emma* to *A Perfect Murder.* With Madden's help, she puts a full-bodied, aching young woman inside her costumes, not only justifying Shakespeare's hunger for Viola but promising much for Paltrow.

Shakespeare is Joseph Fiennes, younger brother of Ralph. Joseph, more slender and dark and willowy than his brother, has had some small parts in films and some large ones in the London theater, including the Royal Shakespeare Company. Now he is (gulp) the bard himself. This is hardly the first time that Shakespeare has been a character in a dramatic work. (Even Bernard Shaw used him—in a one-act play, *The Dark Lady of the Sonnets,* where he implores Elizabeth to found a national theater.) Still, it can't be a role an actor steps into blithely. His best advantage is that, as Bate tells us, little is really known about the man's character. Ben Jonson said he was of "an open and free nature," then added that he has "gentle expressions, wherein he flowed with that facility that sometimes it was necessary that he should be stopped. . . . His wit was in his own power; would the rule of it had been, too." But this semi-generous description, one of the few accounts that survive, isn't of much relevance to an actor who wants to play a Shakespeare who is a model for his own Romeo.

Fiennes carries the day. He is lithe, strong, hot, with an attractive voice. The part isn't widely varied, so his performance isn't, either; but he moves through this film with the surreal effect of a flashing rapier. His Shakespeare puts the seal on the pact between us and the film. "Very well, this is not fact," we concede. "Then let it be gratifying fiction." And it is.

FEBRUARY 1, 1999 | New England. Winter. Snowy countryside, skies black with cold. Hard-bitten folk, surviving. *Ethan Frome. Way Down East.* Ah, it's good to be back in that barren landscape, so fertile for American drama.

Affliction was adapted from a Russell Banks novel by Paul Schrader, who then directed. Another Banks novel, *The Sweet Hereafter,* set in much the same climate and terrain, became a haunting film in 1997. Paul Sarossy, who shot that picture, is also the cinematographer here, with the same ability to make the snow seem part of interiors and to make the exteriors, even with flakes falling, seem no less habitable than warm rooms. Schrader's last notable work, adapted by Harold Pinter from Ian McEwan, was set in the voluptuary Venice of *The Comfort of Strangers;* here Schrader suffuses his film with the smell of wet wool and cheap whiskey and cigarette smoke in the cabs of pickup trucks.

In this atmosphere lives Wade Whitehouse, sole policeman of a small town, separated from his (remarried) wife and their small daughter. He loves the child but bungles her visits with him. He bungles relations with lots of people he would really like to get on with. He is a big man, given to spurts of violence that are almost expected of him by now. Hovering—more than hovering—in the background is his father, as big as he is and even more of a drinker, more violent. Wade has a brother, Rolfe, who (unexplained, though he comes from precisely the same background) is a professor in Boston. Rolfe is from time to time a commentator, through voice-overs, on the story we watch. That story begins with a seemingly accidental death on the first day of the deer-hunting season; from this death, events then lead to Wade's loss of his job, his involvement in more deaths, and his eventual disappearance from the town and from everybody's ken.

Schrader deploys this decline and fall before us enticingly enough to tease us into "if only." We keep wanting to reach into the screen to stop foolish actions. This is a tribute to the director and his actors, because most of these characters, as such, are not deeply interesting, and the overall motion of the story is early manifest. But the principal performances, by Nick Nolte as Wade and James Coburn as his sodden ultra-macho father, provide the film with a rock-hard texture that commands attention. Nolte in particular keeps reaching into niches of feeling that give his blustery brute some poignancy—no small achievement for a character who pulls his own aching tooth with a pair of pliers, swirls some whiskey around his mouth, then keeps going.

In fact, Nolte and Coburn are so powerful that they distort what, we are told, is the story's theme. Both men are physically huge. (Willem Dafoe, as Rolfe, Wade's professor-brother, is not.) We sense that these two men are so strong that they get impatient with restraining that strength, that they contrive occasions just to cut loose. But at the end we get a moralizing voice-over from Rolfe to the effect that what we have witnessed was an instance of a father passing on to a son a tradition of wife-abuse. This is not what we have seen. *Affliction* is about a stratum of society trapped in a societal jet lag, a frontier ethos marooned in a more complex world. Women are used and abused by such men, of course, but so—as we see more often—are other men. And size, the sheer surge of the power to vent impatience and frustration on others, aggravates the trouble. (Perhaps it's because I'm only 5′ 8¼″ that I burrowed out this subtext; still, it seems pertinent to the picture.) Thus, with hardly one sympathetic or admirable action, Nolte's Wade becomes somewhat pathetic.

The Dreamlife of Angels

MARCH 22, 1999 | How did he do it? The question persists after *The Dreamlife of Angels*. Not one story element is fresh, the theme is familiar in any purview of modern society, yet this French film is completely absorbing, almost rudely poignant. How did the director, Erick Zonca, do it? The answer is both simple and deep. He paid no attention to predecessors or echoes: he just wanted, overwhelmingly, to make this film. If he worried about familiarity at all, he clearly felt that his conviction would overwhelm reminders of other films. He was right.

This is Zonca's first feature film—he had made three shorts—yet he wasn't exactly a stripling in 1997 when he wrote it (with Roger Bohbot) and directed it. Born in Orléans in 1956, he went to Paris when he was sixteen to study acting and at twenty moved on to New York to continue acting studies. He didn't enter the film world until he returned to France when he was thirty. He found success with his short films, which is to say he won awards, so he was enabled to make a feature.

The story consists of events, not a plot. Isa is twenty-one years old, on the road, rucksack on her back, traveling because she doesn't want to melt into conventional life. She arrives in Lille, is offered a sewing job on a machine in an assembly line, and accepts it to raise some cash. She is soon fired for inefficiency, but meets a local girl, Marie, who has much the same alienation from burrow life. Marie is apartment-sitting for a woman and her daughter who were gravely injured in a car crash, and she permits Isa to stay with her.

They apply for waitress work but are offered only sandwich-board jobs. Isa accepts. Two men happen along, bouncers at a club, and they all become friends. Marie sleeps with her gent. Then she meets Chriss, a rich young man who owns a couple of clubs, and she really falls for him, responding warmly to his skilled seducings.

Meanwhile, Isa has been reading the diaries in the apartment of the girl who lives there and who is comatose in the hospital. (The girl's mother has died by now.) Isa is fascinated, is drawn to the girl, visits her often. Though the girl is quite unconscious, Isa has a sense, because of the diaries, of connection with her. The odd overtone suggested is that the inert girl has achieved a state that Isa almost envies: to be in the world but safe from it.

Marie's affair with Chriss heats up—for both of them, she thinks, but she is wrong. The results are dire. At the end Isa doesn't hit the road again with her rucksack: she takes a job somewhere else much like the one from which she was fired at the start.

If there is a cellophane-wrapped moral in the film, probably it's that the world is too much with us, late and soon, but that in trying *not* to get and spend, we can lay waste our powers. Still, though this is hinted, the film doesn't stay within that theme's boundaries. It's simply about two young women and some things that happen to them. The real vitality of the film, beneath any adage, is that Zonca cares greatly about Isa and Marie. He worries about them, almost frets about them, chuckles at them, consoles them, is sometimes grieved by them. He is so involved with them that the film allows not a millimeter in which we can doubt that they exist.

Zonca is tremendously justified by Elodie Bouchez (Isa) and Natacha Regnier (Marie), both of whom have previously appeared in films but who have life faces, not film faces. (Minnie Driver as against Michelle Pfeiffer, let's say.) Zonca states that his experience as an actor helped him in his work with Bouchez and Regnier, and they have quite evidently benefited from him. The film exudes an intimacy with the lives of women that such a director as Chantal Akerman evokes in her work. Or that Alain Tanner captured in *La Salamandre,* another account of a young woman's struggle against drowning in the humdrum.

And, to cite one more reference, the very last sequence is a reminder of *Il Posto.* At the end of Ermanno Olmi's agon of a young man being ground into job-burger, rows of men at their desks are drizzling their lives away at grubby routines. At the end of Zonca's film, the camera moves along from Isa's bench in her new job to the faces of other young women stitching away like her. Are we to infer that Isa is either defeated or "adjusted" like her co-workers here? Well, society needs goods and these women need jobs; still, we're allowed to suspect that the world and the human race were not created in order to put these young lives at these machines.

Lastly, the film's title. We see neither dreamlife nor angels; yet it seems reductive to read the title as merely ironic. There is much more in the picture than the obvious fact that the young women are not angels. Perhaps the title suggests that human beings are burdened with dissatisfactions, often inchoate, and that this fact is our best virtue. In any case, whatever the title means, we can all hope that Zonca is thinking of other characters for whom he cares as passionately as he does for Isa and Marie.

An Ideal Husband

JULY 19 & 26, 1999 | In the January 12, 1895 issue of the *Saturday Review* of London, the magazine's theater critic reviewed two new plays. The first was by Henry James, the second by Oscar Wilde. The critic was Bernard Shaw.

Gasping for breath, I go on to note that the Wilde play has now been filmed. Again. It was done in 1947, directed by Alexander Korda; this time *An Ideal Husband* was directed by Oliver Parker. Parker's only previous feature was the Laurence Fishburne *Othello,* a picture doomed before it began, as most Shakespeare films are. The Wilde film had a chance, and by and large Parker has won out.

Parker made his own screen adaptation and — again by and large — kept the twists of the original plot, and of course kept a great many of the epigrams that help to camouflage the arrant plottiness. In Shaw's review, he noted that other London critics complained that "such epigrams can be turned out by the score by anyone lightminded enough to descend to such frivolity. As far as I can see, I am the only person in London who cannot write an Oscar Wilde play at will." Samples of Wilde's sparkle: Lord Goring, the *boutonnière* bachelor who is generally held to be Wilde's dream projection of himself and therefore has most of the wit, is reproved by his crusty father for wasting his time in society. The father says that London society consists of "a lot of damned nobodies talking about nothing." Goring replies: "I love talking about nothing, father. It is the only thing I know anything about." Other characters have unwitting wit. At a later point Goring's father says to him, "Damme, sir, it's your duty to get married. You can't be always living for pleasure."

Parker and his producers have given the picture almost every kind of aid. His adaptation has slimmed down the plot, which helps it in most ways. (A plot strand about a diamond brooch is completely eliminated.) The base is that favorite device of the period, an action in the past that comes back to haunt the present. The mighty Ibsen used it in *A Doll House,* the workaday Pinero in *The Second Mrs. Tanqueray.* Wilde uses it here in terms of blackmail.

Sir Robert Chiltern, a rapidly rising member of Parliament, once sold a state secret in order to get the capital to begin his now-shining political career. Mrs. Cheveley, an attractive "adventuress," arrives in London, from Vienna where she has been making hay, bearing with her Sir Robert's youthful letter confirming his guilt about that secret. She will give the letter to the press unless he reverses a stand he has taken in the House of Commons on a certain matter: his reversal will benefit her financially. Chiltern's problem is compounded because his wife, who knows nothing of that past matter, adores him as a paragon of virtue.

Parker has helped the story by opening it up into varied locations. For instance, a couple of scenes take place in Rotten Row in Hyde Park, with some characters mounted and others in carriages. Also he inserts a visit by some of the people to the first night of *The Importance of Being Earnest.* (Thus, in a neat three-cushion-billiards carom, Wilde comes out for a curtain speech after that play in a film made from another play of his.) Parker has had to maneuver the closing plot mechanics as busily as Wilde did to make things come out right—and to reconcile the adoring Lady Chiltern with her imperfect husband, whose career will now sail on. From Shaw's review: "The modern note is struck in Sir Robert Chiltern's assertion of the individuality and courage of his wrong-doing as against the mechanical idealism of his stupidly good wife, and in his bitter criticism of a love that is only the reward of merit." (This from the man who had already written *Widowers' Houses, The Philanderer, Mrs. Warren's Profession,* and *Arms and the Man.*)

Parker directs skillfully, deploying both wit and drama. The film opens with Lord Goring's servant, facing us, impassively opening the curtain in his master's bedroom to let in the morning light, as in the background we dimly see a naked woman slip out of his lordship's bed and into the bathroom. The scene in which Mrs. Cheveley first confronts Sir Robert with her threat is robust old-fashioned theater, without the *jambon.*

Costume design is always more noticeable in period pictures and, in some ways, more easy to excel in. But nothing can stop us from admiring the clothes here, especially the women's clothes, especially the hats, designed by Caroline Harris, who did Parker's *Othello* and the recent Victorian *The Governess.* And those clothes look especially resplendent in the camera of David Johnson, who shot that *Othello* and who makes us feel that all the night scenes were shot by lamplight.

Then—a big then—there's the cast. Whatever the plot's arthritis, the actors make us glad that the film was done. Begin with the first face we see, Goring's servant, played by Peter Vaughan, who was Anthony Hopkins's father in *The Remains of the Day* and who sets the class stratification of this world before a word is spoken. Goring is Rupert Everett, who quite evidently enjoys the part immensely but who (unlike the man who played the role on Broadway a few years ago) restrains his pleasure so that we can enjoy it too. Excellent, airily precise acting. Chiltern is Jeremy Northam, recently the polished barrister in *The Winslow Boy.* Here he is asked for deeper feelings and very nearly finds them. His wife is Cate Blanchett, who moved adequately through *Elizabeth* and struggled through *Push-*

ing Tin. Here she has considerable wistful charm, a turn-of-the-century woman created by her ideals but more victimized than supported by them. Minnie Driver, as Sir Robert's maiden sister, acts well enough but is miscast. She is simply not the fetching ingenue that the part requires. John Wood, stout oak, is Lord Caversham, Goring's harrumphing father, and makes us wish the part were bigger.

Mrs. Cheveley is played by Julianne Moore. It's higher than high time that particular attention be paid to Moore. We hear, justly, that careers of range and depth are difficult in American films, but occasionally some people manage them. Meryl Streep is a fine instance. Moore is in one way even more adventurous: she takes minor roles when she likes them, like Glenn Close's dim sister in *Cookie's Fortune.* In major roles, she played — unforgettably — Yelena in *Vanya on 42nd Street* and, among others, a sophisticated neurotic in *Safe,* a conventional movie heroine in *The Lost World,* and a regal porno star in *Boogie Nights.* In *An Ideal Husband,* the only American in an English cast, she gives her Victorian *femme fatale* all the burnish of her social position at the same time that, with steel under the silk, she lets us see how hard-won that position has been, what she has had to undergo as a woman in order to make her way; and she conveys it all with stature and grace.

Onward, Moore!

Eyes Wide Shut

AUGUST 16, 1999 | In the spring of 1967, Robert Brustein, then dean of the Yale School of Drama, asked me to do a film course in the following academic year. I was to co-teach: I would meet the class one afternoon a week to deal with history and style, and on another day they would meet a filmmaker who would explore techniques. Brustein and I, both keen on the relatively recent *Dr. Strangelove,* decided to aim high and invite Stanley Kubrick for the filmmaking post. I agreed to approach Kubrick because I knew him slightly.

I had lunched with Kubrick in New York two years earlier. (One remark lingers. I praised Peter Sellers's three roles in *Dr. Strangelove,* and Kubrick said dryly, "Yes, three performances for the price of six.") We had lunched because I was inviting Kubrick to appear on a series about film that I was then doing on PBS in New York; he had seen some of the programs and was sufficiently interested to meet and talk about it, though eventually he declined. A year later, when I went to *The New York Times* as their theater critic—a brief sojourn, as it turned out—I had a warm note of congratulations from Kubrick.

So I now telephoned him, in England where he lived, to offer him the Yale job. He was pleased by the offer itself and, though highly dubious, said he wanted to consider it for a few days. And a few days later he wrote that he was sorry but he had to confirm his doubts. Two reasons were patent: he was now living abroad and he was working on a film. "This obviously makes it impossible." (Despite which, he had wanted to think it over.) "In addition to this," he said, "I have steadfastly avoided talks, lectures, etc., because they tend to formalize my own thinking, which I think would not be a good thing."

This was the last time I heard from him. I was in England fairly often thereafter, but I did not, as he had asked, ring him, because my reviews of his films, from *2001* on, were adverse, increasingly so. Neither of us would have enjoyed a meeting. But I never forgot his statement above because, as it seemed to me, it was almost a prophecy. In one way his thinking became increasingly formalized, came closer and closer to sheer formalism. "The formalist," says Rudolf Arnheim, "emancipates the medium from the content it is supposed to serve. . . . Rather than submerging in the content, form steps between the beholder and the theme of the work." This, it seemed to me, fit Kubrick more and more closely. Isolated—notoriously so—in his country home and in his studio, he became more concerned with filmmaking than with films. Yes, themes can be discerned in his work, and since his death the winkling out of Kubrick themes has bloomed into a small critical industry. Certainly violence and cynical bleakness are patent in his work, but they seem structural conveniences to him rather than burning concerns. From *2001* on, with longer and longer periods of time between pictures, he became centered on the solution of problems, technical and narrative, rather than on creating work aimed at the responses of the viewer. Solipsism became king in the Kubrick studio; formalism became supreme. This is a long way from design, which is a beauty and blessing in art, a means of affecting people. Formalism is a tyranny even when self-imposed, as it usually is.

Now we have Kubrick's final film, finished just before his sudden death (at seventy). It is much too aptly the finale of a declining career. *Eyes Wide Shut* is a catastrophe—in both the popular sense and the classical sense of the end of a tragedy. Everything in Kubrick that had been worming through his career, through his ego, and through his extraordinary talent swells and devours this last film. It is a long slow exercise in self-admiration, in the formal fulfillment of film problems that he had set himself at the expense of the audience's involvement.

Begin with the title. It is completely meaningless before and after seeing the picture. Frederic Raphael, co-author with Kubrick of the screenplay, has written a lively short book about that experience, called *Eyes Wide Open* (!). In it, Raphael tells that they both scrounged for a title and that finally Kubrick proposed *Eyes Wide Shut*. "I refrained from any response," says Raphael, "except that of refraining from response. It was his movie." Later Raphael says, "Can he really consider *Eyes Wide Shut* a poetic title? If it incites him to make the movie, so be it." Raphael's reactions to the title are a neat implicit definition of formalism.

The screenplay is derived from a short novel by Arthur Schnitzler called *Dream Novel*. Raphael synopsizes it in sufficient detail to confirm that the general outlines of the Schnitzler story and of the film are the same. Kubrick wanted the locale transposed from Schnitzler's Vienna around 1900 to New York today, an odd decision for a middle-European escapade. Everything that happens could possibly happen in New York—what couldn't happen in New York?—but the shape and the temper seem less at home here than in *alt Wien*.

A very successful doctor, Bill Harford, and his wife, Alice, are happily married and have a small child. Bill and Alice go to a large, lavish Christmas party, and each of them gets a chance for an affair. Alice rejects her offer; Bill is prevented from accepting his. But both offers raise thoughts of extramarital possibilities in them. Bill investigates those possibilities. (Alice's only venture is to confess a temptation the past summer which didn't actually end in bed but which Bill keeps imagining thereafter as a porno movie.) Bill gets a late-night call to the home of a patient who has suddenly died, and in the dead man's bedroom, his daughter, Marion, throws herself at Bill. He gets away but is so aroused that, while walking home, he lets a hooker take him to her apartment. But nothing happens there, either, because he gets a cell-phone call from his wife.

Yet that same night—with the help of a pianist friend—he sneaks his way into a masked orgy held by very rich men in a Long Island mansion. Costumed and masked—I omit description of the costumier's establishment, which is blatantly an exotic set-piece—he is nonetheless unmasked as an intruder before he can have sex. He just about escapes with his life, or at least that is what he is made to think.

The next day, further heated by a sexual nightmare that his wife recounts about her "lover" and by the porno film that he keeps imagining of his wife and that man, Bill tries to get in touch with Marion. Thwarted, he then tries to visit the hooker he met last night, but she is gone. She had been informed that morning that she is HIV positive, Bill is told by another hooker who tries to persuade him to accept her instead. But he leaves.

All the above has involved death threats to himself and others, Bill thinks, but these threats are shown to be mere concoctions of his fervid fantasy. At the end Bill and Alice are reunited, tearfully, as if each had been through some sexual trial by fire, though in fact neither has actually slept with anyone else and Alice hasn't even tried. They go shopping for a Christmas present for their small daughter, and in the department store, after some homiletic plot-concluding exchanges, Alice says to Bill, "There's something very important we must do as soon as possible." He asks what it is, and she says, "Fuck."

The point of this 157-minute picture seems clear. Every married person has within himself or herself a secret cosmos of sexual imaginings, longings, fantasies, and perhaps extramarital actions. The actual marital life of a husband and wife involves only a portion of the sexual cosmos of each. But Schnitzler wrote this story in 1926, and even then he set it back at the beginning of the century, presumably because he felt it was already a little out of date. Kubrick, who had been nursing this project for years, insisted not only on ignoring Schnitzler's recognition of the necessary pastness of the story, but on transposing it to New York. Thus Kubrick coolly disregarded all that his audience has encountered of enlightenment in these matters in this century, not least in the films of Ingmar Bergman.

Even the elementary matter of credibility is ignored. After that extensive noctural odyssey of Bill's—summoned to a dead man's bedside, embraced by Marion, visiting a hooker, going to a nightclub where he is steered to an orgy on Long Island, renting a costume and mask at midnight, being taxied far out on Long Island, attending the orgy and escaping—he gets home in the morning and, as he falls into bed, merely murmurs to his wife, "It took longer than I thought."

Kubrick's very filmmaking acuteness seems to have been blunted. The scene in the costume shop is a faintly stale reminder of numerous old horror movies (including the mannequin scene in his own early *Killer's Kiss*). The orgy scene is redolent of *Seven Footprints to Satan* (1929) and many a Satanic thriller, especially because of Kubrick's clichéd close-ups of grotesque masks. (The music for the orgy, by Jocelyn Pook, is done on a piano struck, seemingly, with a sledgehammer.) Wit had virtually disappeared from later Kubrick pictures, but here he permits an actor to insert a modernized version of Franklin Pangborn's swishy hotel clerk, a fixture of 1930s comedies. At the end, after Bill has returned his costume but has presumably lost the mask (he has actually misplaced it at home), he returns to his apartment; and Kubrick slips in a shot of the orgy mask on the pillow next to the sleeping Alice before Bill goes into the bedroom, so that when he does go in there, sees the mask, and is shocked, we are not. Worse, fundamentally worse, is Kubrick's insensitivity to the constant abrasion between the whole fabulated escapade and the hyperrealism of the New York setting, characters, and dialogue.

As for that dialogue, it is freighted with repetitions. Examples:

"We're going to the rainbow's end."
"To the rainbow's end?"
"To the rainbow's end."

"I'm just trying to figure out where you're coming from."
"Where I'm coming from?"

"I had you followed."
"You had me followed?"

Nearly three hours of this echo-chamber talk almost makes us beg for mercy, especially when it's all *molto andante*.

Kubrick wanted a married couple for his two leads. He first thought of Alec Baldwin and Kim Basinger, says Raphael, but he engaged Tom Cruise and Nicole Kidman. When Cruise and Kidman were amorously busy in the film, I thought of the former theater stars Alfred Lunt and

Lynn Fontanne, married, who always included a pat on the behind or a touch of the bosom to give the audience a small thrill of private glimpse. That was pretty quaint compared to the Cruise-Kidman behavior, but it was the same principle.

Doubtless this couple would not decline roles just because they are married: it would be a denial of acting ability and adventure. And Kidman is moving, despite her limited voice, particularly in her two long speeches, the remembrances of a temptation and of her nightmare about it. Cruise, a proven powerful actor, seems here to be repressed and contained, deliberately slowed down by the director. His role is much larger than Kidman's and is less vivid. I'd hazard that Cruise was restrained by Kubrick in aid of some pattern the director had in mind, rather than the effect on the audience. More formalism! One other performance must be noted: the Swedish actress Marie Richardson plays Marion, and is excellent in her difficult transition from mourning to sexual outburst.

In the matter of sex, which is the matter of the film, Kubrick tinctures heavily with salaciousness, the particular salaciousness of aging film directors who have the power to display women as they like. Not because the film's first shot is of Kidman undressing—a stunning shot, in fact—nor because of Kubrick's insistence on showing her on the toilet chatting with her husband who is in the bathroom with her, nor of the rat-a-tat of the f-word in the dialogue (hardly a distinction these days), but because of Kubrick's insistence on showing as many naked female bodies as he can possibly crowd into his film. (Something like the latter-day Godard.) For instance, at the lavish Christmas party early in the picture, Doctor Bill is summoned by his host to attend a young woman whom the host has been screwing upstairs but who took a hard drug and is blotto. Any reasonably human person, like the host, would have covered her prone naked body, but Kubrick insists on her nakedness. This, he might have argued, was brutal candor, but it looks like brutal voyeurism.

So this is where the Kubrick career ends, with this technically accomplished, inadequately conceived work. Retrospect is inevitable. A young photographer claws his way into film (he shot his earliest pictures himself, adroitly), makes a war fantasy and two crime thrillers. None of them, as he himself said, is really worth looking at again; but what is extraordinary, and is insufficiently noted, is the change in texture and style from his third feature, *The Killing,* just one more Hollywood film noir struggling for eccentricity, to *Paths of Glory,* a grim drama about heartlessness in the French army in World War I. Of course, Kubrick had more money for that fourth feature, but it was spent by a very different director from the man who had made the third. He had suddenly become a sophisticated and excitingly fluent filmmaker. *Spartacus* was insufficiently appreciated because it is a costume spectacle, but it was directed with muscular imagination. Then came some work on Brando's *One-Eyed Jacks,* which Kubrick quit because, he said at our lunch, Brando was absolutely insane. Then *Lolita,* beautiful, whose only fault is that it isn't really the novel. Then *Dr. Strangelove,* a pinnacle. But then the decline into cinematic display, from *2001* to the end: the preening pride in being figuratively alone and literally imperial. Perforce there had to be stories and actors, but, seemingly, they were only necessary nuisances for Kubrick.

At the last, he had become an advanced cinematic constructor, virtuosic but immured. In another guise, the formalism that he dreaded had prevailed.

American Beauty

OCTOBER 12, 1999 | Six characters are again searching for an author —not Pirandello's people but Alan Ball's. These six are in *American Beauty,* which was written by Ball, and if they are not startlingly original or deep people, they are vivid, principally because the actors who portray them are strong. But at the finish of the picture, we're left feeling that Ball has had a trial run with them: now he needs to go back and really use them to some enlightening and organically whole purpose.

The title is a declaration: it blazons that this is the one thing the film is not going to be about. Ball wastes no time in keeping this promise. The film starts with an aerial view of neat suburban streets, and as the camera moves in, a man's voice tells us that his name is Lester Burnham and that this is his neighborhood. Then he says: "In less than a year I'll be dead. Of course I don't know that yet. In a way I'm dead already."

If we resist an urge to reach for our coats and leave—after this double whammy of facile metaphysics and a prediction of moribund suburban life—*American Beauty* compensates us in some ways, but it never justifies the blatancy of its opening, and it never does anything to freshen what is only one more journey through familiar fortyish unfulfillment. Lester is a journalist (living, as do so many film persons, in a home and style beyond his apparent means) who feels his existence slipping through his fingers. His wife Carolyn has more passion for developing her real estate business than for the man who lies next to her at night. Their daughter Jane, a high schooler, hates them both for the usual adolescent reason: she thinks she's a woman and they think she's a child.

Thus each is tagged, and each is ready for trouble. For Lester, it's the sexy blonde high-school chum of his daughter. For Carolyn, it's Buddy Kane, the handsome real estate honcho of the area. For Jane, it's the boy who just moved in next door. This boy, Ricky Fitts, is the one real surprise in the picture: he is the son of a Marine colonel and, in his introspective way, has found a way of dealing with his two-fisted father that leaves him free to follow his own quirks. His mother has been erased almost into catatonia by the father, but Ricky is quietly surviving.

This supposedly realistic film has more than its share of arrant mechanics. If a middle-aged journalist of some success gets fired, would he then insist on getting a job as a cook in a hamburger joint? Just to flaunt his freedom? Would Buddy Kane, a skillful smoothie, snuggle with another man's wife in a public place? Just because the plot needs the affair to be discovered? Would Lester proceed toward sex with the young blonde on the sofa in his living room—with his daughter upstairs and his wife liable to come home?

Yet these coarsely stitched seams might pass if the stories of all these people moved to some enlightenment or if some new light were shed on old subjects. But all that Ball can tell us is what many American and British and French and Italian films have already expounded. Modern urban-suburban life can be anesthetic; the human spirit often chafes against de-humanizing limits and either explodes or shrivels. Ball has nothing to add.

What's worse, he burdened his script with that zingy opening which he then had to justify. But Lester's death at the end is no kind of summation of what the film is about. It's merely a maniacal affront, irrelevant to what Lester has been through in the story. Worse still, his opening lines and the symmetrical postmortem voice-over make Lester a spirit hovering over his mundane life, with no hint as to why this particular suburbanite has been elevated to an all-seeing view. Except, of course, that the opening and closing were thought to give the film "stature."

The actors deserve better. Lester is Kevin Spacey, who is becoming the new Gene Hackman—a man of ordinary appearance and effect, gifted in a way that makes his ordinariness an asset, an apotheosis of the contemporary. Peter Gallagher, who in contrast has exceptional good looks, struggles with that burden to make Buddy Kane comprehensible, if not appealing. Thora Birch is pathetic and irritating as Jane, and Wes Bentley finds odd mental corners in the loony boyfriend. As his father, Chris Cooper takes good care of the role. Mena Suvari is sufficiently succulent as the quasi-innocent blonde menace.

The really memorable acting comes from Annette Bening as Carolyn. Energized, deep-breathing, wonderfully precise, Bening makes Carolyn flare through the picture. Bening was trained for the theater, and the press notes tell us that she has lately played Hedda Gabler in Los Angeles; her work here makes me regret that I missed her Hedda. Her past films, especially *The American President* and *Bugsy,* showed how incisive her acting can be. This new film suggests that she may be one of the few film women since Bette Davis to have an *acting* career as she ages.

The director is Sam Mendes, the Englishman who quickly made a reputation in the theater with *Cabaret* and *The Blue Room.* I saw the latter and thought that Mendes did ingeniously well by his actors; here, in his film debut, he has sensibly concentrated on his actors. Some newcomers to film directing, after theater acclaim, try to prove themselves cinematically with all sorts of fussiness—odd camera angles, intrusive montage, and so on. Mendes simply tells his story clearly. He was much assisted, I'd guess, by the veteran cinematographer, Conrad L. Hall; but Mendes's real concern was his cast, helping them to dig into themselves.

Now if Ball or someone else would only improve the script—and if they could remake the picture with the same cast. . . .

The Straight Story

NOVEMBER 15, 1999 | The viewer need not know David Lynch's reputation before seeing *The Straight Story,* but it helps. Here is a writer-director celebrated for his eccentricities, his disregard for convention, in such works as "Twin Peaks" and *Blue Velvet,* who has done a picture released by Disney, a picture based on the true story of an old man making a sentimental journey. Anyone ignorant of Lynch who sees *The Straight Story* will need an extra mite of patience to allow its beauty to unfold; others will be curious from the start about why this unconventional filmmaker chose this material, and that curiosity will speed up the unfolding.

The title is not really a pun: it simply uses a fact with a smile. This is a story about a man named Straight. In 1994 Alvin Straight, a seventy-four-year-old resident of Laurens, Iowa, traveled eastward across the state to visit his brother, Lyle, in Mount Zion, Wisconsin. Lyle had suffered a stroke. Alvin wanted to see him before both of them passed on. He wanted to patch up relations with Lyle, whom he loved but with whom he had quarreled badly. Alvin was too infirm to drive a car, so he made the long trip on the only vehicle he could still manage, a lawn mower, to which he hitched a small trailer. It took Alvin many weeks to reach Mount Zion (this name is another useful coincidence), camping along the way and occasionally receiving hospitality from people he met. But he accomplished both his aims. (Alvin died in 1996.)

The story itself is *Reader's Digest* material. But with a concise screenplay by John Roach and Mary Sweeney, distilled in its dialogue and committed to verity of character, Lynch has made a small epic that echoes and enlarges in memory. He begins by insisting on the usual tempo of a Lynch film, an unapologetic *adagio,* implying that anything worth looking at is worth more than a hurried glance, unafraid of the latter-day shrunken attention span. Lynch's measured, attentive gaze assures us that he takes his story very seriously, and, unlike some other Lynch material, this story is so plain, so devoid of grotesquerie, that we soon see why he cannot be anything but serious about it. The subject is homespun, folksy; but to follow it with Lynch is to see Norman Rockwell become Thomas Eakins.

This is a resonant journey through a troubled life, encased in a grand deployment of the American heartland. We move through Alvin's past, including boyhood memories, memories of service in World War II, and the story of the seemingly impaired daughter who lives with him; but it is also a gallery of today's heartland people, including a runaway teenager whom he befriends and a Roman Catholic priest who befriends him (a Baptist, as he tells the priest). It is also, through the camera of the accomplished Freddie Francis, a poignant sprawl in the wide Midwest.

Soon we see that Alvin intends more than a brotherly visit. He refuses proffered transportation along the way because he wants to suffer the hardships of this journey; it is a penance, an expiation of past misjudgments. This journey is a gift that he is fashioning for his brother, as a craftsman might finish a fine object, which he wants to present to Lyle by the very fact of his arrival on this snail-paced lawn mower; so he must make this trip alone, this trip that at first looks ludicrous and cranky but that soon seems a spiritual pilgrimage.

Every detail in the film is perfect. Something that is often overlooked in pictures about rural America is carefully tended here: the people's accents. I'm not able to say that they all speak like Midwesterners, but they all sound credible as country people, and every role, no matter how small, from the dealer who sells Alvin the new lawn mower he needs (Everett McGill) to another old man with whom he exchanges grim war memories (Wiley Harker)—every role is put in place like a small gem in a crown. Harry Dean Stanton, who has perhaps two minutes on-screen at the end as Lyle, is, in a grateful word, fulfilling. Sissy Spacek gives Alvin's daughter warmth and the requisite secret scars.

But all these excellences would come to little without Richard Farnsworth. Born in the same year as Alvin, wrinkled and skinny and white-bearded, quiet yet dogged, Farnsworth performs a miracle. He has been knocking around in films for at least forty years, has been everything from a stunt man to an extra to a minor supporting player, and has sometimes had prominent parts in the Wilford Brimley vein, the by-cracky likable old hick. Here, no doubt aided by Lynch, Farnsworth understands his role as the one toward which his whole life has been winding, as if he were stepping into a better reincarnation of himself. It won't suffice to say that he never makes a false move: the highest compliment I can pay is that he made me think of the great Victor Sjöström in his last role, in Bergman's *Wild Strawberries*. Sjöström played an old professor journeying to a university town to receive an honorary degree, revisiting his life along the way—a valedictory performance by an important figure in film history. Farnsworth, arriving from a quite different past, places Alvin in the same company as Sjöström's professor, an archetypal portrayal of an old man near the end. Farnsworth's voice lingers in the mind. At one point a young man asks Alvin, in a friendly way, what the worst part is about getting old. Alvin says: "The worst part is rememberin' when you was young."

But *The Straight Story* goes past honesty. Without satire, with calm admiration, it presents a national self-image. Every country of which I have any knowledge has such a self-image. America likes to think of its ideal personification as a self-reliant, stubborn, humane yet taciturn, courageous loner—or at least someone who is willing to be alone if the situation demands it. (John Wayne, Gary Cooper, James Stewart.) Lynch's film is bifocal: it treats Alvin with complete authenticity, yet it also sees his story as an ideal—senescent this time, yet essentially the cherished romance.

Congratulations to Lynch and Farnsworth and everyone who contributed to this extraordinary film.

The End of the Affair

DECEMBER 27, 1999 | A new high in irony—sheer gall, really—arrives in *The End of the Affair*. In this adaptation of Graham Greene's novel, the protagonist, himself a novelist, takes his lover to see a film made from one of his books. As they watch the screen, he keeps whispering to her, "Not what I wrote." The film that we are watching, in which he says this line, is not what Greene wrote, either.

In his deep and compelling novel, Greene uses a conventional triangle situation—single man, married woman, her husband—as an armature for an unconventional drama of religious faith, its testing, its agony, its balm, its awe. The story begins in London in 1946 when Maurice Bendrix, the novelist, accidentally meets Henry Miles, the husband of his former mistress Sarah. The account goes back a couple of years to the beginning of the affair during the war; then, in the "present," Bendrix remeets Sarah, whom he has not seen since the affair ended two years ago, and their emotion is recollected in something less than tranquility. She is now gravely ill (we learn later). Her progress toward death and through stages of faith—recovered, questioned, born again bravely almost as a penance—are disclosed to Bendrix through an uninvited reading of her diary.

The "present-day" drama includes a rationalist preacher, whom Sarah visits secretly as a sort of test, and a private detective who leads Bendrix to this preacher. (Bendrix himself has engaged the detective. Henry has confessed to Bendrix his unrest about his wife's odd absences; Bendrix wants to assuage Henry's unrest, but surely Bendrix himself is curious about the secret visits she is making to someone.) It is this detective who purloins Sarah's diary for Bendrix.

Right in the fabric of this understated story of a spiritual pilgrimage, Greene places two miracles, also understated. First, the rationalist preacher has a large, livid birthmark on one cheek; this birthmark disappears after Sarah's death, a dying that is wrapped in religious agon. The medical explanations about the mark's disappearance don't convince, and the rationalist, frightened, abandons rationalism. The second miracle is revealed after Sarah's death. Bendrix meets her mother, Mrs. Bertram, for the first time. She is a Catholic, her husband was not; and she confides to Bendrix that when Sarah was a child, she had her daughter baptized secretly. Mrs. Bertram says that Sarah was a real Catholic "only she didn't know it." The clear implication is that, aware of it or not, Sarah was marked for God and that what happened to her in her last years was her unwitting Catholicism taking over.

And how does the screenplay by Neil Jordan handle these miracles? The rationalist preacher is turned into a Catholic priest whom Sarah visits secretly. The birthmark on his cheek is transferred to the young son of the private detective. (The boy follows his pa around, learning the trade.) Though the boy is of course not involved in Sarah's religious searchings—which Greene's rationalist preacher certainly was—she once happens to kiss his cheek; this "explains" why the mark left his face. Thus Jordan deletes the battle between rationalism and divinity, whose victory Greene assigns to God, and thus the defeat of rationalism is changed to a blessing conferred unknowingly by a woman on her way to paradise.

As for the second miracle—the secret baptism that grew within Sarah into a transfiguring blaze—Jordan omits it completely.

Aside from ravaging the spiritual elements in the novel, aside from other sorts of subtleties that are trashed, Jordan has vulgarized the book's very structure. Toward the end of Sarah's life, Greene keeps Bendrix suspended in a medium of complex emotions, on the periphery of the Miles marriage. One morning when his telephone rings and he thinks that it is Sarah, it is in fact her husband. Bendrix hears something strange in

Henry's voice and thinks that Sarah may have told him about their affair. But Henry has called to tell him that Sarah is dead. "How conventionally we behave at such moments," thinks Bendrix, who, after the shock, simply says that he is sorry. Henry doesn't "fancy being alone," and invites Bendrix over for a drink. In the course of time, Henry invites Bendrix to move from his apartment to some rooms in Henry's house. Bendrix accepts. Husband and lover—Henry now knows of the affair—are united by Sarah's death after she has gone.

This structure, which might even be called another miracle, is not good enough for Jordan. He has Bendrix move into the Miles house before Sarah dies, where the lover helps the husband to tend her sickbed. Greene's delicate suggestion that her spiritual presence lingers on after her death and changes the lives of these two men is cartooned into commonplace sickbed scenes. This change of course enlarges the role of Sarah for its actress and provides her with moments out of *Camille*. Especially since her illness is pulmonary.

Jordan's screenplay is not an adaptation, it is a devastation. It's so drastic that we are left puzzled as to why Jordan, who also directed, wanted to adapt the novel at all if he was going to violate it this way. Greene's book is a work of art about religion, set amid involvements of the most banal kind. If Jordan felt obliged to squeeze and to distort—almost to apologize—for the religious theme, why bother with the book? I never saw the 1955 film of *The End of the Affair,* adapted by Leonore Coffee, directed by Edward Dmytryk. I remember avoiding it because, though Deborah Kerr played Sarah, Bendrix was played by that epicene nonentity Van Johnson. I regretted my decision some thirty years later when Greene said that, of all films made from his religious novels, this was "the least unsatisfactory." Even this restrained praise suggests that, if there was shrinkage of spiritual elements in the Coffee adaptation, at least it didn't result in the dreariness of the Jordan film. The place that Greene gave those spiritual elements is not filled otherwise in Jordan's film: it is simply left empty. Hence the dreariness.

That dreariness is certainly not due to the Bendrix here, Ralph Fiennes. Apparently Fiennes is on his way to supplant Jeremy Irons as the refined, taciturn English sex idol of the day; but he is a skilled, chromatic actor, sensitive to half-tones in feeling and speech. Stephen Rea, an old associate of Jordan's, plays Henry and is miscast. He does not convince as a high-level government official who is dignified yet almost pathetic because of his dulled emotional being.

The real disappointment is Julianne Moore as Sarah. She looks right and sounds right: her accent is as good here as it was in *An Ideal Husband*. But she is frigid. Presumably Moore wanted Sarah's torments and yearnings to be private, as they mostly are in the novel; but she presents very little of the woman who contains these private storms. We get overt revelations from time to time, like the praying that she does after Bendrix is knocked flat by a V-2 bomb in 1944. (His quick recovery is still another miracle that she has wrought — again unwittingly.) But Moore leaves such moments uninflected. "Batter my heart, three person'd God," cried John Donne. Moore conveys small sense of that plea.

Jordan, as director, gives us plenty of other batterings. He loads on fairly explicit sex scenes that tilt the film in quite the wrong direction. Greene, except for one mention of Sarah's experience of orgasm with Bendrix — none with her husband — keeps the emphasis on the specificity of these individuals, not the universals of copulation. Sarah's rites of religious passage, Bendrix's love-hate relationship with God as his rival for Sarah's love, are smothered in the way of all this flesh.

A pleasant final word. The story dwells in two time planes, the time of the affair and two years later, which is "now." The editor, Tony Lawson, slips in and out of the two planes so lightly that past and present seem almost a metaphysical continuum.

All about My Mother

JANUARY 31, 2000 | The recent flood of holiday films swept aside some discussable pictures. One of them is Pedro Almodóvar's latest, and, with the flood now down to a drizzle, there's a chance to look at *All about My Mother*. It's Almodóvar at both the top and the middle of his form, something we may have to become used to.

The term "woman's director," often used in the past for such men as George Cukor and Douglas Sirk, has a resonance with Almodóvar that doesn't apply to the others. They directed what was given them, though no doubt with emendations: Almodóvar is not only the writer of his films, he begins them deep within a seemingly feminine interiority. This is rare among men. Female directors such as Chantal Akerman have made films with the same "insider" view, but Akerman begins with the advantage of being a woman, and, to my knowledge, she hasn't often used this perspective as a vantage point for laughter—at the comic spectacle of maleness and of women dealing with men. Almodóvar is the only male director I know of who can laugh at men like a woman and who can offer men the fly-on-the-wall view of women's privacies. Women have verified this.

This director's particular view—glee in his insight, along with an over-the-top use of it that his female characters seem to enjoy—is immediately announced by his settings. Done here by Juan Pedro Hernandez, every room seems just slightly larger than life, because of the leaping colors. Red is the dominant one here, and it's frequently echoed in clothes. This sort of design has two effects: it dramatizes character, and, in one of Almodóvar's clearest intents, it guarantees that we know we are watching a film. "These are reasonably real people," he seems to say, "but don't forget, they are performing their reality." (Implication: we all do it, even if we happen not to be in a film.)

So much for the top of Almodóvar's form. His middle is another matter. When he began his career, some twenty years ago, with such pictures as *Dark Habits* and *What Have I Done to Deserve This?* and *Women on the Verge of a Nervous Breakdown,* he seemed to burst forth, with satire ablaze, to revenge himself, like a good satirist, on the oppressive stupidities and hypocrisies of society. He was like a mongoose that had been penned up, furious and frustrated, and now had got loose to attack snakes. But, as the years tumbled by, he seemed to run out of hatreds. With most of his work after *Tie Me Up! Tie Me Down!* (the film that donated Antonio Banderas to American dreck), Almodóvar has seemed to be searching for subjects, for targets. The gleaming satirical weapons are still very much there, but he has found less to carve up. In some degree he is now a rebel without a cause.

He can contrive screenplays. For *All about My Mother,* he contrived a good one, a sinuous trip through a series of bumps and surprises that is never tedious. But it all feels devised. Imagine a TV serial in which blue language is common, in which fellatio is viewed as one way for women to make a living and is a subject of hilarity among them, in which a young nun becomes pregnant and infected with HIV—imagine it all treated just as incidents along life's TV highway—and you have the tone of the new film. It has no discernible theme: its purpose is to surprise us with non-soap incidents in a soap opera about women. "Mother" in the title can be taken as Mother Eve. (Almodóvar says he derived his title from *All about Eve,* the Bette Davis picture, of which we get a glimpse.) He apparently just wanted to snuggle down in a nest of frank, unfettered women.

Manuela, about thirty-six, has a hospital job in Madrid. (Cecilia Roth is humane and lovely in the role.) She is a single mother with a seventeen-year-old son. The son is killed in a car crash, and she goes back to her native city of Barcelona to look for the boy's father. Arrived there, she takes a taxi to the Field, a mall for all kinds of hookers. Manuela sees one of them being assaulted, stops the cab and rescues the hooker—whom she knew eighteen years ago. She goes home with the hooker who, not long afterward, is revealed as a transvestite. (Antonia San Juan, very wicked.) What follows is too tortuous for summary. Some fragments: Manuela becomes assistant to an actress in *A Streetcar Named Desire;* she even goes on one night as Stella; the actress (Maria Paredes, neurotic but nice) is a lesbian in love with a junkie; when the young nun (winsome Penelope Cruz) enters the story—her pregnancy still a secret—she takes a hooker to her wealthy mother for a job; the mother is irate that such a woman has been brought to her home; then mom stamps back into her studio to continue her own profession, forging Vermeers.

All of the film—except for the sad moments dropped in like vinegar in a dressing—is brightly, uniquely amusing. It leaves us feeling concessive. If this concoction is the best that Almodóvar can do now, then let us have more. If his original impulses are spent, let us enjoy the afternoon of an ex-faun.

Joe Gould's Secret

APRIL 17 & 24, 2000 | "Ah, did you once see Shelley plain?" asked Browning. Well, not quite, but I did see Joe Gould—more than once. He was a fairly familiar figure in Greenwich Village when I was a student there in the early 1930s, and I sometimes caught sight or sound—or smell—of him. He was a short, whiskery, homeless man, dressed in whatever clothes he could acquire, who was always laden with some sort of package or portfolio, who cadged food in coffee shops and (after the repeal of Prohibition) drinks in bars, who airily asked anyone for contributions to what he called the Joe Gould Fund. He would declaim poems of his wherever possible, and coins would be tossed at him, which he scrambled to retrieve. He would sometimes flap his arms and squawk like a seagull, whose language he claimed to understand. He was writing, according to gossip, *The Oral History of Our Time,* setting down in school notebooks every day every word that he could remember of conversations that he heard. He was well-spoken, intelligent and deliberately loony—that is, he may have been a clinical case, but, if so, he realized that it was an asset to his character and his performance.

My friends and I were fascinated by him in a sad and proud way: sad because an apparently educated man of some capability was cavorting his life away, proud because he was helping to maintain the legend of the Village—the Bohemia once inhabited, right before and right after World War I, by Floyd Dell and Edna St. Vincent Millay and Eugene O'Neill and Maxwell Bodenheim, amid others. That atmosphere had been considerably shrunk by the 1930s as the central figures moved on and the Depression darkened spirits; but Joe Gould made it possible for us to boast to outsiders that the Village still had color.

Many times, as years went on, I have seen retrospectively that I lived through some high moments of social and cultural history and met some memorable figures without being adequately aware of either; but I have never had that feeling about Joe Gould. Not even when Joseph Mitchell published two articles about him in the *New Yorker,* in 1942 and 1964. When I read them, I felt pangs, of course, for the past because it was past; but I still didn't feel latter-day regret for myopia about Joe Gould as I did when I thought of my muffed meetings with, say, Thomas Wolfe or some of the Provincetown Playhouse figures. Now comes *Joe Gould's Secret* to reprove me somewhat.

Only somewhat. Because—which is why this production took considerable courage—the film expends time and talent to explain that Joe Gould (1889–1957) was of virtually no importance. He had all the scruffy habits of a genius who would be posthumously venerated; but he was not remotely such. He was an oddball, not much more. A Harvard graduate, as he occasionally mentioned, an acquaintance of e.e. cummings and the painter Alice Neel, he wrote only snippets of his *Oral History*—and those that were published were essayistic, not the dialogues of which he bragged. His only true distinction was the way he chose to live, when he could have lived otherwise. So this film, with a screenplay by Howard A. Rodman based on the Mitchell articles, is about a man who tried nothing, accomplished nothing, and was distinctive only by virtue of those negatives. The one moment in this picture that comes close to poignancy is the shock to his self-image when he is forced to face that iron fact.

Joe Gould's Secret traces Mitchell's discovery, belatedly, of the secret: that buried in the hirsute enigma is a blank. Mitchell, a *New Yorker* writer, becomes interested in Gould, becomes friends with him, writes his first article—the second was published after the subject's death—tries to help Gould to get his work published, and finds out that, in effect, there isn't any. (A curious epilogue: after Gould's death, Mitchell seemed to want to replace him as a legend. The last article that he wrote was the second Gould piece, and for thirty-two years afterward until his death, he went to his *New Yorker* office regularly yet never published another thing. The Mitchell legend superseded that of Gould.)

Obviously, the interest of this film depends on the performance of Joe Gould, because the only progress comes not from the usual sorts of narrative and conflict, but from traversals of his character, from ventures into the crannies and nooks of his life, from the bravado of his static being. How lucky and smart the filmmakers were: they got Ian Holm for the role. This English actor has had, is having, a career of quiet astonishments—quiet only in the sense that they are insufficiently sung. The first time that I saw him was in a Broadway production of Pinter's *The Homecoming,* where he played the icy psychopath Lenny, a performance that he repeated on film. Here is a handful of his other film roles: Napoleon in *Time Bandits;* Fluellen in Branagh's *Henry V;* the Olympics coach in *Chariots of Fire;* the old New York detective in *Night Falls on Manhattan;* and, in a TV film of his London theater production, *King Lear.* There are many more. Is it possible to describe this actor's existence among us as anything less than a benison?

With Joe Gould, Holm has understood that his character is not just the leading role in the film, it *is* the film. He saw that this fact did not call for surface virtuosity but that everything the character did, said, growled, shrieked and danced had to be rooted in a realized man. Holm doesn't "explain" Joe Gould; no one knew the explanation—not even Joe Gould, I'd guess. Holm proceeds from his perception of a man with no more complete knowledge of self than most of us have, but with inchoate drives, with fears about those drives, and with aggressions growing from that combination. The result is a human oddity who takes a peculiar pride in his panhandling and his rag-wrapped areaway slumbers.

Stanley Tucci plays Mitchell inoffensively and has directed the film with such caution against whopping things up that the pace dribbles at times. This could never be a pulse-quickening picture, but it sometimes takes that point as a license for lagging. Patrick Tovatt supplies a good impersonation of what (by report) Harold Ross, the *New Yorker* editor, was like. The expected warmth comes from Susan Sarandon as Alice Neel, the painter who befriended Joe Gould and did his nude portrait. (With three penises. Talk about generosity.)

Reviewings

Film is only a bit more than a century old, so retrospect has a paradoxical aspect. To look at early films is often to look at work that appeared
during the lifetimes of people we knew; yet so much has changed in
film and in the world in every decade that films acquire "pastness" with
comparative speed. This doesn't necessarily mean that they lose their
effect—sometimes quite the reverse—but it does mean that this art's
present tense and past tense are uniquely interwoven.

A Streetcar Named Desire

NOVEMBER 29, 1993 | Warner Brothers has re-released *A Streetcar Named Desire,* restoring some footage that had been omitted in 1951 because of censor pressure. I hadn't seen it on tape or otherwise since its first showings, so I hastened. I think I spotted the new footage, but much more to the point, I had—thanks yet again to Thomas A. Edison and his fellow inventors—an adventure in time, a chance to bring a piece of 1951 to today. *Streetcar* today looks better, the same and a bit worse.

Tremendous, prime, even better than I remembered, is Marlon Brando's performance as Stanley Kowalski. The role is altered slightly from the original play; still, this is his performance. I had seen it twice in the theater in 1947, and when the film first appeared, I rushed to make sure that it was there. It was; it is.

This wasn't Brando's first screen appearance; he had been in *The Men* (1950) as a disabled war veteran but hadn't had sufficient chance to show his powers. It was *Streetcar* that stamped Brando on the world's mind indelibly. The screenplay, by Tennessee Williams himself, gives Brando a different "entrance" from the play. The play begins with Stanley coming in and tossing a package of meat to his wife. By the time the film was made, Brando had become Brando, and his entrance was delayed. The film opens with Blanche arriving in New Orleans, then finding her sister, Stella, with her husband, Stanley, in a bowling alley near their apartment. Blanche and Stella greet each other while Stanley roughhouses with some men in the distance. We are teased for a moment before the bomb explodes.

Sculptural yet lithe, he irrupts into the film like history taking its revenge. The voice itself is part of that revenge: instead of the round, resonant voice we expect in good actors, this man's voice corkscrews in, incises sideways, then turns into full-bladed flashes of steel. It's a new voice for a new kind of acting. American films, global films, had had plenty of working-class heroes; but here is a man (like Jean Gabin in France) who brings anger with him, anger and genitals. He is furious at the world that has subordinated him. He arrives to change things and to establish a line of change—the hot, hot-tempered "gaudy seed-bearer" (Williams's phrase) whose life can be defined as what he does when he isn't having sex. A basic image of the play is of a wave of latter-day immigration rolling right over domestic Anglo-French gentility; here is that raw new power, rolling tidally.

Vivien Leigh's performance as Blanche Dubois doesn't have equal conviction. Leigh had played the role previously on the London stage, directed by Laurence Olivier, and she brings to the screen a real knowledge of Blanche and of the means to realize it. But—perhaps because she played Blanche first for a director quite different from the director of the film, Elia Kazan—she never seems absolutely at ease. She is always working at the part, with great skill and of course with affecting beauty, but she is never tragic: she is always reaching for the pathetic. What's missing is the blank, frenzied evisceration, the cloak of true-false poetry that (as I remember) Jessica Tandy had in the New York production. When Leigh leaves at the end, it's a pathetically deranged woman being taken to a hospital. With Tandy, it was the netting of a butterfly-tarantula, a victim who assisted in her own victimization.

Kim Hunter, Stella in the Broadway cast, is Stella again. Never a compelling actress, Hunter responds keenly to Kazan here, particularly—I think this is restored footage—when she descends to Stanley in the courtyard below. They have fought; she has fled to friends upstairs. Now, part infant and part stud, he bawls for her in the courtyard below; and Hunter, her breasts and loins warm, comes down the stairs to him.

Karl Malden is Mitch, Blanche's reticent suitor, as he was on Broadway. Often through his career Malden has seemed to use his homeliness the way some actors use their good looks; but here he doesn't make an issue of it, he just plays directly.

Kazan, who did that first theater production and had done six films before this one, is now a part of theater-film history in two senses: he made his mark with a signature style, and that style now has a slight whiff of mothballs. The Actors Studio approach—the version of Stanislavsky called The Method—seems so consciously honest, so determinedly anti-traditional, that in today's perspective, it becomes just another tradition.

In film directing, that style transmutes into heaviness. All through the first sequences in the apartment, the lighting is almost a parody of 1920s German expressionism, with street signs flickering on the faces of people within. Throughout, in that small apartment, Kazan concentrates on actors' movement, rather than on camera movement. Possibly he believes this more "honest" or possibly he wants to re-create theater on film. But often the film looks as if it's being performed in a submarine. And he uses off-screen sounds blatantly, especially the Mexican vendor selling "*flores para los muertos.*"

But the most upsetting element in the film is the screenplay. *Streetcar,* as time has shown, is a masterwork, one of the few great plays written on this side of the Atlantic; and the author of that masterwork, under censorship pressure, was willing to tamper with it significantly. This isn't without precedent. (Ibsen gave *A Doll House* a happy ending for German production. O'Neill altered *Desire Under the Elms,* hoping for a Hollywood sale.) But precedent doesn't really help.

A few scenes are so condensed that they almost sound like synopses, but those aren't the worst matters. Williams made two huge injurious changes. First, Blanche's long speech to Mitch—in which she reveals how she discovered her husband's homosexuality and caused his suicide—is made nonsense. She says that she discovered that her husband was "weak." Not only is the sanitized speech silly, it destroys the complex of sexual relations that leads from the suicide to her promiscuities and on to Stanley, a figure exactly the opposite of her husband.

Second, the ending is changed. Stella punishes Stanley for his rape of Blanche by leaving him. In the play Stella tells a friend that, if she believed Blanche's account of the rape, she couldn't go on living with Stanley. Clearly, for her own reasons, Stella has convinced herself that Blanche's story is a fantasy of the unbalanced. In the film Stella apparently believes Blanche (to underline her story, Kazan has given us a shot of Stanley advancing on Blanche melodramatically), even though there's a quick line later to disavow that the rape ever took place.

The film finishes with Stella's noble, head-high departure. This is not merely a sop to simplistic morality: it contravenes the torrential flow of the work. The play ends with Stella outside, sobbing after Blanche is taken away, and with Stanley going to her and embracing her. "He kneels beside her," says the stage direction, "and his fingers find the opening of her blouse." The play ends in its glandular habitat. The film ends as a tract.

Its re-release, in these greatly shifted times, raises a question: Ought *Streetcar* to be remade more faithfully? (It was redone for TV in 1984: I missed it.) Eventually, it will happen, I suppose, and it may be done well, but I can wait. Maimed though Williams's art is, Brando's is monumental. That's enough.

Nights of Cabiria

AUGUST 10, 1998 | *Nights of Cabiria,* made in 1956 by Federico Fellini, has just been rereleased in a new, fully restored print. It's fascinating. Part of the fascination is in seeing how much of it is intrinsic, untarnished gold; and, as with most earlier works of masters, part of it now is in seeing the hints of the Fellini to come.

Cabiria is a Roman prostitute in the early 1950s. (A fact I've never seen noted: Cabiria is not her real name, just one that she adopted for trade reasons. *Cabiria* was the title of a 1914 Italian film epic, a popular costume drama about a slave-girl of that name.) Fellini's film was made during the flood of post-war Italian neorealism, but it is not a naturalistic study à la Pasolini (though Pasolini did some uncredited work on the screenplay). We know very soon what Cabiria's profession is, and we see her on her favorite street along with other hookers, chatting and squabbling; but we never see her dealing sexually with anyone.

Nor have Fellini and his credited collaborators, Ennio Flaiano and Tullio Pinelli, written a cumulative drama. The film consists of five episodes, like passages in a morality play, in which Cabiria goes from humiliation through several kinds of exaltation back to humiliation again, with a different result. After the first episode she is infuriated; after the last she is, in a certain sense, purged. Thus this account of a prostitute's life is essentially a passion in the spiritual mode, with much along the way—a visit to a shrine, an encounter with a nutty friar, another with a true Christian bringing gifts to the homeless—to counterpoint the theme.

Retrospectively, we can now see evidence of the stylistic Fellini to come. The very first sequence is of people moving and the camera moving with them, as clear a hallmark of Fellini as any. That sequence is mostly in long shot. The place is what were then the fairly empty outskirts of Rome. A young man and woman burst out of a scrubby field where presumably they have been making love — Cabiria and a boyfriend. They run and tease along like any two lovers, laughing and kissing. They reach the banks of the Tiber, with the city across the way. Suddenly the young man grabs her pocketbook and pushes her into the river. The tenor and the surprise of the sequence, plus its integral motion, signal the quality of Fellini's vision — in cinema and in subject.

Here, and all through his career, Fellini makes the most of the fact that he lives in a country where his religion provides him with cinematic décor. The procession of nuns here is like religious processions in others of his films. Another of his passions, the music hall, seen earlier in *Variety Lights* and later, more elegantly, in *8½,* is the setting for one whole episode.

It's generally thought — rightly, I'd say — that Fellini's career is schizoid, the first part neorealist, the second baroque, as his concentration moved from needy people to wealthy ones. But seeing *Cabiria* again suggests that, within the somber neorealist, there was a satirical maker of splendid swirl waiting to burst out.

My one big trouble with this film was and still is Giulietta Masina as Cabiria. She is petite and perky, but her acting is a series of poses and assumptions — what actors call "indicating." Now I'm being winsome, she seems to say; now I'm being plucky. She adopts these attitudes like illustrations in a nineteenth-century textbook of acting. If she were a candid, truthful actress, then the last scene, in which a betrayed and penniless Cabiria is walking back to Rome amid a group of singing youngsters, would be transfixing. As is, all we can see is what it might have been.

Masina's mechanics are hardly a small flaw; still, Fellini's genius is sufficient (though he certainly didn't think of it that way) to compensate for them and to sweep us along.

Touch of Evil

SEPTEMBER 28, 1998 | In recent years some older films have been reconstituted in what was, or ought to have been, their original form. Add to the list the 1958 thriller by Orson Welles, *Touch of Evil.* In charge of the Welles restoration were Rick Schmidlin and the redoubtable editor Walter Murch. They unearthed a mass of production notes and reports, footage from the original negative, and a 58-page memo that Welles had sent to the studio after he saw the producer's cut of the film, a memo that the studio disregarded. Now the picture is available in a form as close as possible to what Welles intended.

On this matter of intent, consider an interesting document that I haven't seen in any book about Welles. When *Touch of Evil* was released in Britain, it was reviewed in the *New Statesman* by William Whitebait. Welles wrote to the magazine about that review, and the May 24, 1958 issue contains his long letter. Here are some excerpts:

> Sir, — Without being so foolish as to set my name to that odious thing, a "reply to the critic," perhaps I may add a few oddments of information to Mr. Whitebait's brief reference to my picture *Touch of Evil* (what a silly title, by the way: it's the first time I've heard it).

He goes on to speak of

> the wholesale re-editing of the film by the executive producer, a process of re-hashing in which I was forbidden to participate. Confusion was further confounded by several added scenes which I did not write and was not invited to direct. No wonder Mr. Whitebait speaks of muddle. . . . Just once my own editing of the picture has been the version put into release [*Citizen Kane,* surely]; and . . . I have only twice been given any choice at all as to the "level" of my subject matter. In my trunks stuffed with unproduced film scripts, there are no thrillers. When I make this sort of picture — for which I can pretend to have no special interest or aptitude — it is not "for the money" (I support myself as an actor) but because of a greedy need to exercise in some way the function of my choice: the function of director. Quite baldly . . . I have to take whatever comes along from time to time, or accept the alternative, which is not working at all.

This letter, though it seems disarmingly candid, is itself a curiosity. Welles complains about the film's title, but he himself adapted the screenplay from a mystery novel by Whit Masterson called *Badge of Evil;* if Welles didn't actually suggest the new title, it still couldn't have seemed so vastly different from the original. Compelled by circumstances to direct thrillers for which he claimed no special aptitude, he nonetheless did three others,

The Lady from Shanghai, The Stranger, and *Confidential Report.* Then there's his general discontent with *Touch of Evil* as released; at about this time he told a group at Oxford that it was one of the pictures that had come closest to his original plans.

These contradictions would just be part of the recurrent writhings of ego-and-commerce at release time except that we're dealing here with a genius, and that the film itself mirrors, in some degree, at some angles, the contradictions between this letter and the facts.

Obviously much has been restored to *Touch of Evil;* it now runs 111 minutes as against the 95-minute version that has usually been shown. Without detailed comparison of the two versions, it's possible to say only that the longer version sustains its texture more consistently than (as I remember) the earlier one. But, grateful though we must all be to the Schmidlin-Murch team, the film itself is—still is—a disappointment. It's a flurry of pressure-cooker baroque, an extreme example of the exhibitionistic hijinks in which Welles could sometimes indulge, apparently intensified here because he wasn't doing what he really wanted to be doing. (*Don Quixote* was much on his mind at the time.) So he showed the commercial people how he could force a piece from their own world to respond to an artist. Or so he seems to have thought.

Welles's screenplay is braided, as thrillers often are, with serious themes, not seriously utilized but flaunted to imply weight—in this case racial conflict, civic probity, personal ethics, and loyalty. The setting is the Mexican-American border, and the two main characters are a sprightly young Mexican narcotics detective (Charlton Heston) and a porcine, sly, local American police chief (Welles). The film opens with a murder-by-bomb—a justly famous three-minute tracking shot in which a bomb is planted in a car, which is then driven a short distance across the border before the explosion. (It's the one truly thrilling sequence in this thriller, made even more effective now because Schmidlin-Murch have removed the credits from this sequence and put them elsewhere.) The search for the perpetrators of the bombing is the meat of the plot.

Much of the action takes place in a relatively deserted motel on the American side. Janet Leigh is Heston's just-married American bride who, quite incredibly, gets herself into taut situations just because the plot demands it. Hubby stashes her in that motel while he is busy; she is harassed there by his enemies. Leigh, here as always, is only an archetypal movie-star puppet. Heston's attempts to be a dashing young man were painful even when he was young. Akim Tamiroff does a rerun of his sleazeball, this time as the head of a Mexican drug gang. Dennis Weaver plays the motel manager, the kind of neurotic never seen anywhere except in thrillers looking for lurid characters. Joseph Calleia, as Welles's sidekick, carries his part like the load of lumber it is. And Marlene Dietrich, delphic in a dark wig, has a few scenes as a world-weary Mexican tart. Dietrich is not expected to be credible in the part, just to appear in it. She does.

All the characters are burdened with the portentous hollow dialogue familiar in thrillers, dialogue that gets quoted in articles about them, usually in italics. For instance, after Welles is killed (his body lies, of course, amid garbage), Dietrich is asked what he was like, and she replies in much-quoted lines: "He was some kind of a man. What does it matter what you say about people?" For tinny wisdom, this is hard to beat.

Graham Greene, when he was a film critic, said that he disliked Hitchcock because "his films consist of a series of small 'amusing' melodramatic situations. . . . Very perfunctorily he builds up to these tricky situations . . . and then drops them; they mean nothing; they lead to nothing." In terms of structure and resolution, this seems to me to apply to *Touch of Evil* even more than to Hitchcock. Further, Welles shoots almost everything from a strained bizarre angle. The lighting, by Russell Metty, is exaggeratedly *noir*. The film moves with a kind of rush, rather than rhythm. All of these points seem to me to underscore the contradictions between Welles's *New Statesman* letter and the facts of the matter.

But the crowning paradox is Welles's own performance. He is excellent. In the midst of the whirling pretentiousness, he is genuine. He creates a parochial god, sure of his parish and his parishioners, cunning, vicious, sad. It's almost like a secret diabolical joke: while everyone else (except Dietrich) is scratching furiously away, he is having a quiet triumph.

Comment

Mozart opera on film, shifts in cultural appetites, the play of film experience on the world's imagination, the complicated matter of historical
accuracy in film—all these subjects confirm that the writer about film
is, willy-nilly, close to the fullest range of contemporary life. Obituary
comment about film figures is different from other such comment. When
a beloved film figure goes, the impact is personal. It involves a sense of
gratitude and of intimacy now heightened rather than breached because
the figure is only literally gone.

The Abduction from the Theater Mozart Opera on Film

THE YALE REVIEW, WINTER 1993 | "Whenever I go to an opera," said Lord Chesterfield, "I leave my sense and reason at the door with my half-guinea, and deliver myself up to my eyes and ears." What would he have said about opera on film? Would his eyes and ears have insisted on some recourse to sense? Obviously opera is a hybrid, a marriage of theater and music, but can a marriage accommodate a third partner with a third set of conventions? Would Lord Chesterfield have thought the triad more aesthetically scandalous than sensorily engaging?

Many modern observers do so consider it, and, in my view, they are essentially right. The only occasions when the combination succeeds are, to be tautological about it, when it succeeds. From the start, film hungered after opera, even in the days of silent pictures. The opera star Geraldine Farrar made a film of *Carmen* in 1915; *Der Rosenkavalier* was filmed silently in 1926 (under the supervision of Richard Strauss and his librettist Hugo von Hofmannsthal). These are only two instances of the continual attraction that opera has had for film, an attraction based on the belief that if the theater itself could nourish film, so could this hybrid form of theater. With the advent of sound, operas on film have become, if not numberless, so plentiful that they are not worth trying to count. The film world is ravenous, even for this improbable fare.

The opera house itself relies on a centuries-old set of conventions between stage and audience. We know that people in the world around us don't sing their conversations, and we also know that if we accept these conventions, we profit in beauties. But the film art has its conventions, too: whatever its stylistic variations, film asks its viewers to accept lights and shadows on a screen as manifests of realism — that is the mode toward which film consistently tends. Accepting that contract, the film audience, too, is rewarded with beauty. But nothing in opera, nothing whatsoever, tends consistently toward realism. (*Verismo* at its most intense is still a long way from realism.) To transfer opera to film is to obfuscate the fundamental contracts of both arts. One fights the other.

It's worse. When we go to an opera or a film, we know the contract of conventions in advance. But a viable contract that covers all films of operas has yet to be drawn up. Almost every director who films an opera has to try to find his or her own solution to the problem by creating the contract between this particular film and its audience. This is so generally true that it might as well be stated as a fact: every film of an opera needs to write its own contract with the audience. Therefore the audience, as it prepares to watch an opera on film, must ask itself, whether consciously or not: What is the contract this time? What conventions are we expected to observe here? In very large measure, the success of the enterprise depends on the viability of that contract.

Mozart has, inevitably, proved irresistible to filmmakers, and they have operated under a variety of audience contracts. Here I will examine three films of Mozart operas. My purpose is not to draw overall conclusions— I doubt that any such will ever be drawn—but to determine how each director conceived his contract.

The Magic Flute, directed by Ingmar Bergman

The first point to be noted here, for it is the source and genesis of this film, is the curious imbalance of Bergman's career. Here is an artist who is securely established as one of the greatest directors in film history, yet he has spent only about a quarter of his professional life in film. He has done most of his directing in the theater, where he has put on plays ranging from Athens to Broadway, as well as operas and operettas. Twice he had hoped to do productions of *The Magic Flute,* and he even used an excerpt from the opera in his film *Hour of the Wolf.*

In 1972, when Swedish television asked him to make a film of the opera, he was at the height of his theater and film careers. We can infer from the result that he determined to use both aspects of his experience. He could have had no interest in merely photographing a theater performance; on the other hand, he also wanted to avoid the desperate pretense that what we are seeing is not an opera at all but a "real" drama—despite the fact that, in this stubbornly realistic medium, actors have to sing their feelings and thoughts.

Bergman, genius that he is, devised a quite new contract with his audience. He provides a vicar for the audience itself, an on-screen audience that watches the performance he is filming. He goes further by taking us backstage from time to time, allowing us to see both sides of the stage. Thus the performance of Mozart that we see is held in two beams of vision, one from behind and one in front. The camera consequently creates a fourth dimension, in which the other three dimensions — stage, backstage, audience — come together to highlight both the conventions that underlie cinematic art and the beauty to which this convergence can lead. In this way, Bergman creates a unique arrangement with his viewers that is at once intimate yet lofty.

He began by devising a theater production of *The Magic Flute* solely for use in this film. (It has never been put on elsewhere.) Then, almost as an ironic touch in this late twentieth-century venture, he put that production in an eighteenth-century theater located in the palace of Drottningholm outside Stockholm. (The grounds and the auditorium that we see are at Drottningholm. For technical reasons, the stage was replicated in a Stockholm film studio.)

After a brief prelude in which we see the palace woods and hear a few twilight bird calls, we move into the opera house, where we see the audience listening to the overture. Soon after the performance starts, we are briskly introduced to backstage life when Papageno, lounging in his dressing room, almost misses his first entrance. Thus, before long, the four elements are fused: the audience in the theater, the opera performance, the world of the performers, and the film that encompasses all these. Now must be added a fifth element, ourselves, the audience for whom it has all been done. We are given a godlike vantage point, and our overview completes a work that is larger than either a theater performance or an orthodox film.

We come then to Bergman's view of *The Magic Flute* and his complex approach to it. Obviously he knows the opera's history; its use of Masonic symbols; its susceptibility to charges of antifeminism today; its mixture of German opera and singspiel; and, in the Queen of the Night's two great arias, its Italianate flavor. His comprehension of all these elements is reflected in his production, but he attends this approach with another — what can be called, with the dignity it deserves, a child's view of *The Magic Flute*.

Bergman has told us that he fell in love with the opera when he was twelve years old and that it has haunted him all his life. When he first saw it, he assumed, though it is not in fact the case, that Sarastro was the father of Pamina and that he stole her from her wicked mother for her own good; and this early assumption Bergman retains in the film, adding some rearrangements in the second act that are consonant with his boyhood vision. Thus this sophisticated film, without being coy, is the realization of a youthful point of view.

Bergman underscores this view in several ways. During the overture we see many members of the audience; we are given several glimpses of the film's cinematographer, Sven Nykvist, and, during the coda, a very swift look at Bergman himself; but the image which recurs most often, both during the overture and the performance itself, is that of a child. She is Bergman's daughter, Linn, and she quite clearly serves as a deputy for the boy Bergman seeing *The Magic Flute* for the first time.

Other evidence abounds of the child's-eye view. The libretto of the opera contains a number of maxims for human behavior that, despite the celestial music to which they are set, can strike the listener as a bit didactic. Bergman has these maxims inscribed on banners, and this display has a double effect: it renders them, with gentle humor, as Aesopian morals fitting a cautionary tale, and it shows Bergman's awareness that he is dealing with consciously crystallized innocence. And then there are the animals. When Tamino first plays his flute, animals appear, enchanted as they once were by Orpheus. But these are animals from the Peaceable Kingdom—large, funny, friendly creatures from the nearest marvelous toy shop. When Sarastro appears, he is in a chariot drawn by two toy lions; when he descends from the chariot, his first action is to kiss a child. Throughout the film, we are reminded that there are children in the Drottningholm audience and that within each member of the audience everywhere there is a child. One of the triumphs of this film is the way that Bergman merges a full rendition of the work's profundities with his still-persisting childhood view of it.

One more point to be noted: light. In Bergman's work generally, light is almost choric; it not only fits the moment but underscores it without straining to do so. In *The Magic Flute,* however, he uses light quite differently. The world outside the theater, the audience, and the backstage areas are all lighted in a relatively realistic manner; but in the performance of the opera on stage, Bergman uses theatrical light—changes of intensity and shade within a scene, different faces seen in different ways. (In one sequence, for example, the Queen of the Night changes from her usual self into an older, fiercer woman—presumably her hidden self—and back again.) All through the film Bergman seems to exult in doing precisely what he could not do when making realistic films: using light in the same sheerly instrumental way that he had employed in the theater.

This film, then, is the fruit of Bergman's double career. Out of all the elements described above, including his particularized view of this opera, he creates a new form that is impressively complex yet utterly lucid. The contract that Bergman offers his viewers is at once an invitation to the making of an opera performance, to the making of a film of that performance, and to a vantage point that acknowledges the ridiculousness of the project while lavishing gratification on us. We are swept away by delight and cozy conspiracy. This is Bergman's mastery, simultaneously cunning and straightforward.

Don Giovanni, directed by Joseph Losey

Losey's approach is diametrically opposed to Bergman's. Losey wants the audience to forget, if possible, that it is watching an opera performance; his intent is to make his *Don Giovanni* just another film among films, except that in this case the actors sing.

To put his approach in perspective, let us first look at the work itself, a treatment of one of the basic myths of the Western world. So rooted is that myth in our culture that it comes as a surprise to note that Don Juan made his first appearance in a Spanish play published as recently as 1630. Some elements in his character and adventures caused him to be taken up immediately—one can say immediately—in other countries. The Italians wrote plays about him, as did the French. Molière's *Don Juan,* in my opinion his best play, was written in 1665, only thirty-five years after the Don's first appearance. Other plays followed, continuing to, though not concluding with, Bernard Shaw's *Man and Superman.* But Wolfgang Hildesheimer writes: "Without Mozart, without the proportions and dimensions he brought to the figure, Don Giovanni would scarcely be the archetype he is now, with a history so well explored." Shaw would have agreed.

Mozart was not the first to write an opera about the Don. In fact, he and his librettist, Lorenzo da Ponte, were discussing possibilities for a new collaboration when they learned of an opera about Don Juan that had been produced in Venice only a few months before, with music by Giuseppe Gazzaniga and a libretto by Giovanni Bertati. Mozart and Da Ponte decided to write a *Don* of their own. Da Ponte leaned on Bertati's libretto; Mozart, we may assume, had no need of help from Gazzaniga.

Why were they so interested? Why has the Don Juan myth persisted? Is it only that men get an empathic thrill out of a man who is arithmetically stupefying in his success with women, or that women can't help feeling, perhaps against their will, that there is something diabolically appealing in such a man? If so, why Don Giovanni? Stories about libertines are not hard to find. For instance, there are several operas about Casanova, but Casanova is not exactly a fixture in Western mythology. Surely there must be something more to Don Giovanni than his libertinism.

Losey, though otherwise he falls short, has some sense of a theme deeper than amorous athleticism. In the first scene of the opera itself, there is a murder; and in the last, divine retribution. But Losey frames both scenes by showing us a blazing fire in the first and in the last moments of his film. Losey also adds to his cast a new, silent character: a servant dressed in black, who is seen frequently throughout the film, apparently to remind us that though the Don may frivol, fate has not forgotten him. This story of a man of the world is enclosed in the embrace of an unseen world.

But there is even more to the Don's story—an element that is not only nonreligious but antireligious. Molière's Don Juan is a man who knows of that larger, unseen world and deliberately chooses to challenge it. Shaw said of Mozart's work, "Don Juan is a tragic hero or he is nothing: his destiny is announced by Mozart from the very first chord of the overture." All three of these great artists have seen in the Don a good deal more than a philanderer. My favorite passage in Da Ponte's libretto comes near the end, at the appearance of the stone guest, the statue of the Commendatore. The statue says: "Don Giovanni, you invited me to supper, and I am here." To which the Don replies: "I would not have believed it. But I'll do my best. Leporello, set another place." That seems to me a heroic reply, by a man who is not to be frightened out of his disbelief by a ghost, even a petrified one.

This opera about a man who makes love incessantly as part of his belief in the right of human beings to control their own lives was filmed by Losey in 1979. Compared to Bergman's audience contract for *The Magic Flute,* Losey's is disappointingly torpid, even though he had assistance in devising it. Rolf Liebermann, the former director of the Hamburg and Paris opera houses, is credited with the film's basic concept—a puzzling credit, because it is hard to see that there *is* a basic concept. The film was shot in and around several gorgeous Palladian villas near Vicenza in northeastern Italy, and no matter what else happens or fails to happen cinematically, a few architectural flowers of the Italian Renaissance are put at our disposal. But though Losey has some awareness of thematic depth in the work, he shows no firm, problem-solving filmic intent. This, despite the fact that he is an experienced theater director and an even more experienced film director, the maker of such notable films as *Accident* and *The Servant.* So unhappily do opera and film collide in this *Giovanni* that we often ask ourselves why these actors are singing, a question that in itself points to the enterprise's lack of success.

Instead of aiding the film, the camera almost seems to be discomfiting it. The disguises in Act Two, when Leporello and his master exchange clothes, seem silly here. Losey has them use hand-held Venetian masks, but these masks only emphasize that the opera stage doesn't need them and that in film they don't much help. The insistent camera is additionally cruel in a way that wouldn't apply on the opera stage. It comes in close to the baritone and seriously questions his reputation for success with women. It also makes it hard for us to accept that this Zerlina is a young and innocent village maiden.

But aside from such matters—and there are many more—how does Losey try to deal with his elemental problem, the opera-film conflict? He knows that, in cinema terms, opera is relatively static; therefore he takes primal measures, almost primitive measures, to avoid stasis. He moves. He moves everyone and the camera as much as he possibly can, hoping that continual shifts of angle and of background, that brief tours down gorgeous corridors and majestic stairways will give the film a vital mobility. But since most of the movement seems a hasty addition to the scene rather than a part of it, we are so conscious of the fight against a conventional opera performance that we almost long for a conventional opera performance.

To help fulfill his desperate need for motion, Losey invents business for the performers. For example, after "Là ci darem la mano," it's impossible for the Don to take Zerlina to his castle because they are already there, courtesy of Losey's devisings. Instead, the Don takes her into a bedroom where, with open doors, they proceed to make love until they are interrupted by Donna Anna. But this added business makes it hard to understand why, a bit later, when the Don takes Zerlina into another bedroom, she screams, as the libretto requires. The two bedroom scenes just don't mesh. Furthermore, in the second act, an ensemble, singing away, moves into a large salon. Suddenly there is a group of people sitting in the room and watching them. The ensemble performs for these people. Who are they? Why were they seated there waiting? Only because Losey is feverishly trying to satisfy what he assumes is our appetite for constant visual variety.

Other instances could easily be added, but it is clear enough that Losey is caught in the crunch—he's not the first film director nor the last to have this problem—between opera and film. Like many directors before and since, he opted for the most obvious means of dealing, or trying to deal, with it—that is, he has chosen to pretend that his film is not an opera. But, though he attempts to beguile our eyes, they will not allow us to accept his contract with the audience.

The Marriage of Figaro, directed by Peter Sellars

Peter Sellars's approach to *Figaro* is generally thought to be so antitraditional that it may be as well to begin by noting how snugly it fits into a latter-day tradition, one that originated in the theater. His version of *Figaro* began production, in a direct historical sense, on May 1, 1874. That was the date when a company of actors from the provincial German city of Meiningen made their debut in Berlin. Their appearance was soon widely noted because it proclaimed to the world the arrival of an important new profession in the theater, that of the director.

Movement toward that profession had been visible earlier in Germany and England, but it wasn't until the duke of Saxe-Meiningen insisted on ensemble playing in his personal troupe in his small capital, insisted on one central vision to govern a production by that troupe, that the idea of directing as we know it became a permanent part, an expected part, of our theater. Since classical times, productions had been organized according to the traditions in a particular theater or according to the wishes of leading actors. After the duke sent his company to Berlin and then on a series of extensive tours, those circumstances began to change.

What the quality of the theater had been before and why the new profession arose where and when it did are fascinating subjects, but they are too complex to explore here. Let us note, however, that when the profession arrived it quickly took hold throughout Europe and America. For the next twenty-five years or so, directors devoted themselves to reforming or initiating productions according to the expressed or implicit wishes of the author.

Most directors still practice their professions that way. But around 1900 some directors began to have a new sense of authority—in the literal sense of being authors themselves. The arts of performance, as distinct from the arts of playwriting and opera-writing, had obviously always been present and essential; but now that their profession had become established, some directors began to feel that the performance arts should be exalted in order to make the production itself of supreme importance. They felt that the text of the play or the opera should be treated not as the production's reason for being but only as one of the contributory elements—like the acting and design and lighting—and that all these elements should now become components of a superseding art: the director's.

One of the most famous statements of this view came from Gordon Craig in 1905:

> The theater must in time perform pieces of its own art. . . . When [the director] interprets the plays of the dramatist . . . he is a craftsman; . . . when he will have mastered the actions, words, line, colour, and rhythm, then he may become an artist. Then we shall no longer need the assistance of the playwright—for our art will be self-reliant.

The history of directing in the twentieth century quite clearly is divided between those directors whose aim is "to interpret the plays of the dramatist" and those who, without absolutely discarding the dramatist, nonetheless use his work to serve their own purposes rather than his.

Peter Sellars, from the very beginning of his fulminant career, has been a fervent member of the Craig school. He began in the theater but lately has turned to opera because, he says, opera gives him more opportunity "to explore a secret world." Whether or not the theater really affords less opportunity, opera has certainly given Sellars plenty of chances to explore his own secret worlds.

I saw his production of *The Marriage of Figaro* on stage in the mid-1980s, and I went through my usual set of reactions to an unusual production of a familiar work. First, I asked why. Why had the setting been changed to the fifty-second floor of the Trump Tower in New York with costumes to match? Second, I got pleasure out of the imaginative use of modern artifacts that Sellars chose to accommodate Mozart and Da Ponte: for example, Cherubino's hockey stick and sweater mark him as a youngster full of physicality; even his much-discussed solo sex miming seemed to fit up-to-the-minute, overbrimming youth. Third, I began to relish the whole transposition as a new plane on which to enjoy the opera. Fourth, I became conscious of matters that simply couldn't be transposed. For instance, at the end of the first act, to what army does a count residing in the Trump Tower send the troublesome Cherubino? Fifth was the first reaction all over again: why?

If I couldn't find a completely satisfactory answer, at least Sellars had one for himself. He told us that he was using an eighteenth-century work to comment on America today—class, power, corruption, and more. Well, those matters certainly need comment. But we might ask how the Mozart–Da Ponte work managed to survive to our day, before Sellars came to its aid, if it hadn't been pertinent all along. Still, even if his argument had a touch of rationalization as well as reason, there was no denying—on the contrary, one could rejoice in—his vitality. And politics are hardly absent from *The Marriage of Figaro*, as Bernard Shaw observed:

> It is true that Mozart made no attempt to write political music in the sense of expressing not only wounded human feeling but the specific rancor of the class-conscious proletarian; but the wounded feeling is provided for very plentifully if only the conductor will allow the singer to put it in instead of treating him as if he were one of the second violins.

Read *director* for *conductor,* and we might agree that Sellars, consciously or not, followed Shaw's advice more vigorously than Shaw could have foretold.

At the least, and it is surely not a little, the Sellars approach energized his whole cast, who performed with great enjoyment of both the music and its novel presentation. This approach also helped that last scene, which is chockablock with masquerades and disguises—a notorious headache to opera directors. Sellars didn't completely clarify the last scene, but at least we could see what was originally intended.

Sellars later filmed his theater production of *Figaro* for television, and therefore had to make a contract with a film audience. The first point to be noted about this film of a radical production is that, as film, it is in no way radical. Bergman's *Magic Flute,* built around a relatively orthodox theater production that was conceived especially for the film, is much more adventurous cinematically. For example, during the *Figaro* overture, Sellars gives us a sequence of shots of people on Fifth Avenue in New York at Christmastime, a sequence that merely establishes place and season. During the *Magic Flute* overture, Bergman presents a collage telling us that this work grips all kinds of present-day people and that a little girl will figure prominently among them. Bergman's overture effectively *begins* his production. Sellars's overture is only a conventional preface *before* his production begins.

Bergman's contract with his audience, as we have seen, entails the amalgamation of five components virtually to compose a new form, unique and unrepeatable. Sellars's task is more limited: he is to record a particular theater production. Without referring to an actual theater—the audience, proscenium, and so forth—he preserves the lateral, mostly two-dimensional essence of a theater production. He does this without stultifying the performed opera but also without pretending that this is simply one more film. His frankness and his skill make his contract succeed.

His chief instrument is his vantage point. Sellars opts to work in close, as close as possible—a technique superbly suited to film and television. In a way, this choice justifies the film by amplifying the chief merit of his original production: its liveliness, and its enlivening of the cast. His stage production (and consequently his film) had no trace of stiff opera singing accompanied by studied countenance and gesture; he evoked from his people the emotional verity of each moment. In this film those qualities are even more striking. The finespun, intricate interplay of the performers reflects the finespun music.

When Stanislavski was working with opera singers, he said:

> How lucky you singers are. . . . The composer provides you with one most important element — the rhythm of your inner emotions. That is what we actors have to create for ourselves out of a vacuum. All you have to do is to listen to the rhythm of the music and make it your own. The written word is the theme of the author, but the melody is the emotional experience of that theme.

In Sellars's theater production, it seemed as if he had overheard Stanislavski. In his film of that production, he seems to take this advice even more to heart. Even his editing is brisk and bright and underscores the rococo plot. Sellars cuts frequently from one character to another, not only to keep the plot's complications clear but also to use the kinetics of the film to mirror the interweavings of intrigue. By the time we get to the last scene, the editing, like the performances, seems to have the pulse of the music.

Here, then, is an authentic twentieth-century production that derives fundamentally from the directorial explosion of 1874. Eighteenth-century opera, ultramodern theater, and film: to engage all three, it takes serene self-confidence and conviction, qualities that Sellars does not lack. His very daring in this engagement is part of his audience contract and helps to keep us involved even when we have reservations.

The three examples above, chosen to exemplify certain approaches to filming operas, of course do not begin to exhaust the possible approaches to this hybrid genre. Bergman's work can hardly even be called an approach; it is sui generis. Most films of operas, however, are simply records of actual performances or specially arranged performances for filming, with occasional arthritic attempts at cinematic limbering. They make Sellars's filming of a theater production seem all the more exceptional and all the more welcome. (The most successful attempt in what might be called

the Losey vein—"This isn't really an opera at all, friends, it's just a film"—
the most successful attempt that I know of is not with a Mozart opera; it
is Francesco Rosi's 1984 film of *Carmen*. Rosi treats the opera as if it were a
musical conceived for film, directs it under the influence of such excellent
Hollywood musical directors as Stanley Donen and Vincente Minnelli,
and manages to articulate *Carmen* in lithe and sinuous cinematic form.)

Mozart lives, films live, directors live, and the three will certainly continue to encounter one another. Few of those films can succeed aestheti-
cally: the union is too strange. But if those few are exceptions, we can
console ourselves by remembering that it is the exceptions that sustain
any art or combination of arts. And when the usual kind of filmed opera
is patently unsuccessful, we can at least amuse ourselves by imagining
what Lord Chesterfield might have been thinking: possibly of his mis-
spent half-guinea.

All the World's a Film

SEPTEMBER 4, 1995 | Whenever I teach a course in the history of
film, I begin with *The Great Train Robbery*. Edwin S. Porter's eleven-minute
work, made in 1903, was not the first to use editing or the first to use a
popular play as its source, but Porter certainly advanced the art of editing,
and his film illustrates a transition in audience expectations.

Porter's editing helped to free film from the strictly linear story and
showed, among other things, that different simultaneous time strands are
part of its power. The transition embodied in Porter's film is fascinating:
some of the fourteen scenes are patent theater imitations, with painted
scenery and with actors playing in profile, while others are as "real" as
anything done today. Some scenes, for instance, are on top of a rushing train, with the actors moving as naturally as the moment requires.
Porter clearly was counting on an audience conditioned by a lifetime of
theatergoing, expecting scenery that looked like scenery yet eager for the
new. (This paradox continued for years. In 1920 Griffith made *Way Down
East,* in which there are scenes shot in an actual blizzard, yet the heroine's
bedroom has snow painted on the windows.)

Porter dramatized the transition further. The interior of the railroad depot is a patent canvas-and-paint job with a window, yet at one point a real locomotive goes past the window drawing a real train. (Double exposure, of course.) Porter assumed, correctly, that audiences would welcome the contrast.

Imagine being a member of that audience. People could have had as much as eight years of filmgoing experience by then, mostly of non-fiction films, but now they were entering a dimension in which everything in the world could become a character in a story. A breeze, a leaf, a raindrop, a ship at sea could become a member of the cast. (Even today those facts have not lost a tickle of the metaphysical.)

But one particular moment in Porter's film is my chief reason for showing it. The matters mentioned above have been much discussed: that one moment has been neglected. Robbers stop the train out in the countryside. (Porter cleverly films the train at an angle, not straight across the screen, to give the composition perspective.) At gunpoint, the passengers are forced to disembark and line up against the train, hands raised, while the robbers go down the line taking money and jewelry. One of the passengers, a man in a derby, is apparently eager to protect his belongings. He runs. One of the robbers shoots him in the back. He falls.

This, I believe, is an evolutionary moment in the history of film, one that revised concepts of space in drama. That passenger doesn't run right or left: he runs, at a slight angle, directly toward us, toward the camera.

If this had been a scene in a play and the actor had run toward the footlights, the audience would instantaneously have expected him to leave the fiction and join the facts—themselves. Equally swiftly they would have thought that the actor or director was out of his mind. But Porter surmised that his audience, prepared perhaps by the verism of the train itself, would be ready to enter a new realm.

What was that realm? The length and breadth of the world itself. The universe. Universes yet unknown. When an actor leaves the stage, he steps out of the play. When an actor leaves a film shot, in any direction, we simply assume that he is continuing on in the rest of the world. Even when an actor walks out of a set in a studio, we don't envisage him as walking "off-stage" as we do in the theater. We don't think of the camera as seeing only what it ought to see at any moment, with something quite different bordering it on every side. We conceive that the camera at any moment is focused on one fragment of immensity. Porter's fugitive wasn't heading toward the end of anything: if he hadn't been killed, he might still be running.

The theater has its own powers, some of which are shared with film, some not (like a centrality in language). But the theater has never been greatly concerned with verity of place and has rarely used such verity successfully. Eisenstein began his career in the theater, and in 1923 he staged a play called *Gas Masks* in the Moscow gasworks, but this production only signaled to him that he belonged in the cinema. Today there are theater productions called "site-specific," but they are often accommodations to the place where the production is being done, rather than works that began by choosing the site as integral. I've seen — taken part in — productions of *A Midsummer Night's Dream* and *As You Like It* and *The Tempest* on a wooded hill, but the trees and grass never looked real in the beams of the spotlights. The stage lets a play concentrate on matters other than "placeness." Film always has "placeness" at its careless command.

In 1952 André Bazin, one of the most visionary of critics, wrote a two-part essay called "Theater and Cinema" in which he said:

> The stage and the decor where the action unfolds constitute an aesthetic microcosm inserted perforce into the universe but essentially distinct from the Nature that surrounds it. It is not the same with cinema, the basic principle of which is the denial of any frontiers to action.

Inevitably Bazin saw the matter in humanist terms:

> On the screen man is no longer the focus of the drama but will become eventually the center of the universe. The impact of his action may there set in motion an infinitude of waves. The decor that surrounds him is part of the solidity of the world.

I don't know if Bazin ever saw *The Great Train Robbery;* still he describes it. That fleeing passenger set in motion an infinitude of waves.

Career Note: The slain passenger was played by a salesman turned actor named Max Aronson, who, within a few years, became the first cowboy star, Bronco Billy Anderson.

DECEMBER 11, 1995 | *The following is the text of a talk given at the U.S. Holocaust Memorial Museum in Washington on November 9, 1995 in a discussion of the use of the Holocaust on stage and screen.*

When people question the propriety of the Holocaust as a subject for art, they are rarely concerned with painting or music or poetry or fiction: they mean theater or film. Few, as far as I know, have ever questioned the fitness of Anselm Kiefer's paintings or Arnold Schoenberg's music or Nelly Sachs's poetry or Piotr Rawicz's fiction on this subject. It is the practice of enactment that disturbs, and even then, the disturbance comes more from film than from theater.

Here is a paragraph that can serve as a text. It comes from a recent book called *Flickers* by the English critic Gilbert Adair. Says Adair:

> A few shameless miscalculations aside . . . *Schindler's List* was not at all the disgrace one had every right to expect. It was still, however, a monstrosity. It was, after all, a Hollywood film like any other film (the first words one saw on the screen were "Amblin Entertainment") and it was shot like any other Hollywood film. It had . . . a cast, probably, of thousands. And what I see when I watch the film, what, hard as I try, I cannot prevent myself from seeing, is that cast being put through its paces on some foggy, nocturnal location, put through its paces by the boyishly handsome director in his snazzy windcheater, his red N.Y. Yankees baseball cap, his granny glasses and his beard.

This paragraph—I've condensed it: there's more in the same vein—is well worth examining.

First, it's about *Schindler's List*. If one is to discuss the proprieties, aesthetic, social, moral, of making fictional films about the Holocaust, this is the prime instance because it looms so large in the filmgoing experience of so many and because it has drawn more attention than any other fictional film on the subject. *Schindler's List* emphasizes strongly some difficulties that a fictional Holocaust film faces.

Second, Adair is frank about the surprise involved. I went to the film prepared for offense and was disarmed within two minutes. John Gross, who wrote the most intelligent favorable review of the film that I have read, in *The New York Review of Books,* spent the first six paragraphs of his long critique adjusting to the fact that he had liked it. It had come bearing the stigma of Spielberg's previous success.

Third, the provenance was Hollywood. If we can fantasize that this film, exactly as it is, frame by frame, had arrived from another source, I believe that its reception would have been more cordial in certain resistant quarters. If the opening credit had said Film Polski or Sacis or some other foreign brand name instead of Amblin Entertainment, it's a fair guess that fewer nerves would have been grated right at the start. I can't remember that any European film, of the dozens that have been made about the Holocaust, has aroused strong opposition. It's also interesting to note that, when a book on the Holocaust comes from a publisher who has made millions on lesser books about lesser subjects, few literary critics are offended because the name of that publisher is on the book.

I don't understand what Adair means when he says that *Schindler's List* was shot like any other film. If he means that its techniques and visual values were crassly commercial, the point is severely arguable, beginning with the fact that, in an age insistent on color, Spielberg shot the film in black and white. Then there is the recurrent image in Adair's mind of Spielberg dressed as he usually dresses when working. This, of course, is a response to the fact that the film was made by a personality famous in popular culture. It makes me wonder whether Adair and similar critics would have liked *Schindler's List* better if, before shooting started, publicity photos had been distributed of Spielberg dressed somberly for work.

But it is Adair's comment on the cast that, I believe, is the base of all that troubles him and commentators like him. All his complaints rest ultimately on the issue that the film, though basically factual, was re-created by actors. Claude Lanzmann, who made *Shoah,* believes that re-creating the Holocaust is impermissible, "is tantamount to fabricating archives." I note that Marcel Ophuls, who made *The Sorrow and the Pity,* disagrees vehemently with Lanzmann; still, despite this welcome reassurance, let's investigate what I take to be the root causes underlying both Lanzmann's and Adair's views: causes that are present in all fictional Holocaust films but which, in a large-scale, lavishly promoted film—in what Adair says is "after all, a Hollywood film"—become most apparent and most abrasive: causes with a vivid history.

That history begins many centuries ago, with the first appearance in Western culture of a practice sufficiently formalized to be called acting, the profession of the actor. The earliest recorded criticism was adverse. Twenty-four hundred years ago Plato opined that mimesis, impersonation, was a danger to the state; and he has had many supporters in subsequent centuries. All through the chronicle of the theater, periods recurred when, under a political or religious or social aegis, the theater was attacked as a breeder of troubles. In a distinguished book called *The Anti-theatrical Prejudice,* Jonas Barish articulates the long record of this prejudice in the Western world. Let's content ourselves here with just one example, a famous one: in the eighteenth century, Rousseau, who had already achieved success as a playwright, turned bitterly against the theater as a source of moral imbalance.

Surely, what underlies this prejudice to a great degree is a factor that is not always emphasized: the power of the actor himself. Usually the objections focus on the contents of plays, sometimes on the very existence of the theater as an institution. Discernible throughout, however, even when the plays are pablum, is some fear of the art of acting.

In a penetrating study titled *The Actor's Freedom,* Michael Goldman says:

> Any playwright, actor, or director knows that aggression is an essential ingredient of drama. But not perhaps for the reasons familiarly proposed [conflict in the text of the play]. . . . Rather, the importance of aggression has more to do with the aggression the actor himself must use to assume his role and maintain contact with his audience. The effort to set actors loose, to harness and encourage their terrific energies, requires . . . an aggression that must be felt in every turn of dialogue, in every corner of the play.

If this thesis is credible, as I take it to be, such aggression is amplified in film, by technological and other means, to a degree that would have made Rousseau's hair curl.

Indeed, the arrival of film in this century, its emplacement in human consciousness to such overwhelming effect, has greatly reduced the power of the theater actor's aggression—comparatively, at any rate. I am not arguing the superiority of one art, as such, over another: I don't accept such hierarchies. But in sheer numerical terms, let alone psychological or social ones, the sway of film has increased at the expense of the theater's sovereignty. Actors in the theater these days rarely achieve the mystical powers of many film actors, powers that are not necessarily identical with talent. The theater actor in our time is, in Goldman's sense, much less aggressive. Consequently, and I believe it is consequent, objections to plays about the Holocaust are rare.

When the Holocaust is the subject of a film, a re-created film, this resident power of the screen actor is even more disturbing than usual. The innate aggressiveness of the actor, which we might see as an emotional invasion for the purpose of conquest, seems even more invasive when it succeeds. To be moved by an actor practicing his or her profession by portraying a Holocaust victim can seem — before, during or after the event — obscene.

I underscore that I am not castigating *Schindler's List*. My opinion of the film is close to Lawrence L. Langer's. He notes that "some relics of Hollywood infiltrate" the film, but he says, "*Schindler's List*, like all serious art, invites us to join in the creative process by speculating about the riddle of human nature without expecting simple answers, or perhaps any answers at all." I am here trying to investigate not any "relics of Hollywood" in the film, but an inescapable component of *Schindler's List*, a component that, recognized or not, has been, I believe, a major factor in much of the reproof it received. Plato would have recognized that factor: impersonation.

When we read a novel or a poem, no one obtrudes between what the author presents and what our response makes of it. In a film, much more imperially these days than in the theater, someone has learned words and rehearsed actions in order to enthrall us. In a Holocaust film, even if it is as close to fact as Spielberg's, someone is devising strategies for his or her own creative purposes. Elsewhere, in the general course of cinematic events, that can be an enrichment. Kenneth Branagh did more for the character of Henry V than most of us can do for ourselves by reading the play. But this enrichment can seem out of place in Holocaust material.

Further, there is our awareness of careers. When we see Actor A in a Holocaust film, unless he or she is a newcomer, we can see the performance as an event in Actor A's career, which would be normal and possibly pleasant in other roles but here can seem exploitative. When Ralph Fiennes appeared as the Nazi commandant in *Schindler's List*, he was completely unknown in the United States. For us, Fiennes began and ended with the Nazi commandant, thus — territorially, we might say — he seemed different from the other two leading actors. To see the film again now, after Fiennes has appeared in other pictures, is in some measure to see him in changed perspective.

The ideal in this regard is Falconetti as Joan of Arc in Dreyer's great film of 1927. Though she had been a working actress in the Paris theater, this was her first film, so world audiences had no mundane Falconetti appearances as background. She never made another film, thus Falconetti is fixed forever as martyr and saint, unsullied by career.

Compare that fact with what we know and knew about Liam Neeson and Ben Kingsley in Spielberg's film. Both of them had appeared in lesser films and most certainly have appeared in lesser films since. We may have admired their performances in *Schindler's List,* as I certainly did, but we couldn't help seeing them move ahead in the lives of Neeson and Kingsley. At the least, we laid on them, consciously or not, an obligation never to appear in any film of lesser seriousness than this one. When they did, as inevitably they had to, some of the public took it as a kind of betrayal, as a confirmation of the opportunism that they suspected in Spielberg's picture.

Thus it is, I believe, that in the paragraph cited earlier, Gilbert Adair finds *Schindler's List,* though better than he expected, nonetheless monstrous. The ancient discomfort with the actor's powers, the intrusiveness of impersonation, the use of the film as a professional stepping-stone for its makers, all these matters bother Adair — and others. Does this mean that there can never be a totally accepted fictional film — from Hollywood or some other famously commercial source — about the Holocaust? That it will be resisted whatever its quality? I think that this will probably be the case during the lifetimes of those who were contemporaries of the Holocaust or those whose close relatives and friends were involved in it.

I have to hope that no one will ever be able to look at the Holocaust with complete objectivity, but it will take several generations before audiences can confront re-creations of it as they confront a film on any profoundly grave subject. At such a time, the aggression of the actor in a Holocaust film will operate no more disturbingly than it usually does, without the immediate resentment and hurt that must so often intervene today.

What's Left of the Center?

SALMAGUNDI, SUMMER 1996 | In 1974 an extraordinary French film arrived, directed by Bertrand Blier and adapted by him from a novel of his own. In America it was called *Going Places,* but the title in France, where it had been a big success, was *Les Valseuses (The Waltzers).* This is French slang for the testicles. It's a pity that the American distributor couldn't have found some sort of vernacular equivalent, perhaps drawn from sport — such as *Base on Balls.* The saltiness might have underscored certain qualities in the film, qualities that make it a good place to begin an inquiry into current relations between art and morality in the world of performance.

Going Places follows the escapades of two young men as they wander around France without plan or purpose other than to gratify themselves in any way they choose. They are intelligent and acute. They have nothing, and they care about nothing, except themselves. They steal or appropriate whatever they want, in goods, cars, sex.

The very opening of the film is a historical marker. Pierrot pushes Jean-Claude in a supermarket cart as they pursue a stout woman who has just been shopping. Jean-Claude keeps reaching toward the woman's behind, trying to pinch her as she hurries. This sequence, as was clear to many in France and to some in this country, was severely iconoclastic. In 1960 Jean-Luc Godard had made *Breathless,* the film that virtually ushered in both the so-called New Wave of cinema and the ambiance of youthful revolution that swelled rapidly in that decade; and one of the most publicized facts about the making of *Breathless* was that, for his traveling shots, Godard had put his cinematographer in a shopping cart and pushed him about in it. This pragmatic informality had struck everyone as a witty, direct assault on conventional filmmaking, the *cinéma de papa,* which would have required an expensive dolly and a special crew. Godard's slash through studio convention was applauded as a break with stuffy procedure.

Yet, only fourteen years later, here was Blier mocking Godard's mockery, telling us by implication that the high-spirited 1960s had by now fallen into the dusty files of failure, the sorry ledger of all the failed revolutions of the past. *Going Places* implies further that the very idea of revolution is passé: all that is left is the moment, and the moment ought to be amusing. In *Breathless,* though the protagonist kills a policeman at the start, Godard dares to have him engage our sympathy, especially at the end when love leads him to death. In *Going Places* there is no attempt at sympathy for the criminal pair, and there is certainly no love.

Here are some other things that happen in *Going Places.* The two young men watch a young woman nurse her baby in an otherwise empty railroad car, then use that intimacy as a means to seduce her. They lure a sixteen-year-old girl away from her parents and initiate her into sex. They wait outside a women's prison for a released prisoner on the assumption that such a woman will be sex-starved; and thus it proves. But they don't exploit only women: when no woman is around, they utilize each other sexually.

There is more in the same greedy gratification tenor: indeed, almost everything in the film is of that tenor. But the references I've given are enough to fix the film's moral stance. It has none. *That* is its moral stance. Moral considerations of any kind, traditional or new, are treated as irrelevant, encumbering, ridiculous.

It's possible to say that *Breathless* is one of the last serious films that can be called modernist. Though its cinematic techniques—which I haven't discussed—were radical and its attitude toward social convention was daring, still it was true to certain old values of loyalty, of affection. *Going Places,* however, can be seen as one of the first postmodernist films; and postmodernism is a school on whose banner is inscribed absolutely nothing. Except perhaps skepticism. The whole point of the banner, to put it too simply but perhaps not untruthfully, is to decry the idea of banners.

In temporal perspective *Going Places* can be seen as one of the early eruptions into the film world of themes that had been gestating for two centuries. Lionel Trilling, who never saw *Going Places,* nonetheless hinted at its origins in the eighteenth century when he said of Rameau's nephew: "His thwarted passion for what society has to offer goes along with a scornful nihilism which overwhelms every prudential consideration." Irving Howe said that Rameau's nephew became, in the nineteenth century, the Underground Man:

> Here he assumes his most exalted guise. . . . He scrutinizes his motives with a kind of phenomenological venom, and then, as if to silence the moralists of both Christianity and humanism who might urge upon

him a therapeutic commitment to action, he enters a few relationships with other people, relationships that are commonplace yet utterly decisive in revealing the impossibility of escape from his poisoned self. In the twentieth century the underground man comes into his own. . . . Thus far, at least, it is his century.

In *Going Places* the up-to-the-minute Underground Man goes even further: he is less venomous than cheery. Diderot's and Dostoevsky's versions were men reactive to the insults and injuries of society and history. Blier's young men think it tedious to fret about those insults and injuries. Even more than for their recent forebears, this is their century. For they have a new and terrifying freedom—freedom from anger. Anger is an exponent of concern. Nothing, except interference with their pleasure, can make these young men angry. They float.

By now, something over twenty years later, *Going Places* is, morally speaking, unexceptional. In film after film—and I'm limiting my comments to films and plays—we have grown accustomed to protagonists who, though they may have loyalties within a group, have nothing that could be called overall moral direction.

This is a profound change. Cast a cool eye over theater history. To speak only of plays since the Renaissance, dramatist after dramatist plumbed moral depths but always gave us a reference point, a moral center in his work, possibly as reassurance but certainly as benchmark against which the depths could be measured. Jonson's *Volpone,* Etherege's *The Man of Mode,* Sheridan's *The School for Scandal* are only a few of the past works that are scathing about scummy behavior but that also present other possibilities. However, by the time we get well into this century, with some of the plays of, say, Edward Bond and Harold Pinter and Joe Orton and Sam Shepard, the idea of moral-reference characters verges on the risible.

This latter-day development argues that we have changed; that our age-old expectation of a link between art and moral reassurance is problematic. Now if we read a review telling us that a play or film is "life-affirming," we immediately suspect saccharine untruth. Marilynne Robinson wrote recently about "the general sense that we are suffering a radical moral decline which is destroying the fabric of society, seriously threatening our sense of safety as well as of mutual respect and shared interest." It seems to me indisputable that this sense is widely pervasive. Films that deny this sense make us wary. But—and this is my chief interest here—films that exploit that sense of moral decline create a curious double response in us.

First, there is escapism. Not the kind in which we flee our immediate world with some marvelous mate but one in which we stay close, more intensely, within our world and dive into strata of it that are outside our own patterns of behavior. It's a relief (to be candid about it) to relax once in a while, to wreak a limited vengeance on our ideas of order. An example from childhood. When we were children, our parents made us obey certain rules, keep certain hours, do our homework. How we envied those other children, down the street or across town, whose parents were more lax and let them wander. Now we can join those others. We, like them, can go to see *Pulp Fiction.*

Quentin Tarantino's film, almost devoid of moral qualm, is smoothly, humorously, cleverly made. So we don't have to feel that we're suspending cinematic standards while we watch it. We can sit in front of it for two hours, we people who have jobs and pay taxes and insurance premiums, and we can murder without tremor. Gangster films of the 1930s, no matter how gory, always ended with some sort of justice. But *Pulp Fiction*—and *Bad Company* and *Prizzi's Honor* and many, many more—invite us to kick off our moral shoes and relax, without any bow to eventual justice. A laudatory review of Tarantino's film in the *New York Review* ended: "Over and over again we were provoked into responding, but we didn't have to feel a thing." That comment is true, as far as it goes: it is true about the first effect of such films.

But there is a second effect. Let me begin comment about it with a reference to that insufficiently recognized philosopher of drama, Bert O. States. In his book *Irony and Drama,* States defines irony as "an unlimited capacity to negate, or oppose, ideas," and subsequently he talks about the new place that irony has taken in the drama of this century. Previously, he says, "from the Greeks through Shakespeare to Ibsen and beyond," drama thrived on "the character-driven plot." This mode is "no longer of much use" to the modern ironist. The character-driven plot "is replaced by what might be called the author-driven plot in which the author becomes the silent and invisible antagonist of his own fiction."

Tarantino is most certainly an ironist. He is thus, by States's declension, the antagonist of his own fiction. He cannot be called a mere exploiter:

his filmmaking is too good. Since he cannot rationally want the whole world to behave the way his characters do, he is an ironist. And since he puts no other kind of person in the film, he is its antagonist.

But, in my view, Bert States's proposition has expanded. Possibly because Marilynne Robinson's precept is valid, possibly because ultimately —even if not immediately—some desperate hope in us objects to the moral vacuity on the screen, we join Tarantino as antagonists to his picture. The author-driven plot becomes the author-viewer-driven plot. That reviewer of *Pulp Fiction* stopped too soon. She did have to feel something at the last. She felt different from the characters up there. However uncomfortable the phrase may be, she felt morally superior to Tarantino's characters, and she joined him in opposing them. Or she wouldn't have been able to write her review, even one in which she says she didn't have to feel anything.

So this second effect of the morally anarchic film is paradoxical. Bertrand Blier and Quentin Tarantino, just to pair those two out of many, know that we will not have committed murder on our way to the theater and that we will have paid for our tickets. They cannot, in any range of reason, hope that we will change the way we live for the way their people live. Consciously or not, they rely on us in a way that the morally sound film does not. They rely on us to function as antagonists. If the Good Guys have left the screen and only the Bad Guys are up there, there are still Good Guys in the theater, enlisted by Blier and Tarantino. The Good Guys are us.

Marcellino

FEBRUARY 3, 1997 | The obituaries for Marcello Mastroianni that I saw mentioned some of his roles (a few of those notices did *not* use the phrase "Latin lover"), and they noted admiringly, even affectionately, that he was one of the few foreign male stars to win international fame. But the obituaries omitted one rather relevant fact: he was a magnificent actor.

This omission was partly his own fault. Mastroianni disliked arty posturing; he liked to feed the press disparaging remarks about himself, just to puncture conventional hype. (The headline on *The New York Times* obit called him a "Self-Deprecating Charmer." Try to think of another important actor to whom that phrase could possibly apply.) He once told an interviewer that he'd had a dream in which all the producers of his films realized that they had been bamboozled and descended on him to get their money back; and he said, "Ha, ha! I've spent it all!" But his dislike of pretentiousness couldn't keep some of us from taking him as seriously as he must, privately, have taken his work—in more than 120 films.

I first saw him on stage, in Visconti's 1956 production of *Death of a Salesman,* in Rome. Mastroianni played Biff (pronounced Beef), and although there was a touch of marinara in this Brooklyn young man, he was outstanding. He had already done several theater roles for Visconti—"I discovered him," the director once boasted to me—in Shakespeare and Goldoni and Chekhov. The first time I saw Mastroianni on screen was in a comedy called *Too Bad She's Bad.* He is a hardworking Roman taxi driver who falls in love with Sophia Loren, discovers that she's the daughter of a professional thief, Vittorio De Sica, then sets out to reform her and her whole family. Delightful.

By then Mastroianni had become someone to watch. But more: the films that came along in those extraordinary years soon marked him as a phenomenon. When postwar Italy produced its great wave of scintillating film directors, it also produced an actor who could serve those directors with a wide range of Italian experience that evoked response throughout the world. In the course of his career Mastroianni also made films in Britain, America, Greece, Portugal, Brazil and France. But it was as an Italian that he shone.

Think of his range of characters: one of the birdbrained burglars in *Big Deal on Madonna Street;* the novelist at the existentialist bottom in *La Notte;* in *A Special Day* a harassed but courageous homosexual in Mussolini's Italy. In 1960 he became, one may say, Fellini's vicar in *La Dolce Vita,* continuing with *8½, City of Women, Ginger and Fred.* For De Sica he explored the rooster element of Italian maleness in *Yesterday, Today and Tomorrow* and *Marriage Italian Style.*

Some of the films in his life—more than some, actually, but who wants to be overly rigorous at a time like this?—he probably accepted just because he wanted to keep working and they were the best available scripts. But lately and gratefully I saw again one of his best, Monicelli's *The Organizer.* (The original title is better—*I Compagni. The Comrades.*) It's a story of labor struggles in Turin around 1900, centering on a textile factory. Workers' unrest is smoldering there because of the fourteen-hour day, with one half-hour break. Mastroianni tumbles off a freight train, a scruffy, bearded, itinerant socialist professor, who lost his teaching job because he is an agitator and now travels from one trouble spot to another. Comical as a scratcher and moocher, unshakable as a man committed to principles of justice, and quite conscious of both qualities, he brings the incipient workers' unrest to a blaze by organizing a strike.

In his key scene, he is informed belatedly, after thirty-one days of the strike, that the workers are weakening, are voting to call off the strike. He is in his long underwear when he learns of this meeting, throws on some clothes and grabs a bicycle to rush there and save the strike. (The comic element.) He arrives just in time to rally the workers—not only to continue the strike but to occupy the factory. (The evangelist element.) Anyone who has seen *The Organizer* will treasure the whole film, and Mastroianni's whole performance, but this scene in itself shatters the argument that first-rank acting, large in every way, is not possible on screen.

With actors who mean much to us over the years, a nearly personal bond develops. When someone told me—at a screening, aptly enough—that the news of Mastroianni's death had just been announced on the radio, I suddenly felt sad. Bereaved. I thought of him not in any of his roles, but in Fellini's *Intervista,* the autobiographical fantasy-documentary made in 1987 in which he and Mastroianni play around together, two old friends and collaborators, full of an admiration for each other that doesn't need to be spoken. Throughout their scenes Fellini calls him "Marcellino." Like many many others, I'm sure, I realized that, without knowing it, I had been calling him Marcellino for years.

In Memoriam

AUGUST 4, 1997 | In March 1934, when I was a drama student in New York, I went to see Sidney Howard's play *Yellow Jack.* Afterward I went backstage to meet a friend in the cast, an old actor, and we went to a bar next to the theater. Soon two younger members of the cast came in, one of whom was quite tall, and my friend introduced us. The taller man was

James Stewart. We all chatted for a while, then I moved to leave. Stewart reached out his long arm; and we shook hands and wished each other luck.

A Lost Love?

SEPTEMBER 8 & 15, 1997 | In 1966 I published an article called "The Film Generation," which was prompted by the then immense appetite for film in young people. In 1985 I published an article called "After the Film Generation," which was prompted by the dwindling of that appetite. I hazarded some reasons for the steep change in a relatively brief time: the thinning of the flow of excellent films that came from Europe and Japan in the 1960s and early 1970s; the effect of film courses, which, for non-specialists, now seemed to finish off their interest, just as literature courses so often do for non-specialists; the decline of university film societies from alertness to crowd-pleasing; and the rise of rock, of which I knew and know nothing but which had clearly attracted many of the intelligent young. In 1993 I reprinted that second article in a collection and noted that, eight years later, the condition had not brightened.

Recently, comment in this threnodic vein has increased, usually concentrating less on the quality of new films than on the dwindling appetite among young people. The most trenchant comment, predictably enough, came from Susan Sontag, who last year published an article in *The New York Times Magazine* called "The Decay of Cinema." (In fuller form, under the title "A Century of Cinema," this article appears in the "Movies" issue of *Parnassus*.) Sontag centers her elegy on what she calls cinephilia (more or less what I had called "appetite"): "if cinephilia is dead, then movies are dead, too." And other voices have joined the mourning chorus.

Disagreement followed, of course. For example: Laurence Goldstein and Ira Konigsberg have edited an anthology called *The Movies,* drawn from two special issues of the *Michigan Quarterly Review,* and they say in their introduction, "This book has been assembled in order to assert the opposite point of view" from Sontag's, to locate "dynamic forces certain to impel filmmakers and audiences alike toward a continuous series of satisfying encounters in the dark."

It's my own dilemma that, by now, I find weight in both views. Sontag's view is easy, terribly easy, to support. Film books, which once were prominent in bookshops, are now stuck in the back, and there are fewer of them. Bright university students, whose predecessors cared about the best films of the present and past, now don't even know that they haven't seen those films. Earlier in this decade I spent four years teaching the history of film to undergraduate film majors, most of whom had never heard of Ford or Bergman or Kurosawa, though some of them thought they had heard of Chaplin. Those majors, who knew all about lenses and tape transfers, resented having to watch silent films or sound films in black and white. And as for subtitles. . . .

Thus the cinephilia situation is worse than when I began lamenting it. All the reasons I offered still hold, and there is also, as I have heard from students, the eagerness of some film teachers to cater to students' predispositions or gender or ethnicity or whatever, rather than assuming that the purpose of education is to broaden.

There's another factor that is a heavy blow to cinephilia. The latter-day economics of the film world have greatly constricted film availability. In the past the best foreign films and the most adventurous American films admittedly never got the distribution of the Hollywood biggies, but now the situation is much worse, because costs are so much higher and distributors are even more reluctant to take chances on films of limited appeal. (This caution has worked backward to reduce drastically the number of foreign films imported every year.)

Too many times I write here about a film, domestic or foreign, that may not get adequate distribution in the United States. I must recognize, as best I can, the good work being done in film; anything else would be an offense to readers and to the art of film. (Otherwise the weekly *Variety* box office report could replace this column.) But it is wrong, culturally and morally wrong, that so many of the people who might respond to those films are going to have a tough time getting to see them. Tapes eventually help, but not always—and not in theaters. There's a difference.

The situation is inarguably dark. But is it black? I think not. First, much of what we read and see conveys that there are people in this country ready to respond to art (certain mole-like film students excepted). Some resident theaters report upturns in attendance. Museum attendance has long been prospering. Those aren't just numbers, those are people.

Second, the dire conditions noted above leave us with a large question. If film prospects are so cloudy, why do gifted people go on making films? Let's limit ourselves to American films, and let's omit the interesting films that come along occasionally from mainstream sources, and still we can cite — only since last August — such films as *Manny and Lo, Walking and Talking, Sling Blade, The Daytrippers, Chasing Amy, Traveller* and *In the Company of Men*. Except for *Sling Blade*, how many of those films reached or will reach anything like the number of people who could have responded to them? (And wouldn't this response, this confirmation that film is accomplishing beauty and relevance, have done a good deal to resuscitate cinephilia?)

The people who made those films knew very well the conditions they were facing. Why did they proceed anyway? Well, in a sense, they were stuck. Stuck with filmmaking talent. Like composers who write symphonies and operas despite the conditions of the musical world, these filmmakers knew that not to make films is a species of suicide. What these people and their colleagues here and abroad are hoping for is the closing of the gap — between their work and the public for whom they have done it.

Can that gap be closed? Without being overly roseate, we have a right to hope so. First, we can at least acknowledge that the gap exists, which means, primarily, recognizing that good films are being made here and abroad (even though the cornucopia of foreign films no longer overflows). The trouble is not that modern filmmaking is arid. The good work arrives and, in reasonable measure, keeps arriving. But where does it go? "Only connect!" said E. M. Forster. We might purloin the phrase for the film world's banner.

Two suggestions. Universities have some responsibility and opportunity here, and I don't just mean film departments, though they could lead. Administration and faculty people could do much to see that students get, through film series, enlightenment about current and past film equivalent to programs about other arts and world affairs. Second, film theaters around the country, in college towns and elsewhere, have a chance to help and perhaps even profit. Whatever happened to special weekend midnight showings?

Optimism is possibly too grandiose a term to use here. Persistence isn't.

Notes on a Visit

FEBRUARY 16, 1998 | Recurrently the film world is assayed by an outsider—a "let me set your house in order" visit from an eminence in another field, usually an historian or sociologist or literary light. The latest example is an article called "Clio at the Multiplex" by Simon Schama in the January 19, 1998 *New Yorker,* in which, beginning with *Amistad,* he presents what he sees as vulgarizations, lapses, and achievements in some historical films.

Schama, whose brilliance as an historian needs no endorsement here, follows form: he presents his bona fides the way visitors often do, by mentioning a number of films he has seen, together with his enthusiasm for some of them. He concludes: "The most enduring historians have always valued the necessary alliance between picturemaking and argument." This has certainly been proved in such books as his own rich *Landscape and Memory* and Martin Meisel's superb *Realizations* (which studies relationships between narrative, pictorial, and theatrical arts in nineteenth-century England). No conceivable dissent on that conclusion. It is some of Schama's suggestions en route, for the improvement of *Amistad,* that provoke discussion.

He objects to the closing speech that Steven Spielberg gives to John Quincy Adams before the Supreme Court, with its "ringing appeal to ancestor worship." Schama's ground is that "the case turned neither on the morality nor on the legality of slavery in America, but on the slave *trade* on the high seas." Technically this is true, but it ignores the massive subtext of the film. The real antagonist in this drama—one might almost say protagonist—is the United States of America. *Twice* the lower courts had decided in favor of the Africans' freedom, and *twice* the government of this country persisted in trying to keep them in slavery. Adams's appeal to the Supreme Court to remember the founding principles of the United States, despite the slaveholders among those Founding Fathers, may not be historically exact, but it is dramatically and thematically apt.

Then, says Schama, there is "an opportunity that Spielberg passes up." Spielberg omitted the fact that one of the Supreme Court justices died in his sleep before Adams had finished his address to the Court, which in actuality stretched over two days. (The justice died during the intervening night.) What, really, was this opportunity that Spielberg passed up? The chance to splay the narrowing focus that he wanted as the film approached its climax by spreading the Supreme Court hearing over two days, in order to include a historical datum of absolutely no relevance to that climax.

And, according to Schama, that wasn't Spielberg's only omission. "At the climax of the true Amistad history, Spielberg missed, somehow, an astounding story that ought to have been a director's dream." What is this dream story? A few days before the Supreme Court hearing, Adams was descending from his carriage near the Capitol when his horses were startled by the testing of a Colt rifle nearby. The coachman was hurt by the horses and died of his injuries the next day. "For the devoutly religious statesman," says Schama, "there could have been no more shocking witness that Providence was watching over the unfolding drama."

I have pondered that sentence considerably and am still unable to understand why the death of that coachman assured Adams that Providence had an eye out for the fate of those Africans. It may be, as Schama says, that this confluence of "Colts, carriage horses, and Calvinism" is "the kind of historical collision undreamed of in scriptwriters' fiction," but it's easy to see why they dream otherwise—when the historical collision has no dramatic relevance to the story and is no kind of textural increment.

All these criticisms by Schama seem to fall into one of two categories: either they reveal a questionable sense of dramatic/cinematic structure, or they are meant to display reaches of historical scholarship beyond that of Spielberg and his colleagues. Or, of course, they may fit both categories.

What disturbs further—and, admittedly, this goes deeper into the area of subjective response—are some of Schama's admirations. He holds up Scorsese's *Kundun* as a counterexample to *Amistad,* calls it an "undersung masterpiece" among historical films, and says that "Scorsese has invented a disconcerting visual language that flows naturally from his subject and does the necessary work of shaking the audience loose from habitual expectations of what a history movie is." I'm a longtime admirer of Scorsese, not least of the film about a spiritual leader that he made before *Kundun. The Last Temptation of Christ* seemed to me to do a great deal more "shaking the audience loose from habitual expectations" than *Kundun,* and not just because Jesus was more active in the world than the Dalai Lama. *The Last*

Temptation was a true Scorsese film: this vigorous, individualistic director presented *his* Christ just as innumerable painters and sculptors have presented theirs. *Kundun,* on the other hand, is nervously bland, a series of respectful episodes. Schama finds in it elements of Satyajit Ray and Olivier and *Gone With the Wind.* Perhaps; but this in itself proves little more than, say, finding reminders of Max Ophuls (which one can do) in a recent Dutch blob called *The Dress.* For me, to exalt *Kundun* as a prime instance of historical filmmaking is to cede the field to *National Geographic.*

To be sure, Schama names other films, all made outside Hollywood, that are indeed "powerful history movies, created in the poetic, not the instructional mode"—works by Visconti and Jancsó and Rossellini and Tarkovsky and Herzog and, most acutely, Yves Angelo's *Colonel Chabert.* But then Schama clouds matters again by equating the quietly fierce filmmaking vision in Angelo's film with the style of *Kundun.* As it happens, I recently saw *Colonel Chabert* again and am left aghast at this equation with Scorsese's picture.

I had better say I'm not trying here to assert that only a professional film critic has the right to express opinions about film. Such arrogance would be bootless, anyway. So many people are affected by film that these visitors to film criticism, basically, prove a cultural phenomenon. Early in this century it was a standing joke that everyone had two professions, his own and theater criticism. The change in the second profession corroborates a fact: film is one of the few universal cultural linkages that the human race currently possesses.

I am merely pointing out that, when a person of large reputation in another field decides to pay a little attention to the film world in order to set it right, it is not obligatory to be humbled by the honor of his or her attention; it is not obligatory to be awed by a judge whose opinions must be considered sounder than ones we're used to because they come from outside the moiling world of film.

Kurosawa

OCTOBER 26, 1998 | In 1981 I had the honor to introduce Akira Kurosawa at a press luncheon given by Japan House in New York. I remember saying that my job seemed superfluous, introducing that man to that audience, but that I was happy to have the privilege of doing it anyway. Now, with this comment following Kurosawa's death, I feel somewhat the same: he is known, esteemed, mourned. Still, I'm glad to have the privilege of saying a few words about him.

He was born in 1910, and after some training and work as a painter, at the age of 26 he answered an ad by a film studio looking for assistant directors. He had to submit an essay discussing what was wrong with Japanese films. After a few months he was called for a second round of testing—scenario writing, an oral exam, and more. The details are in his autobiography; but what strikes an outsider is that a newcomer's entry into Japanese film life, at least in those days, was organized and systematic. He was hired and was assigned to assist an experienced director, Kajiro Yamamoto, who soon recognized the younger man's qualities and did much to teach and advance him in their years of collaboration.

Kurosawa made his first film in 1943, when he was 33. *Sanshiro Sugata*, though much concerned with the judo tradition, was clearly the work of an individual talent. The career broadened as it moved. Japanese elements—kabuki, noh, samurai, postwar Japanese problems—are strong throughout; but he is known, rightly so, as one of the most Western of Japanese directors. He drew on Shakespeare (*Throne of Blood, Ran*), Dostoyevsky (*The Idiot*), Gorky (*The Lower Depths*), not to mention Ed McBain (*High and Low*) and the influence of Simenon (*Stray Dog*). His directorial style reflects his admiration of Eisenstein and Ford.

Yet those facts, though certainly relevant, don't convey the shape, the quality of his career. Like other giants in film history, Kurosawa seemed to grasp these contributory elements along with the core of this (relatively) new art and shape them all to his needs, his discoveries, his troublings. To see a retrospective of his work, which I have done twice nearly completely, from the beginnings through *Drunken Angel* and *Rashomon* and *Ikiru* and *The Seven Samurai* to *Red Beard* and *Kagemusha* and *Ran,* is to see that, like every genius, he invented his art. Of course his work can be analyzed, and analysis can enlighten, but it can't finally explain the result of the coalescence of all those elements, the transmutation that made him unique, imperial. Mozart dedicated six quartets to Haydn, from whom he learned, but what he learned was more about being Mozart.

Fundamentally, most importantly, as with all great artists in every art, there is a sense of hugeness in Kurosawa. Whether he is creating the saga of seven sixteenth-century samurai on the cusp of a different Japan or accompanying a mortally ill civil servant in modern Tokyo, the inner dimensions are immense. This is the world's great egalitarianism: the secrets in every human being, perceived by true art, are immense, spatial.

To remember Kurosawa is to remember that sense of aperture, of exaltation. It is to remember the dying civil servant in *Ikiru,* sitting on a swing in the playground that is the only real achievement of his drab life, singing in the gently falling snow. In that simple image is absolutely everything.

Books

To begin, the pollination of poetry by film, an insufficiently noted loveliness. Then, some lives. Inevitably, if we are taken by artists, we want
to know more about them than the works themselves can provide. This
impulse is often questioned; at least two answers are possible. First, we
want to know about the ways in which these artists are like us, the qualities they share with us — in short, the gossip. Second, we want to know
about their differences from us. It is not that we expect talent (the inexplicable) to be explained. But the fulfillment of talent is, in our society,
always a tale of at least some heroism. Good luck usually figures, but
good luck is happenstance. Determination, which is will, cheers us.

The Faber Book of Movie Verse*

APRIL 11, 1994 | Much is written about the ways that film has contributed to the shaping and subject matter of fiction, but there is little about the ways that film has touched poetry. This is strange for at least two reasons. First, film has been the subject of a notable amount of poetry and has been a wellspring of metaphor for poems that have nothing directly to do with film. Second, poets were among the first to respond to film with serious criticism. The first American book of film aesthetics was *The Art of the Moving Picture* by Vachel Lindsay, published in 1915 (republished in 1970 with an introduction by yours truly). Lindsay subsequently wrote some film criticism for *The New Republic*. Others who wrote film criticism back then were William Ellery Leonard, H. D. and Carl Sandburg.

The impact of film on poets has long needed celebration, and at last it has been provided by the poets themselves—through the agency of Philip French and Ken Wlaschin. They have edited *The Faber Book of Movie Verse* and were aptly qualified to do so. French is the long-term film critic of the (London) *Observer* and the author of several film books and literary studies; Wlaschin ran the London Film Festival for fifteen years, now does similar work for the American Film Institute and has published poetry and novels. French has provided the book's informative introduction and the notes on film facts for the poems that can use this help.

Together French and Wlaschin offer a testament of poets to their bewitchment by film from its first days—even earlier than that. (The first poem is by Austin Dobson, b. 1840, whose "The Toyman" is about the thaumatrope, a persistence-of-vision device that preceded film.) The book contains 340 poems by 227 English-language poets, an important qualification because it's reasonable to infer that a significant number of poets in other languages have responded comparably.

---

*Published by Faber and Faber.

The editors have divided their anthology into eight sections "organized on a partly chronological and partly thematic basis" and worth noting in themselves: The Silent Cinema, Hollywood, Movie Houses and Movie-going, The Stars and the Supporting Cast, Behind the Camera, Films and Genres, Movies as Metaphors, TV, and The Afterlife of Movies. I began by looking for some favorites, and they are all present: Hart Crane's "Chaplinesque," the earliest beautiful poem I know that was inspired by film, Randall Jarrell's marvelous ramble through memory, "The Lost World," Robert Frost's wry and cautionary "Provide, Provide."

But how many there are—by well-known poets—that I had either forgotten or never read. Vernon Watkins's "Elegy" in memory of Pearl White. Jean Garrigue's "Movie Actors Scribbling Letters Very Fast in Crucial Scenes." Roy Fuller on Leni Riefenstahl's *Olympiad* ("No art can hide the shocking gulfs that gape / Even between such bodies and their world"). Robert Lowell's unusually light "Harpo Marx" ("your hands white-feathered the harp"). Richard Wilbur's even lighter "The Prisoner of Zenda," about the 1952 version with Stewart Granger as the dashing impostor, Rudolph Rassendyll:

> One redeeming factor,
> However, is that the actor
> Who plays the once-dissolute King
> (Who has learned through suffering
> Not to drink or be mean
> To his future Queen),
> Far from being a stranger,
> Is *also* Stewart Granger.

A few cavils about the better-known poets. Why include Lowell's "Scar-Face" and Wilbur's "Beasts," which have no demonstrable connection with film? And why Stephen Spender's decrepit "The Truly Great," just because Spender said elsewhere that the closing images were drawn from Eisenstein?

But especial thanks to the editors for unearthing lovely poems by less-known people. A few examples. Michael McFee's "Buster Keaton":

> Into the frenzy of falling bodies
> and chaos of pastry, apollonian

and sober even as an infant,
he came, just as decades later
he would calmly step into a frame
and never leave.

Edwin Morgan's "Five Poems on Film Directors"—Antonioni, Grierson, Warhol, Kurosawa, Godard—each of which epitomizes a cinema style in prosody. Israel Halpern's poignantly symbolic "Lead Star Lovers" ("We met on the cutting room floor / Examining one / Another's rushes"). Al Young's chuckly "W. H. Auden & Mantan Moreland," which arose from the fact that the poet and the black comedian died on the same day. They meet in paradise and exchange dictions.

Not surprisingly, there is something more than a sprinkling of poems about war films. They range in time and point of view. Teresa Hooley, in "A War Film," sees the Mons Retreat of World War I in a newsreel "as in a dream," but an unforgettable one. Decades later, Lucien Stryk, a World War II veteran, reveals in "Watching War Movies" how his experience altered the course of his life. By now, film has become in some degree an artifact of war, and in some degree the reverse is also true.

The closing poem, more than fittingly, is Mona Van Duyn's "Endings," which begins with "setting the VCR when we go to bed / to record a night owl movie." Next evening "we" watch; apparently her companion gets impatient with it, but the poet insists on seeing it all:

For what is story if not relief from the pain
of the inconclusive, from dread of the meaningless?
. . . . I'll follow, past each universe in its spangled
ballgown who waits for the slow-dance of life to start,
past vacancies of darkness whose vainglory
is endless as death's, to find the end of the story.

Stipulate that the French-Wlaschin selections vary in quality—a bit more widely than we normally expect in anthologies. Nonetheless, this book goes on the shelf next to Geoffrey O'Brien's *The Phantom Empire* with the same gratitude for an affirmation: not all poetic responses start in Yeats's "foul rag-and-bone shop of the heart." Some of them start at the movies.

MAY 1, 1995 | Books by film directors are plentiful. They come in several types: autobiographies (Buñuel, Powell, Renoir and—preeminently —Bergman's *The Magic Lantern*); theoretical-philosophical work (Eisenstein, Pudovkin, Bresson); and books "by" the director that are really book-length interviews with him (preeminently *Bergman on Bergman*). Now Sidney Lumet has added to this library a fine professional autobiography. There's little of his personal life in it except as it connects with his films.

Making Movies is full of energy, enthusiasm and wisdom wrung from experience. As Lumet promises at the outset, there are no scandals or exposés; and as can be seen fairly soon, there isn't much that is truly new about the techniques and problems of filmmaking. But what is here is his own in the sense that he has won it with struggle and aspiration.

Sensibly, helpfully, Lumet divides his book into chapters that treat the various aspects of his job topic by topic: "The Director," "Style," "Actors," "The Camera" and so on—thirteen in all. In each chapter he draws instances from his films to illustrate. Each chapter tells us some familiar things and some fresh things, but it's all engrossing because he speaks so fervently and opinionatedly about matters on which he has earned the right to opinions. Besides, his writing is swift and clear. I had the surreal sensation of gobbling up the book.

In the camera chapter, for instance, he cites examples from his films of how he chose the cinematographer and visual approach best suited to the material and theme. (Theme, which underlies the material, is very important to him.) In the chapter on style, a tricky and touchy subject, he takes a few swipes at critics who pronounce on the matter without much knowledge of the specific problems of the picture.

Deserved swipes, probably. But one response is possible. Lumet refers to those who say they can always recognize a style and give Matisse as an instance: "Of course you can [recognize a Matisse]. It's the work of one person *working alone!*" But isn't a film director ultimately working alone? "There are no minor decisions in moviemaking," he says. Aren't those decisions—the artistic ones, anyway—usually made by the direc-

* Published by Alfred A. Knopf.

tor? Doesn't the profile of those decisions, added to his own work, result in a style?

In case any of us still have doubts about the complexity of filmmaking, here is the first paragraph of Chapter 7, "Shooting the Movie," which arrives after a lot of other points have been discussed:

> Sets, clothes, camera concept, script, casting, rehearsals, schedule, financing, cash flow, insurance examinations, locations, cover sets (interiors that we shoot if the weather is wrong for exterior shooting), hair, makeup, tests, composer, editor, sound editor have all been decided. Now we're shooting the movie, at last.

And that list is incomplete. Some of the items he mentions elsewhere are trucking and catering. And out of this quasi-controlled maelstrom, we expect works of art. What's amazing is that we occasionally get them.

The chapter that struck me particularly is the one on actors, in which he describes his rehearsals. He rehearses for two weeks before they begin shooting, which is by no means customary even among directors with big enough budgets to afford it. Lumet, born in 1924, began in the theater. Both his parents were actors in the Yiddish theater, and he himself made his first appearance there at age five. Twice he played the boy Jesus (in English): in *The Eternal Road* when he was thirteen and three years later in Maxwell Anderson's *Journey to Jerusalem*.

Out of this background has grown both his high regard for actors and his high reputation among them. Performances are usually good in his films even when the picture as a whole falters. (Armand Assante in *Q & A*, Rebecca De Mornay in *Guilty as Sin*.) He always rehearses the script in sequence. "This is because movies are never shot in sequence. . . . Rehearsing in sequence gives the actors the sense of continuity, the 'arc' of their characters, so they know exactly where they are when shooting begins, regardless of the shooting order." This is so sensible that it ought to be obvious, but, for many directors, it isn't.

Like most (though not all) directors, Lumet has improved with age. His earliest films, from *Twelve Angry Men* through *Long Day's Journey into Night,* seemed to me the work of a man who (in 1957) had come from theater and TV and felt compelled to prove that he understood cinematic possibilities. But inevitably, for a serious and gifted person, experience produces confidence, which produces simplicity. Which meant, for Lumet, the skilled and prudent use of those possibilities. *Murder on the Orient Express, Dog Day Afternoon* and above all, *The Verdict,* are film-directing at its best this side of genius.

And now he has written an amiable, fascinating book.

*Wilder Times: The Life of Billy Wilder**

JULY 1, 1996 | In Filmland's army of public personalities, the front rank is made up of actors, past and present. Then there is a second rank, smaller yet vivid: directors. Among those "public" directors, to speak only of Americans, are Cecil B. De Mille (the no-frills tycoon proving that down-to-earth businessmen could direct), John Ford (the taciturn saloon pal obliquely admitting to artistry), and John Huston (the loquacious, elegant, man-of-the-world artist). And there's Billy Wilder.

One of the assets of Kevin Lally's biography is that he appreciates Wilder as a public character. Lally is the managing editor of *Film Journal International,* and his book has the tone of an extended magazine article, pleasant journeyman prose dispensing manifold facts. Extraordinary perception is not Lally's hallmark, but he does have enthusiasm and ease — and an eye for the Wilder persona. Lally is especially attentive to the formation of that persona as his book travels the long, long Wilder way. (June 22 is the director's ninetieth birthday.)

He was born Samuel Wilder to a Jewish family in Galicia, now a part of Poland that was then part of the Austro-Hungarian Empire. His mother, who had spent some time in America and had been memorably struck by a Buffalo Bill show, called her son Billie. (Later he changed the spelling.) Thus, from the start, Wilder was in a sense cross-pollinated with a second culture. When he was four, the family moved to Vienna — the father was a hotelier — and when he was ten he watched the funeral procession of the Emperor Franz Josef, a fact that reminds us yet again how short and how long a century is.

At eighteen Wilder left school and became a journalist, specializing in interviews. Vienna teemed with glittering people, politicians, artists and,

*Published by Henry Holt.

in the cradle of that science, psychoanalysts. Alfred Adler spoke to him at length. Sigmund Freud showed him the door.

Before he was twenty, Berlin called—the hub of Germanic culture. There he winkled out different jobs, including journalism again and some ballroom dancing for hire; and he soon entered the busy Berlin film world by a back door, ghostwriting for scenarists who were stuck for ideas. Then he and some other young men, Fred Zinnemann among them, scraped and hustled to make a film of their own, *People on Sunday* (1930). This friendly yet wry look at Berlin's Sunday diversions attracted attention—it's still worth seeing—and it lifted Wilder into the corps of professional screenwriters. Mostly he worked on comedies, and they brought him a sporty car, luxe quarters and attractive girlfriends. The adjectives could be redistributed.

Came Hitler. Went Wilder, the day after the Reichstag fire. The first stop was Paris—he knew French—where he cowrote and codirected a film, with the seventeen-year-old Danielle Darrieux in the cast. Through a friend who had preceded him to Hollywood, he was offered a writing contract with Columbia Pictures, although he had almost no English. Lally quotes him: "My dream all along was to get to Hollywood, which would have happened even without Hitler." In January 1934, he sailed for America.

His initial screenplay proposal was turned down. "It did not work anyway," says Wilder, "even if it had been in perfect English." His job ended; hard times, really hard, arrived. In one of the more familiar Wilder stories, he shared a room in Hollywood with Peter Lorre, and they also shared a daily can of soup, while English was being learned. Then, through the friend who had brought him to Hollywood, Wilder was hired to collaborate on the script of a musical, *Music in the Air*. It starred an actress he would encounter again, Gloria Swanson. Fortune began to smile, then grinned. Jobs bubbled up; along with his increasingly patent gifts, he acquired a well-earned reputation as a furiously hard worker. To him, working on a script meant total immersion, day and most nights. Always he collaborated. He says he did it because he was weak in the new language, but he had almost always worked with collaborators in Europe. We can assume that to him film writing meant a dialogic process, even when dialogue wasn't being volleyed back and forth in verbal tennis. He liked to have a partner even when depressing stretches of silence were being weathered.

In 1938 he joined up with Charles Brackett, who was fourteen years older and markedly different in background. Brackett was a Harvard law graduate who had been a theater critic for *The New Yorker* and had written novels that brought him west. The odd couple fared fabulously. They wrote, among other films, two adaptations from European sources for the director who had long been Wilder's idol, the light-fingered Ernst Lubitsch, also out of Berlin, who had been brought to Hollywood in 1922 on a red carpet and was now monarch of the comic-romantic field. Their two jobs for Lubitsch, *Bluebeard's Eighth Wife* and *Ninotchka,* sent the Wilder-Brackett stock soaring.

In 1942 Wilder was permitted to direct a Wilder-Brackett screenplay, *The Major and the Minor.* The story was built on a motif that became a Wilder fingerprint: masquerade. Ginger Rogers, for plot reasons, has to travel on a half-fare railroad ticket, posing as a twelve-year-old. Male complications ensue. Owing to the film's saucy tenor, Wilder began to be seen as a persona—an adroit Continental, possibly a successor to Lubitsch himself.

Much of Wilder's subsequent career contradicted this boulevardier image. He often made dark, even grim pictures. (So had Lubitsch, especially in Germany.) Wilder's very next film was *Five Graves to Cairo,* about the North African campaign in World War Two, with Erich von Stroheim as General Rommel. (Stroheim had long sold himself in America as an Austrian ex-officer of lofty lineage, but Wilder recognized the way he spoke German—the accent of the "rougher suburbs" of Vienna. Apparently Wilder said nothing about this real-life masquerade. Professional courtesy?)

Then came *Double Indemnity,* adapted from James M. Cain. His collaborator, for this film only, was Raymond Chandler, who later said that working with Wilder "was an agonizing experience and has probably shortened my life, but I learned from it as much about screenwriting as I am capable of learning." The Wilder intensity again. Further down the list of shadowy films came *Sunset Boulevard,* for which Wilder tried to engage Pola Negri before he approached Gloria Swanson. (Negri had starred for Lubitsch in Berlin.) Others on this darker list were *The Lost Weekend,* the trajectory of an alcoholic; *Ace in the Hole,* about the crass exploitation of a disaster; a courtroom drama called *Witness for the Prosecution;* and *Fedora,* about a famous woman's buried secrets.

These dark films often had non-Hollywood flavor, even some of those drawn from American sources. Instance: *The Lost Weekend* came from an American novel, yet, as Lally says, the camera work shows more German expressionist influence than any other Wilder picture. Still, it was chiefly the comedies that nourished Wilder's growing *flâneur* image. (And, unlike any other director, sparks of Wilder's personal wit found their way to the public and amplified the figure of the suave European. About an actor in one of his films who had to sing a song, Wilder said that he had "the musical ear of Van Gogh.")

Wilder parted from Brackett in 1950. After five pictures with other partners, he joined up with I. A. L. Diamond, who was fourteen years younger and the foreign-born son of immigrants from Romania. This team, with one exception, wrote every Wilder picture thereafter, most of them based on European sources. Walter Matthau, who was in several of the later Wilder films, said that Wilder insisted on fidelity to the script. "Actually he was a director because he wanted to protect his writing." The remark doesn't do justice to Wilder's directorial polish; but Wilder did insist that the Wilder-Diamond dialogue be followed exactly as written. No free-hand riffs.

The Continental patina became inseparable from Wilder, not only because so many of his story sources were European, but also because so many of the films dealt with American values thumping against European values. (*The Emperor Waltz* put Bing Crosby at the court of Franz Josef.) And Wilder often used European colleagues. As his art director he frequently engaged Alexander Trauner, born in Budapest (not Vienna, as Lally says) and based in Paris, whose awesome career included *Les Enfants du Paradis, Hôtel du Nord* and *Le Jour se Lève*. The scores of many Wilder films were composed by Miklos Rozsa, also born in Budapest; several were written by Frederick Hollander, born Friedrich Holländer, who had written Marlene Dietrich's songs in *The Blue Angel*.

Wilder, enthusiastically American, clearly needed the support, perhaps the comfort, of European stimuli. His work became an analogue of himself: born abroad, flowering in Hollywood, and eager to make both elements apparent. In this he differed from his revered Lubitsch, whose Hollywood screenplays hold few American ingredients. Lubitsch remained a (very welcome) visitor. Possibly the difference between the two men rose from the fact that Wilder, unlike the early-arrived Lubitsch, was a Hitler refugee and began his American life in a nimbus of grateful wonder.

I've recently seen five Wilder films again, and, together with fairly clear memories of many other Wilder pictures, they point to some conclusions. First, he is enamored of two recurrent themes: masquerade, as noted, and the protagonist who is either a worm that turns or an antihero who alters. Some have seen these themes as psychological hints about Wilder himself. Allowing for the fact that such choices carry implications, I would view them more as congenial professional tools than as Rorschach tests of the Wilder psyche.

Other matters emerge. The performances by children are dreadful (Fred MacMurray's kids in *The Apartment,* James Cagney's in *One, Two, Three*). Wilder seems impatient to get the kids' stuff over and done with. Then there are the Jewish characters, two in *Some Like It Hot,* three in *The Apartment.* They are all played hammily, almost as caricatures. Possibly there was no connection here with Lubitsch in Wilder's mind, but those Jews made me think of the caricature Jew that Lubitsch wrote and himself played in the early films of his Berlin days.

One happier Lubitsch reminder is the so-called "touch" for which he was celebrated. Theodore Huff defined it as a "swift innuendo or rapier-like 'comment' accomplished pictorially by a brief camera-shot or telling action, to convey an idea or suggestion in a manner impossible in words." Two such "touches" in Wilder are a bit with Las Vegas waiters in *Kiss Me, Stupid* and a bit with football team employees in *The Fortune Cookie.* The very fact that it would take a long paragraph to explain each "touch" is a tribute to what is condensed there.

Fusing away culturally, Wilder often uses a device that I think of as American, the double take—the glance at something or the hearing of something that doesn't register immediately. The person proceeds, then is hit by a large belated reaction. Examples: Jack Lemmon's discovery of Shirley MacLaine in his bed in *The Apartment;* in *One, Two, Three,* Cagney's learning that his ward is married.

Wilder, to whom film is a habitat, likes intrafilmic references, which are tickling if they are picked up, harmless if they are not. In *Some Like It Hot,* George Raft gibes at a gangster for the same coin-flicking trick that he himself used in *Scarface,* and the actor he taunts is the son of Edward G.

Robinson, famed for his own gangster roles. Cagney has two film quotes in *One, Two, Three:* when he thinks his hash is settled, he says, "Is this the end of Rico?" (Little Caesar's last line), and he reprises his own grapefruit bit from *The Public Enemy.*

Precision is such a passion of Wilder's that it's especially shocking to note some poor performances in his films. In the five recently re-seen, some of the acting is better than I remembered. Shirley MacLaine's elevator operator in *The Apartment* encloses an authentic person in its quietness. In *One, Two, Three,* Arlene Francis's harried yet cool wife is buoyed up by years of Broadway know-how. As her husband, however, the usually excellent Cagney is blatantly under the director's orders to keep the farce fast. Cagney's best acting always seemed based on a private rhythm in his head: his roles seemed danced. He never quite found the rhythm for this part. And in *Kiss Me, Stupid,* four of the five principals, Dean Martin, Kim Novak, Cliff Osmond, and Ray Walston, are painfully bad. Wilder says he knew early on that this film was a disaster, but a director of his skill could have done something more even with those wretched people.

Still, that film and *The Apartment* and *One, Two, Three* might have misfired in any case because the European-American fusion falters. (Wilder and Diamond set the Cagney picture, taken from Molnar, in Berlin, but its principals and its nature are American.) Names and places and jobs are easy to change, but mental creases are harder to iron out. *Kiss Me, Stupid* was taken from an Italian play, in which a husband uses his wife as bait for a business venture. I dare say that such a maneuver has happened sometime, somewhere, in the USA, but Wilder's characters just don't fit the plot. It's as if the characters themselves were playing roles in a local production of a European play.

Yet—resoundingly—much of the time the transatlantic fusion succeeds. *A Foreign Affair,* set in the postwar ruins of Berlin, confronts that fusion directly. Marlene Dietrich is a German survivor who now must survive the American occupiers. Poignantly, the picture blends the temper of an old culture, weary of its weariness, and a newer, brighter culture, deservedly triumphant yet wearing its triumph in a slightly *nouveau riche* way. If the viewer happens to know that Wilder's mother and grandmother and stepfather were incinerated at Auschwitz, it gives the film a steep dimension. But even those who don't know those chilling facts can still sense the basic daring: the exiled Wilder returning to the blasted city in which he once gamboled, insisting that no culture is monochrome and that, if life goes on at all, it is, among other things, funny.

In Wilder's masterpiece, *Some Like It Hot,* a film that will last as long as the medium lasts, the bicultural fusion is perfect. Wilder and Diamond found their premise in a German film of the 1930s, which they jettisoned completely except for that premise: two male musicians forced to masquerade as women in order to join an all-female band. Wilder and Diamond "Americanized" the film perfectly through the device that compels the men to masquerade. Accidentally the musicians witness the St. Valentine's Day massacre in Chicago in 1929; the killers want to rub them out, so, in order to flee, the two men dress in drag and go with the band to Florida.

To me, it's a masterpiece for a primal reason: not for its bicultural fusion or its slice of American social history, valid though those reasons are — or for the psycho-sexual implications that have been found in the cross-dressing — but simply because every time I see it (certainly twenty times by now) I laugh. It also has considerable pathos, which also always affects me, but it is unfailingly comic. What more is true of, say, *Lysistrata?* When we scrutinize the picture's comic perfection, we discern the technical mastery that creates its comic power. The structure, the dialogue, the timing are immaculate. The performances shine: Jack Lemmon and Tony Curtis were never better, before or after. And the crown of the film is the small miracle that Wilder wrought with Marilyn Monroe.

She had worked for Wilder once before, in *The Seven Year Itch,* where she had been little more than an ambulatory pin-up. Here Wilder and Diamond accomplished something more complex and interesting: a self-portrait. They used Monroe herself as the matrix of her role. Twelve years after the film's release, I wrote a long article about it and queried Wilder for some particulars, all of which he supplied cheerily. Then I asked whether he and Diamond had been thinking of Monroe for the singer right from the start. This time he seemed to be replying through his teeth: "We didn't think of Marilyn Monroe when we started plotting *Some Like It Hot* — about halfway through we signed her and went back to fit her unique requirements as always."

The trouble that Monroe made during the shooting is notorious, but Wilder and Diamond did more than meet her requirements, and Wilder, as director, did even more. They found in Monroe herself the sex and pathos and ditsy comedy. This self-portrait, perhaps unknown to Monroe, makes it her only appearance that is a complete performance, and seals the American perfection of the picture.

Wilder's last film, *Buddy Buddy* (1981), was adapted by him and Diamond from a French comedy. Lally says truly: "The main problem with *Buddy Buddy* is that it just isn't very funny." It feels as if Wilder was now relying on bicultural fusion, rather than relishing it. Well, all careers undulate; and with the more notable ones, a character usually emerges through the ups and downs. So with Wilder. Possibly the most salient aspect of his character is a paradox. Embracing Hollywood, in itself and as an epitome of America, he nonetheless wanted his films to contradict it, at least partly. He wanted to create an atmosphere of deft European theater and film in his pictures, almost of cabaret wit. Ensconced in a huge heterogeneous country, smack in the middle of a mass art, he wanted to make films for an audience as homogeneous as he dared to imagine it.

Yes, he often said that he wanted to make pictures for the mass public, but he often wants also to beguile that audience into a new concept of itself. He wants it to think of itself as people who know one another and can exchange winks. Even when he is deepest in America, whether the film is shadowy or bright, we seem to hear Wilder saying, "Listen, I have a little story to tell you, let's sit down in this café."

David Lean *

OCTOBER 14, 1996 | David Lean began life as a dunce. His kindergarten teacher told his mother that she was afraid he would never be able to read and write. He managed to disprove that prediction, but otherwise there was little sparkle. He munched through schooling, entered his father's accounting firm at the age of nineteen, in 1927, and quickly showed no aptitude for the work.

The most striking thing that had happened to him so far was his discovery of film. His Quaker family had forbidden the cinema, but at thirteen, with his mother's connivance, he began to go, to respond. Still, the move toward working in films didn't originate with him. An aunt visited

* Published by St. Martin's Press.

the Lean home in the dull London suburb of Croydon after he had begun accounting, saw all the film magazines now openly on view, and suggested the film field for him. Lean père, possibly not unwilling to get David out of his office, gave him an introduction to accountants at the Gaumont studio. So in 1928 the son became a runner-and-teaboy at Gaumont, unpaid. Before very long they paid him ten shillings a week.

The raise was the least of it. Lean had found his habitat. In the earlier years of this century, something magical happened to some men. The arrival of the film, its invention and proliferation, transformed them. Many of the early directors came from one kind of artistic background or another, but some of them had no such background or ambition. Josef von Sternberg might have spent his life in the lace business; Howard Hawks might have remained an engineer, and William A. Wellman an aviator if film hadn't existed, hadn't drawn them to artistry in this new medium. Lean might have browned out his life as a London accountant.

Kevin Brownlow's munificent biography, *David Lean,* brims with the details of the life Lean did live. Brownlow is an accomplished film historian whose work is in both books and documentaries, and the first notable point about his new book is a film analogy. This volume about Lean suggests a latter-day film epic by Lean: it is large, long and beautifully produced.

It began as an autobiography, on which Brownlow was helping Lean. They began work in January 1990; Lean died in April 1991. He had given his aide a great deal of material in conversation, and Brownlow decided to press on in the mode of oral history. His own writing is lively, though not much more; but he has interviewed almost everyone available who was involved in Lean's life and work. In his introduction Brownlow says: "I know this will not be the last biography of David Lean." I can't see why not.

At Gaumont, Lean soon became a cutter—what we now call an editor. He rose rapidly in the profession. By the time that Gabriel Pascal had conned Bernard Shaw into giving him the film rights to some plays, Lean was the desired editor for *Pygmalion* (1938) and *Major Barbara* (1941). By the time Noel Coward was to direct his film *In Which We Serve* (1942), he sought out Lean and soon made him co-director. On Coward's next two films, *This Happy Breed* and *Blithe Spirit,* Lean was sole director. By 1946 Lean was considered, after Carol Reed, the best director in England. He was thirty-eight.

Film by film, Brownlow takes us through the entire Lean career, with dozens of photographs inset in the text and with many full-page photographs, thirty-two in black and white, sixteen in resplendent color. The pages teem with instances of Lean's directorial vision and command. Like most modern biographers, however, Brownlow is reluctant to omit anything he has researched. Some long letters and memos could have been condensed. We get potted biographies of quite incidental people; we get plot summaries of sources, let alone the films. The endnotes are a touch prolix. (When T. E. Lawrence appears, we're told that he was born in 1888. An endnote adds that it was August 16, Napoleon's birthday.) But, if the Brownlow cornucopia overflows, at least it's full.

Lean's private life, colorful in itself, is counterpointed with his work. He was married six times. One of the reasons for this marital marathon was that he was prodigiously attractive to women—a tall, slender man with the face of a gentle hawk—long before he was rich and famous and of course no less so later on. Women besieged him, making constancy difficult, particularly during the first clump of marriages. Not contradictorily, perhaps, he could be rather a cold man. He walked out on his first wife and their infant son and wasn't in touch with them even when the child needed an operation and the wife had a car smash. But the lengthy list of Lean's frigidities, familial and otherwise, is paradoxical against his many generosities—again not only when he was rich and famous. Though Brownlow mercifully doesn't wallow in psychobiography, he does often aptly try to connect some choices in Lean's film material with his background and temperament.

Anyone who has been moved by Lean's work—and who else would read this book?—will relish the "backstage" anecdotes. Examples: the beloved Robert Donat was chosen and tested and found wonderful to play Willie Mossop in *Hobson's Choice* (1954), but the strain of testing brought on a recurrence of Donat's asthma, and the insurance company would not pass him. John Mills was summoned and was at his best; but Robert Donat! Marlon Brando accepted the role of the lover in *Ryan's Daughter* (1970), but commitments intervened. He was replaced with a pipsqueak who helped to doom this ill-considered venture.

With actors, Lean was generally edgy. Excepting a few—Katharine Hepburn, Charles Laughton, Celia Johnson—he was uncomfortable with them. Considering that he was a man who loved to be rid of his actors, to finish shooting and to closet himself with bits of film in the editing room, it's extraordinary that he evoked so many memorable performances. There are dozens: I cite one. Peter O'Toole as Lawrence.

Any record of a busy director must include the projects that didn't come off. Two in Lean's life are especially poignant because, later, other people used the subjects. He wanted to do the life of Gandhi with Alec Guinness; and in the fourteen-year interval between *Ryan's Daughter* and *A Passage to India* he spent several years on a two-film project about the *Bounty* incident, which he planned to treat quite differently from the Laughton-Gable picture. Both screenplays were completed by Robert Bolt, who had written *Lawrence,* and were praised by every producer who read them. In New Zealand a $2 million facsimile of the *Bounty* was built—of steel, with invisible motors. A $3 million hotel was built in Tahiti to accommodate the cast and staff of the film. But the enterprise simply disintegrated. A very thick book could be compiled of the interesting projects that prominent directors planned and didn't accomplish.

What, finally, if that word is ever possible in artistic comment, is Lean's stature? André De Toth, a vivid director himself, who assisted for a time on *Lawrence,* told Brownlow that Lean "was a great master of yesterday . . . David was a slow river. . . . He was never a mountain stream. But I think he was one of the really great men." Not far off the mark, as I understand De Toth. Lean was not much of an innovator, but a master of what was known.

He paid his debt to film for giving him his life. At his best, he created works that could exist only as films. I've just re-seen *A Passage to India;* and, in my view, anyone who objects to it because of its adaptation of Forster must also object, on the same ground, to the Bizet–Meilhac–Halévy *Carmen* for its adaptation of Mérimée, to the Balanchine *Don Quixote* for its adaptation of Cervantes. To compare Lean with those creators in process and intent seems to me just: his film, adapted from Forster, is in itself a complete, sophisticated work of art. With this picture and with his adaptations of Dickens and T. E. Lawrence and Pierre Boulle and others, Lean honored the art that made him an artist.

Auguste and Louis Lumière: Letters*

JUNE 2, 1997 | All of us who are keen on the history of film—and, I'd guess, some sane people as well—will be grateful for *Auguste and Louis Lumière: Letters: Inventing the Cinema*. The letters were edited and annotated by Jacques Rittaud-Hutinet, aided by Yvelise Dentzer, and translated by Pierre Hodgson. Louis's grandson, Maurice Trarieux-Lumière, has written a fascinating preface.

The Lumière brothers were born in Lyon—Auguste in 1862, Louis in 1864—sons of a prospering manufacturer of photographic equipment. Auguste was educated in medical sciences, but he never lost involvement in his brother's passion for photochemistry. (Color photography was one of their early interests; they helped to develop it.) In later years Louis always objected strongly when Auguste was omitted as his collaborator, even though Auguste did considerable work in other fields.

To a degree unknown to me elsewhere, the brothers shared their lives. They married two sisters, and, says the grandson,

for decades, the two brothers and their families shared the same house in Lyon [the capacious villa that is now the Institut Lumière] and until Louis left for Paris when my grandmother died in 1925, they took every meal together . . . eating in each other's rooms in alternate weeks. They worked in the same factory that they had established with their father.

Among their non-photographic achievements, Louis invented the loudspeaker, and Auguste "published nearly 60 books and hundreds of articles" in the fields of biology, physiology, pathology. During World War I, Louis subsidized a hospital with 100 beds while Auguste underwrote the radiological treatment of the patients. During World War II, Auguste concealed a German Jewish doctor, then smuggled him off to South America, where, in a Lumière laboratory, he furthered experimentation on Auguste's enquiry into substances to help scar tissue formation. Louis died at eighty-two, Auguste six years later.

And what else did the Lumière brothers do? They invented the cinematograph.

* Published by Faber and Faber.

These letters to and from friends, associates, competitors, customers, are vivid backstage glimpses of the world in which film came into being — before the Paris debut in December 1895 and the global flood almost immediately thereafter. Some technical matters are discussed about cameras and projectors, with small diagrams, but mostly there is excitement, always expressed in language as graceful and curlicued as old-time Palmer penmanship. And of course the brothers soon expanded into filmmaking, short pictures that are large treasures.

Of all the dozens of matters treated in these letters, one subject is salient. Credit for pioneering in cinema is usually apportioned to Thomas A. Edison in America, Max Skladanowsky in Berlin, Robert William Paul and William Friese-Greene in England, and the Lumières. Edison certainly was demonstrating motion pictures in 1893, Skladanowsky showed film of a kind in Berlin in early 1895, and the two Englishmen, working separately, made important strides. But Paul tried to buy film from the Lumières in November 1895; in January 1896, Edison cabled the Lumières and offered to buy "a fully equipped plant for the manufacture of cinematographic films" (the offer was declined); and in 1935 Skladanowsky wrote to Louis, calling him "my great contemporary, who solved once and for all a problem with which independent workers had been struggling in four countries . . . the famous inventor of the Cinematograph." Though the Lumières were not alone, the matter of primacy seems now to be settled.

What men, Auguste and Louis. Look at the photo of the two of them; in early middle age, on the book jacket. Then look at the photo of them facing page 157, white-haired, still affectionate brothers. What men.

Bernard Shaw on Cinema[*]

MARCH 16, 1998 | Bernard F. Dukore is a preeminent Shaw scholar who has contributed greatly to the (still-continuing) taxonomy of Shaw's career. There is so much material on so many subjects that various editors have arranged in books — Shaw on religion, Shaw on doctors, Shaw on Ireland, etc., etc. — that one might think the field exhausted. Wrong. (We

[*] Published by Southern Illinois University Press.

can almost hear Shaw chuckling as he says it.) Dukore's major editorial work so far is his four-volume edition of Shaw's theater criticism, which may be briefly described as a blessing. But Dukore has also done a lot of work on Shaw's writings for and about film, and this goes on.

In 1968, Dukore prepared an edition of the screenplay of *Saint Joan* that Shaw wrote in 1934–36. (He tells us that Otto Preminger didn't even know of the existence of this screenplay when he directed his 1957 film of *Joan* from Graham Greene's flaccid version.) Subsequently Dukore edited *The Collected Screenplays of Bernard Shaw;* and two years ago he edited the correspondence of Shaw and Gabriel Pascal, the entrepreneur who produced three films of Shaw plays.

Now Dukore presents *Bernard Shaw on Cinema.* Here are 107 articles, interviews, and letters to the press that are concerned with film. The order is chronological, 1908 to the year of Shaw's death, 1950. Through the book we can glimpse the arrival of film in the world, particularly from a playwright's view, and how it became established as an immense factor in a playwright's thinking.

Shaw's besetting sin, and virtue, is apparent from the beginning of the book: nothing ever happened in the world that he somehow hadn't expected and couldn't explain. With our superior hindsight we can see how slow he was to recognize that there is a distinct art of film, but his belief that, from the start, he knew more about filmmaking than most filmmakers was, and to some extent remained, justified. What he quickly perceived and argued on all his life was the special problem of censorship that film entailed.

It's well known that Shaw was a fanatic about photography. (The papers that he bequeathed to the London School of Economics include at least 10,000 of his photographs. That is not a misprint.) What Dukore explores is the surprising extent to which Shaw was involved with film. In 1946 he was asked, "If you had your time over again, would you write for the screen rather than the stage?" The answer was simple: "Yes." (In 1908 Tolstoy made a comparable comment vis-à-vis his plays.) As it was, in addition to earlier screen adaptations of his work, from 1937 to 1945 Shaw wrote only one new play, *In Good King Charles's Golden Days,* which he intended as a film; the rest of that time he spent on screenplays, including *Pygmalion,* which won an Oscar.

The extent of Shaw's film curiosities, animosities, admirations is well displayed in this collection. There's one pleasantly surprising conversation, with the actor Adolphe Menjou in 1928, about the advent of sound — which Shaw had predicted twenty years before. Presumably he knew Menjou through the latter's appearance in Chaplin's *A Woman of Paris*.

Shaw's enthusiasm for Chaplin winds through the book like a bright ribbon. (In Volume Two of the *Collected Letters* is one that he wrote to Thomas Hardy's widow after Hardy's funeral: "If only you knew how I wanted at the end to swoop on you; tear off all that villainous crepe . . . make you come off, *with him,* to see a Charlie Chaplin film!") On the cover and the title page of Dukore's book is a photograph taken on Shaw's California visit in 1933, at a luncheon given for him by Marion Davies. On his left are his hostess, Louis B. Mayer, and Clark Gable. On his right is Chaplin.

Index